THE BEATLES

An Illustrated Diary

H.V. Fulpen

Plexus, London

All rights reserved including the right
of reproduction in whole or in part in any form
Copyright © 1982 by Har Van Fulpen
English translation copyright © 1983, 1998 by Plexus Publishing Limited
Published by Plexus Publishing Limited
55a Clapham Common Southside
London, SW4 9BX

British Library Cataloguing in Publication Data.
A catalogue record for this book is available from the British Library.

ISBN 0-85965-274-2

Printed and bound in Great Britain by
Hillman Printers, Frome, Somerset.

10 9 8 7 6 5 4 3 2

'Tell me what you see.' John, George and Ringo, June 1963.

'Thank You Girl'

The preparation of a book like this requires access to an extensive and comprehensive collection of Beatle material. I've been compiling such a collection since 1963, and over the years I've been assisted by many friends, colleagues, relatives and fan club members. To them, for their invaluable assistance, this book is dedicated.

It would be impossible even to *attempt* to thank each of them individually. But I'd like to name at least a few of the people whose contributions were especially important, people like Jan Tijmes, Jan van der Bunt, Raymond Richard, Bertus Elzenaar, Henk van der Woude and, of course, Fred Frank, who sold me his enormous Beatle collection when he got married. My parents, my wife Annemieke and, lately, even my daughter Michelle and son Daniël have also supported me in keeping my archives up to date.

A special word of thanks goes to four friends from England who have regularly provided me with information from their direct contacts with the Beatles: Freda Kelly, Allan Williams, Bob Wooler and Dezo Hoffmann.

Lydia and Josh Pachter were extremely helpful in the preparation of the book, and the biggest contribution of all was made by Piet Schreuders (who illustrated the Dutch Beatles Fan Club magazine in 1968–69 and designed this book). Piet has been much more than a designer, though: his memory, his precision, and his excellent ideas were always available to me, especially at those moments when my own supply of those qualities seemed lacking. Without his co-operation, many of the most interesting facts, comments and illustrations in this book would be missing.

Any material reproduced from Merseybeat is by permission of Bill Harry.

FOREWORD

I was never very interested in history at school. Memorizing dates was the worst: I could never get those damned numbers to stick in my head.

And yet, I've been walking around for years with the idea of writing a history book somewhere in the back of my mind: a history book about the Beatles, a book in which all the important events in the lives of four of the most influential musicians the world has ever known would be neatly catalogued by day, by month and by year.

Is there really a need for such a book?

I think there is.

For example, there are the millions of younger people who didn't become Beatle fans until after the group's break-up in 1970. They find it fascinating to go back and see exactly how the Beatles came to be, how their career progressed, how and when they made their records and performed their concerts. For those fans who are too young to remember the phenomenal rise and the devastating disintegration of the Beatles, this book will be important and valuable.

For older fans – those who were in at the start and still around for the finish – and for those who have an interest in the history of popular music, it is time to bring all the relevant facts and figures together, once and for all. Pick up a few different books about the Beatles and leaf through them: the disagreements over dates, names and other information are legion. Not only are the authors confused, but even, on occasion, are the main characters themselves – John, Paul, George and Ringo.

John Lennon especially made countless misleading statements during interviews about the history of the Beatles; not surprising, by the way, when you consider everything the group did and experienced in just a few short years. They say that a year in the tropics counts for two – well, a year as a Beatle must have counted for at least *ten* . . .

Of course, John wasn't the only one to make mistakes. For

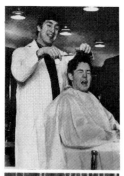

instance, in her book, *A Twist of Lennon*, Cynthia Lennon not only misquoted her own wedding day, but also reported that John was not present at the birth of their son because 'he was on tour with the Beatles'. This explanation has since been cited in a number of leading books about the group, and it certainly *sounds* convincing – until you do a bit of research and discover there *was* no Beatle tour under way when Julian Lennon was born!

So, out of my desire to correct some of the errors, I've finally developed an interest in history after all. In *The Beatles: An Illustrated Diary* a large number of inaccuracies are at last corrected – although I don't pretend to have set *all* of the confusion to rest. The sharp-eyed fan may well find that I've slipped here and there myself, and for that I apologize in advance.

As the former head of the Dutch Beatles Fan Club, I had a unique collection of material available to me during the compilation of this volume: dozens of books, tapes, letters, fan club magazines, press releases, newspaper clippings and magazine articles from all over the world, personal notes, scrapbooks, official publicity photos and amateur snapshots.

Many of the pictures I have chosen to include in the diary are well-known; for that reason, they've been reproduced here in a small format. However, for the first time, they are arranged chronologically, and they tell a coherent and cogent story. There are also many photos which appear in print for the first time in this volume, so even the most devoted of fans should be ready for some surprises. (Sometimes the quality of the images is less than perfect: I've included such shots anyway because of their documentary importance. Some of them have been even enlarged from bubblegum cards!)

The diary section has been kept fairly general. I've left out a lot of information which I consider to be unimportant, although it's easy to get into a lengthy discussion of what is and isn't important when it comes to the Beatles. The average reader probably doesn't really care whether or not George Harrison showed up for his nephew's seventh birthday party on January 15, 1967 – but to the true Beatlemaniac such a titbit may well be crucial, if only to demonstrate that George wasn't *somewhere else* on that day. In order to avoid distracting from the story of the band's rise and fall, I've chosen to leave out that kind of specialized data, along with the hundreds of occasions when fans reported sighting or photographing one or more of the boys. I've got it all filed away in an intricate card index at home, though, and if there's ever a demand for it perhaps someday I'll put out a book in which *all* of it is recorded.

The Beatles: An Illustrated Diary is meant for everyone who loves the Beatles – in other words, for everyone. In addition to the diary and the photographs, there are also many chapters in which specific aspects of the Fab Four's lives and careers are treated in greater detail, with comprehensive text and lots of pictures.

For those who wish to steep themselves in the musical world of the Beatles, the albums and singles are, happily, available. But all of us who lived through the Beatles years know that John, Paul, George and Ringo were more than mere musicians.

The Beatles entertained us, yes. But they also surprised us, even shocked us from time to time. They made us laugh, and they moved us to tears. Their approach to life and to love was an inspiration to millions.

Much of it is available in their music. The rest, I hope, is available in the pages of this book.

H. V. Fulpen

Contents

THE STARS ARE BORN

February 18, 1933	Yoko Ono (in Tokyo, Japan)
September 19, 1934	Brian Epstein (in Rodney Street, Liverpool, England)
September 10, 1939	Cynthia Powell (in Blackpool, England)
June 23, 1940	Stuart Sutcliffe (in Edinburgh, Scotland)
July 7, 1940	Richard Starkey (at 9 Madryn Street, Dingle, Liverpool, England)
October 9, 1940	John Winston Lennon (in the Oxford Street Maternity Hospital, Liverpool, England)
September 24, 1941	Linda Eastman (in New York City, New York, USA)
November 24, 1941	Randolph Peter Best (in Madras, India)
June 18, 1942	James Paul McCartney (in Walton Hospital, Rice Lane, Liverpool 9, England)
February 25, 1943	George Harrison (at 12 Arnold Grove, Wavertree, Liverpool, England)
March 17, 1945	Patricia Anne Boyd
April 5, 1946	Jane Asher (in London, England)
August 4, 1946	Maureen Cox (in Liverpool, England)

1948

THE FIFTIES

24 May 1956

15 July 1956

Early 1957

Late 1958

1950	Julia Lennon teaches her only son, John, to play the guitar. Julia herself plays banjo, and teaches John fingering which is, in fact, inappropriate for a guitarist. John's first guitar is purchased through a mail-order catalogue for £10.
September 10, 1950	Brian Epstein, aged 16, goes to work in his father's furniture store at a salary of £5 per week.
1953	School report of John Lennon, aged 13: 'Hopeless. Rather a clown in class. He is just wasting other pupils' time.'
1956	Influenced by Lonnie Donegan's success, John forms a skiffle group, the Quarrymen, named after Quarry Bank Grammar School, where he is a student. The other five members of the band are Gary Vaughn, Ivan Vaughn and Eric Griffith on guitars, Colin Hanton on drums and Pete Shotton on washboard.
May 24, 1956	The Quarrymen's first performance, from the back of a truck, at an open-air party in Roseberry Street, Liverpool.
June 15, 1956	The Quarrymen perform at a garden party across from St Peter's Parish Church in Woolton. At the party, Ivan introduces John to Paul McCartney and Paul teaches John several new guitar chords. Shortly after this event, Paul will join the group.
October 31, 1956	Mary Patricia McCartney, Paul's mother, dies of cancer, aged 47.
1957	George Harrison is introduced to the Quarrymen at the Morgue Club, Old Roan, Liverpool, and plays two numbers for the band: *Raunchy* and *Guitar Boogie Shuffle*. Richard Starkey works at Hunt's Sports Equipment Store in Speke. With his friends Eddie Clayton and Roy Trafford, he forms the Ed Clayton Skiffle Group. Harry Epstein, Brian's father, launches the first branch of the North End Music Stores (NEMS) at 50 Charlotte Street, Liverpool, with singer Anne Shelton a special guest at the opening. Brian goes to work in the shop as a record salesman. The title song of the BBC television series 'Ivanhoe' is sung by Dick James, backed by the George Martin Orchestra. The Quarrymen take on Nigel Whalley as their first manager.
January 16, 1957	Alan Sytner opens a jazz club in the basement of a warehouse at 8 Mathew Street, Liverpool: the Cavern Club.
July 15, 1958	In Menlove Avenue, Liverpool, Julia Lennon is struck and killed by an automobile.
August 29, 1958	Mona Best, Pete Best's mother, opens a music cellar, the Casbah Coffee Club, in the basement of her home at 8 Hayman's Green, West Derby, Liverpool 12. The Les Stewart Quartet, with George Harrison on guitar and Ken Brown on drums, is asked to play on opening night, but at the last moment the group quarrels and breaks up. George introduces the Quarrymen to Mrs Best, and he, John and Paul play together for the first time at the opening, with Ken on drums. The programme includes Paul singing *Long Tall Sally* and John singing *Three Cool Cats*.

September 1958	At the Liverpool College of Art, John meets Cynthia Powell in a lettering class.
late 1958	John, Paul and George play together as the Rainbow, and John and Paul give one unsuccessful concert as the Nurk Twins in Bending, Berkshire.
1959	John meets Stuart Sutcliffe in a pub in Rice Street, Liverpool. Brian Epstein opens the second NEMS record stores at 12–14 Whitechapel, Liverpool. Anthony Newley is the special guest at the opening.
June 1959	The boys appear as Johnny and the Moondogs in 'The Carroll Levis Discovery Show' in Manchester. In order to catch the last train from Manchester back to Liverpool, they miss the second half of the show.
July 1959	John and Cynthia share the first dance at a college party celebrating the beginning of the summer vacation. That night they sleep together in Stuart's room, and from then on they are almost inseparable.
December 25, 1959	Richard Starkey gets a set of drums for Christmas.

early 1960	Against his parents' wishes, Richard Starkey quits his job as a waiter and goes to Hamburg, West Germany to work full-time as a musician with Rory Storm's band.
May 5, 1960	Singer Billy Fury needs a back-up band, and the Quarrymen audition for the spot before impresario Larry Parnes, as the Silver Beatles, with Johnny 'Hutch' Hutchinson on drums. The audition takes place in the Wyvern Social Club (later the Blue Angel) in Seel Street, Liverpool; although Parnes turns them down for the spot behind Billy Fury, he hires the group to back Johnny Gentle.
mid-May 1960	Johnny Gentle and the Silver Beatles tour Banff, Stirling, Nairn, Inverness and other parts of Scotland, with Tommy Moore (a fork-lift truck driver from Garston Bottle Works) replacing Johnny on drums. Paul uses the name Paul Ramon, George calls himself Carl Harrison and Stuart is Stu de Stael.
May 25, 1960	A performance by Rory Storm and the Hurricanes marks the transformation of the Cavern Club from a jazz club to a beat club, and the many Liverpool beat groups (such as Kingsize Taylor and the Dominoes, Cass and the Casanovas, Willie and the Seniors, the Chants, Freddie Starr and the Midnighters, Faron's Flamingos, Gerry and the Pacemakers, Billy Kramer, the Mersey Beats, the Swinging Blue Jeans and the Searchers) now have a new place to play in addition to the Casbah, the Iron Door and the Jacaranda. Bands average £5 per night at these clubs.
June 6, 1960	The Silver Beatles and the Pacemakers perform at the Grosvenor Ballroom in Wallasey.
August 16, 1960	Pete Best becomes the band's new drummer. By now they are calling themselves, simply, the Beatles.
August 18, 1960	The boys arrive in Hamburg, where they have been hired to play a long engagement at the Indra Club. Owner Bruno Koschmider has just changed the Indra from a strip joint to a beat club, a change which surprises and disappoints many of his customers. After a few evenings, Koschmider moves the Beatles to his Kaiserkeller, located at Grosse Freiheit 36. They play four and a half hours per day for Koschmider's patrons, and the five Beatles (John, Paul, George, Stuart and Pete) split a salary of £120 per week. Before leaving for Hamburg Paul had written to his school to explain his absence: 'Dear Sir, I've got a great job in Germany and I'm earning £15.'
October 16, 1960	After the expiration of their contract with Koschmider, the Beatles try to get a gig at the Top Ten Club, also in Hamburg. Koschmider doesn't want them working for his competitors, though, and accuses them of arson. On October 16, the boys are deported by the German police.
December 1960	The Beatles return to Hamburg to play at the Top Ten Club. Art student Klaus Voormann brings his fiancée Astrid and, later, a crowd of fellow students to hear them.
December 24, 1960	Performance at the Grosvenor Ballroom, Wallasey.
December 27, 1960	The Beatles play at a 'Welcome Back from Germany' concert in Litherland Town Hall, Hatton Hill Road, Litherland, near Crosby. Bob Wooler billed them as 'direct from Germany' – as a result many in the audience thought they were German! Owner Brian Kelly pays them £6 for this performance, but afterwards is so enthusiastic that he books them for a series of dates at £8 each. Neil Aspinall, a book-keeping student, attends this concert; he will later become the band's chauffeur, then their road manager.

5 May

17 August

December

December

Ivan Vaughn

Pete Shotton

Stuart Sutcliffe

THEY MISSED THE MILLIONS!

In 1956, while still a student at the Quarry Bank High School, John Lennon formed a skiffle group called the Quarrymen with fellow students Colin Hanton, Gary Vaughn, Ivan Vaughn, Eric Griffith and Pete Shotton. Their manager was Nigel Whalley.

In 1957, Richard Starkey started the Ed Clayton Skiffle Group with his friends Eddie Clayton and Roy Trafford.

In 1958, George Harrison, Ken Brown and Les Stewart set up the Les Stewart Quartet (although they hadn't yet come across a suitable fourth for the band).

And the same year, Paul McCartney joined the Quarrymen after having been introduced to John by Ivan Vaughn.

On August 29, still in 1958, John, Paul and George played together for the first time, with Ken Brown on drums.

John, Paul and George went on to become Beatles, but what ever happened to Ken Brown? And, for that matter, what ever happened to Pete Shotton, Ivan and Gary Vaughn, Colin Hanton, Eric Griffith, Nigel Whalley, Roy Trafford, Eddie Clayton and Les Stewart?

It's a hard question to answer.

At one point, John bought a supermarket for Pete Shotton to run, and he later arranged to have the former Quarryman appointed manager of the Apple Boutique. Paul's friend Ivan Vaughn married a girl named Janet who taught French at a school in London; not much more than that is known about him, but it was Janet who, in 1965, suggested that Paul use the words *'ma belle'* in a song he was writing: she translated the fourth line of the song's lyrics into French and came up with a title: *Michelle*. Ken Brown became a London milkman. And of the other members of the Quarrymen, the Ed Clayton Skiffle Group and the Les Stewart Quartet, little or nothing is currently known.

But this roster of unremembered names is not a complete listing of the men and managers who missed the Beatle millions.

There was also Stuart Sutcliffe, John's friend and fellow student. Stuart was not a very good guitarist, but he was a friend and he owned a very good guitar, so he became a member of the group. During performances he generally stood with his back to the audience,

1958: George, Paul, Ken Brown and John in the Casbah Club.

Johnny 'Hutch' Hutchinson

Ken Brown

Allan Williams

in order to hide his lack of skill. He left the Beatles in June of 1961, staying behind in Hamburg with Astrid Kirchherr, his fiancée, when the other boys returned to England. On April 10, 1962, Stuart died of a brain tumour in Hamburg. He was 21 years old.

And there were the drummers:

lots of drummers. After Colin Hanton and Ken Brown came Norman Chapman, who played with the boys for three months before being called up for military service. Next, Johnny 'Hutch' Hutchinson was brought in to play the drums for the audition in front of Larry Parnes; Parnes sent the group on a concert tour of Scotland with singer Johnny Gentle and drummer Thomas Moore. Moore had a steady job driving a fork-lift truck, and he used up some of his holiday entitlement to go on the Scotland tour; afterwards, he left the Beatles and went back to his regular job. Meanwhile, manager Allan Williams had arranged a series of performances for the band in Hamburg, so yet another new drummer was needed. The job went to Pete Best, who first played with the Beatles on August 16, 1960, and stayed with them for exactly two years. He was finally fired – to be replaced by Ringo Starr.

While in Hamburg and calling themselves the Beat Brothers, the Beatles recorded a single as singer Tony Sheridan's backing band. The single's success led to a contact with record-store manager Brian Epstein, who asked Allan Williams if he could take over as the group's manager. Williams had just quarrelled with the boys, and he was happy to be rid of them. Not only did he miss the Beatle millions, he even turned down the small amount of money which Brian offered him for the right to manage the group!

Eventually, Williams decided that it was time to cash in on his one-time connection with the Beatles, and in 1975 he wrote a volume of memoirs titled *The Man Who Gave The Beatles Away*. After the publication of his book, he resumed regular communication with the members of the group. He organized a drive to erect a statue of the Beatles in Liverpool, was involved in the release of the album *The Beatles Live At The Star Club*, and has been a frequent guest at Beatle conventions around the world. In December of 1980, he performed the opening ceremony for a Beatles Museum in Mathew Street, Liverpool, not far from the site of the Cavern Club. The museum is the brainchild and property of Beatle fans Jim and Liz Hughes.

Hayling Supermarkets Ltd, Hayling Island, Hampshire: managed by Pete Shotton.

1961

April

April

October

January 25, 1961	Performance at Hambleton Hall, Liverpool.
February 24, 1961	Performance at the Grosvenor Ballroom, Wallasey.
March 21, 1961	The Beatles perform for the first time at the Cavern Jazz Club.
April 1961	The band leaves for their third trip to Hamburg, again to play at the Top Ten Club, this time for three months. Without Stuart, they record two songs for Polydor Records (*My Bonnie* and *The Saints*), as Tony Sheridan's backing band. Bert Kampfert produces the session, for which the band receives £10 per person; the record will be released in Germany in June. Cynthia and Dot, Paul's girlfriend, come over from Liverpool to spend their Easter vacation with John and Paul.
June 1961	The Beatles return to Liverpool, but Stuart stays in Hamburg with Astrid Kirchherr and enrols in the Hamburg Academy of Art.
July 1961	The Beatles and Gerry and the Pacemakers play together (as *one* group, the Beatmakers) at the Litherland Town Hall.
July 6, 1961	The first issue of *Mersey Beat*, a Liverpool newspaper covering the local music scene, hits the news stands. It includes an article by John, mock-reporting on the history of the Beatles.
July 14, 1961	Performance at the Cavern Club.
July 21, 1961	Lunchtime performance at the Cavern Club.
August 5, 1961	Performance at the Cavern Club.
August 31, 1961	In Liverpool, Bernard Boyle, Jennifer Dawes and Maureen O'Shea found the first Beatles fan club.
September 1961	Nine performances at the Cavern Club and four at the Litherland Town Hall. The Beatles are on their way to being the most sought-after band in Liverpool.
October 1961	John, Paul and Jurgen Vollmer vacation in Paris. Jurgen becomes the first person to wear his hair in the soon-to-be-famous 'Beatlecut'.
October 28, 1961	Raymond Jones visits Brian Epstein's record store, looking for a copy of *My Bonnie*. Brian doesn't have the single, but promises to order it. He discovers that, although the record was recorded and released in Germany, the Beatles are a local group and play regularly at the Cavern Club.
November 9, 1961	Brian goes to the Cavern Club and meets the Beatles; in their dressing room, Paul plays their German single for him. Brian's memory of the visit: 'Inside the club it was as black as a deep grave, dark and damp and smelly, and I regretted my decision to come.'

November 10, 1961	Several major Liverpool groups participate in the 'Operation Big Beat' concert at the Tower Ballroom in New Brighton. The Beatles, Gerry and the Pacemakers, Rory Storm and the Hurricanes, the Remo Four and Kingsize Taylor and the Dominoes perform. Between their 6.30 and 10.30 spots, the Beatles play an 8.30 gig at the Village Hall in Knotty Ash.

8 December

late November 1961	The band is now playing quite regularly, and Neil Aspinall buys an old delivery van for £40 and begins transporting the boys and their equipment for £1 per night. During the day, Neil works as an assistant accountant for £2 10s 0d per week, but he soon leaves this job to work exclusively for the Beatles.
December 1, 1961	Performance at the Tower Ballroom, New Brighton.
December 3, 1961	The boys meet with Brian Epstein in his office at NEMS, and Brian proposes himself as the band's new manager. By now, NEMS has sold over 100 copies of the imported German single.
December 8, 1961	Performance with black vocalist Davy Jones at the Tower Ballroom, New Brighton.
December 13, 1961	In the Casbah Club, the Beatles sign a contract naming Brian as their manager. The contract is drawn up by Rex Malin, and Alistair Taylor signs as a witness. Brian himself does not sign; he will later say that he *never* signed a contract with the Beatles, preferring to leave them completely free to fire him if his services were ever to become dispensable.
December 15, 1961	Performance at the Tower Ballroom, New Brighton.
December 23, 1961	Performance at the Cavern Club. Mike Smith of Decca Records is in the audience, at Brian's invitation. He likes the group, and soon arranges an audition for them at Decca.
December 24, 1961	Stu and Astrid arrive in Liverpool.
December 27, 1961	Performance at the Cavern Club.
December 29, 1961	Performance at the Cavern Club.

December

December 31, 1961	The Beatles travel to London for their Decca audition, and spend the night at the Royal Hotel in Woburn Place, London, WC1. Bed and breakfast for one night cost them 27/6 (£1.37½p) each.

The Cavern Club

John and Pete Best in the Cavern.

In the late fifties and early sixties, the 'beat' scene in Liverpool was an underground scene – literally – as young people gathered in dim, dank cellars used as 'beat clubs' to hear the raucous music which was sweeping the globe. One of these cellars, the Cavern Club, was to become legendary as the home of the Beatles.

On January 16, 1957, Alan Sytner opened the Cavern Jazz Club in the basement of a warehouse at 10 Mathew Street. The property had previously been used as a wine store; before that it had been an egg packing station. In 1959 the club was taken over by Ray McFall. The Cavern hosted jazz combos for its first three years; then, on May 25, 1960, Rory Storm and the Hurricanes appeared as the first beat group to play at the club. The emphasis quickly shifted, from exclusively jazz to a mixture of jazz and beat: on a typical Saturday evening in the autumn of 1961, an all-night session featured the Panama Jazzmen, Kenny Ball's Jazzmen, Mike Cotton's Jazzmen ... and the Beatles and the Remo Four.

The club grew increasingly popular, and most of the important Liverpool bands appeared there: Gerry and the Pacemakers, Karl Terry and the Cruisers, Pete Mac-Laine and the Dakotas, Dee Young and the Pontiacs, Alby and the Sorrals, Ian and the Zodiacs, Johnny Sandon and the Searchers, Mark Peters and the Cyclones, Clay Ellis and the Raiders, Kingsize Taylor and the Dominoes, Ken Dallas and the Silhouettes, Billy Kramer and the Coasters, plus the Bluegenes, the Big Three, the Statesmen, the Mersey Beats, the Undertakers, the

Mathew Street before a lunchtime session.

Picture of The Big Three in the Cavern.   *1966: The Cavern Club, after its reopening.*

Pressmen, the Four Jays, the Collegians, the Spidermen, the Four Mosts, the Strangers, Group One, the Echoes, the Zenith Six – and, of course, the Beatles.

The Cavern was open seven days a week. There were two shows a day, one around noon and one in the evening. The lunchtime sessions were extremely popular, but paid very little: the average group hardly earned enough by *playing* at lunch to *pay* for lunch.

Brian Epstein attended the Beatles' lunchtime concert on November 9, 1961, intrigued by the requests he had received for *My Bonnie*, the single recorded in Hamburg by the band with Tony Sheridan. He later described the Cavern as 'dark, damp and smelly'. In fact, the cellar was so damp that the cheap amplifiers used by the groups that played there were constantly short-circuiting; and it was

so stuffy that members of the audience regularly fainted.

Brian became the Beatles' manager and the group's popularity soared. They continued to appear regularly at the Cavern Club and it was not long before there were long lines of fans queueing up along Mathew Street on the days when the Beatles were scheduled for a lunchtime session. On one occasion George Harrison discovered three girls forming the beginning of a queue long before the club was due to open, and as it was bitterly cold he bought coffee for them.

Even as their fame spread beyond the Liverpool city limits and across England, the Beatles kept returning to play at the Cavern, which as a result was able to attract such major artists as the Rolling Stones, the Who, the Animals, the Shadows, Wilson

Pickett and Ben E. King.

But all good things have to come to an end some time, and the end of the relationship between the Beatles and the Cavern Club came on August 3, 1963, when the boys gave their 292nd and final performance in the Mathew Street cellar.

As the big London recording companies lured more and more beat bands away from Liverpool, the Cavern Club found it increasingly difficult to draw either artists or audiences. The Radio Luxembourg programme broadcast from the club was cancelled. The original stage was broken up into a thousand pieces and sold to Beatle fans. And on February 28, 1966, heavily in debt, the Cavern Club was closed.

Restaurateur Joseph Davey bought up the property some six weeks later, and on July 23 threw a gala reopening party with Harold Wilson, former prime minister and member of parliament for the Liverpool constituency of Huyton, and the Mayor of Liverpool in attendance. But the Cavern's days of glory were over.

On May 27, 1973, the club was moved across to the other side of Mathew Street, where it remained in business through 1976. Today, the sign above the door reads Revolution Club, and there is a plaque by sculptor Arthur Dooley bearing the faces of John, Paul, George and Ringo.

The original Cavern Club was pulled down during the construction of a new subway line, and today there is a parking lot where 10 Mathew Street once stood.

FROM

THE CAVERN - LIVERPOOL

"The Birthplace of THE BEATLES"

COMES THIS GENUINE PIECE OF THE

CAVERN CLUB STAGE ON WHICH

THE BEATLES

PERFORMED 292 TIMES DURING THE PERIOD

1961 TO 1963

Photo Sessions: 1961

The first professional photographs of the Beatles were taken in Hamburg by Astrid Kirchherr and Jurgen Vollmer. Astrid took pictures of the boys at a fairground, at a deserted railway yard, and in a studio at her home; most of Jurgen's shots were of the group on stage.

In December 1961, when Brian Epstein took over the management of the Beatles, he hired well-known Liverpool wedding photographer Albert Marrion to shoot a series of official publicity pictures. Over the phone, Brian just told Marrion that he wanted pictures of a 'group', and Marrion of course assumed that Brian was talking about a wedding party!

Marrion's first session with the Beatles saw John, Paul, George and Pete posing in leather jackets, and resulted in the famous photo used on the cover of *Mersey Beat*'s January 4 'Beatles Top Poll!' issue. Brian was not satisfied, however – he wanted to move the boys away from their 'leather' image, and hired Marrion to do a new set of pictures, showing the four lads uncomfortable and awkward in neckties and new dark suits.

The Beatles were frequently photographed during their lunchtime performances at the Cavern Club, too, especially by Dick Matthews, fulltime photojournalist for *Mersey Beat*.

Photo: Marrion   Layout: Swerdlow

The Beatles
Fan Club presents
**An Evening
with John,
George, Paul
& Pete**

Guest Artists
will include
The Four Jays
and the Beatles'
favourite
Compere
Bob Wooler

the Beatles for their fans

At The Cavern
7-30 pm Thursday
5th April 1962   Tickets 6s 6d

Purchasers of tickets
will receive a
FREE photograph,
and may apply for
free membership of
the Fan Club

Tickets available
from NEMS
Whitechapel or
Gt Charlotte St
and at The Cavern
Club

For this advertisement in Mersey Beat, *layout man and Beatle fan Alan Swerdlow used the already-clichéd pose which had appeared in the January 4th issue of the paper.*

Dissatisfied with their 'leather boys' image, Brian had the boys rephotographed by Albert Marrion, this time in suits and ties. The Beatles are clearly ill at ease in their new clothes.

21

1962

4 January

24 March

29 March

January 1, 1962	The boys spend part of New Year's Day auditioning in the Decca studios in West Hampstead, London. They play *Like Dreamers Do, Money, 'Til There Was You, Sheik of Araby, To Know Her Is To Love Her, Take Good Care Of My Baby, Memphis Tennessee, Sure To Fall, Hello Little Girl, Three Cool Cats, Crying, Waiting, Hoping, Love Of The Loved, September In The Rain, Besame Mucho* and *Searchin'*.
January 4, 1962	*Mersey Beat*'s readers select The Beatles as their favourite Liverpool group. The paper's January 4–18 issue carries the headline: 'Beatles Top Poll!'
January 6, 1962	Performance at the Cavern Club with the Collegians.
January 10, 1962	Performance at the Cavern Club with the Strangers and Gerry and the Pacemakers.
January 12, 1962	Performance at the Cavern Club with Mike Cotton's Jazzmen.
January 17, 1962	Performance at the Cavern Club with the Remo Four and Ian and the Zodiacs.
January 24, 1962	The Beatles sign a new managerial contract, not with Brian Epstein personally but with Brian's NEMS Enterprises.
February 1962	Fan club president Roberta 'Bobbie' Brown gets engaged and turns over her duties to Freda Kelly.
February 24, 1962	Performance at the Cavern Club.
February 28, 1962	Performance at the Cavern Club with the Searchers and Gerry and the Pacemakers.
March 1962	Dick Rowe and Beecher Stevens of Decca Records reject the Beatles, telling Brian: 'Groups of guitars are on the way out, Mr Epstein. You really should stick to selling records in Liverpool.' Brian unsuccessfully attempts to interest Columbia, HMV and EMI in the group, yet remains confident enough to declare: 'One day they will be bigger than Elvis Presley.'
March 23, 1962	Performance at the Cavern Club with Gerry and the Pacemakers.
March 24, 1962	Afternoon performance at the Jazz Club in Heswall, in the Wirral. At their evening performance at the Women's Institute in Barnston (for which they receive £25), the Beatles wear grey suits with velvet lapels, made for them by Burton's Multiple Tailors, and the Leather Age is over.
March 28, 1962	Performance at the Cavern Club with Gerry and the Pacemakers and the Remo Four.
March 29, 1962	Performance at the Odd Spot with the Mersey Beats.
March 30, 1962	Performance at the Cavern Club with the Dallas Jazz Band.
April 2, 1962	Performance at the Pavilion Club with the Royal Show Band.
April 4, 1962	Performance at the Cavern Club with the Dominoes and the Four Jays.
April 5, 1962	Prior to the band's departure for their fourth trip to Hamburg, a seven-week stint, a fan club evening is held at the Cavern Club.
April 10, 1962	John, Paul and Pete fly to Hamburg, where, the same day, Stuart Sutcliffe dies of a brain tumour at the age of 21.
April 11, 1962	George, Brian and Stuart's mother, Mrs Millie Sutcliffe, fly to Hamburg.
April 13, 1962	First of a series of performances at the newly-opened Star Club, Grosse Freiheit 39, Hamburg.
April 1962	Back in England, Brian meets music publisher Syd Coleman and plays the boys' Decca audition tapes for him. Coleman, enthusiastic, introduces Brian to George Martin, who promises an audition with Parlophone.
May 9, 1962	Brian sends a rather premature telegram to *Mersey Beat* announcing that the Beatles have signed a contract with Parlophone Records.
June 4, 1962	The boys return from Hamburg and celebrate the news of their upcoming audition for EMI-Parlophone with Brian at the National Milk Bar.
June 6, 1962	The Beatles audition for Parlophone in EMI's number 3 studio in London, playing *Love Me Do, P.S. I Love You, Ask Me Why, Hello Little Girl, Besame Mucho, Your Feet's Too Big* and other numbers. George Martin tells Brian that Pete is an inadequate drummer.

June 9, 1962	A 'Welcome Back From Germany' evening is held at the Cavern Club, with Gerry and the Pacemakers as special guests.
June 11, 1962	The Beatles and a busload of fans travel to Manchester, where the band plays in a BBC radio programme, 'The Beatles in Concert'.
June 15, 1962	Performance at the Cavern Club with the Spidermen.
June 16, 1962	Performance at the Cavern Club with Tony Smith's Jazzmen.
June 19, 1962	Performance at the Cavern Club with the Bluegenes and Ken Dallas and the Silhouettes.
June 20, 1962	Performance at the Cavern Club with the Sorrals and the Strangers.
June 21, 1962	Performance at the Tower Ballroom, New Brighton, with Bruce Channel. Channel's harmonica player Albert McLinton provided John Lennon with free tuition on the instrument.
June 22, 1962	Performance at the Cavern Club with the Cyclones.
June 27, 1962	Performance at the Cavern Club with the Big Three.
June 28, 1962	Performance at the Majestic Ballroom, Birkenhead.
June 29, 1962	Performance at the Tower Ballroom, New Brighton.
July 1, 1962	Performance at the Cavern Club with Gene Vincent.
July 21, 1962	Performance at the Tower Ballroom, New Brighton, with Bruce Channel, Howie Casey, the Big Three and the Four Jays.
July 26, 1962	Performance at Cambridge Hall, Cambridge, with Joe Brown and his Bruvvers.
July 27, 1962	Performance at the Tower Ballroom, New Brighton, with Joe Brown and his Bruvvers.
July 28, 1962	Performance at the Majestic Ballroom in Birkenhead and, the same evening, at the Cavern Club.
August 1, 1962	Performance at the Cavern Club with Gerry and the Pacemakers.
August 5, 1962	Performance at the Cavern Club with the Saints' Jazz Band.
August 8, 1962	Performance at the Cavern Club with Shane Fenton (real name Bernard Jewry, better known as Alvin Stardust, husband of Lisa Goddard).
August 16, 1962	At the band's request, Brian tells Pete that he will be replaced by Richard Starkey as soon as Richard, by now calling himself Ringo Starr, finishes his tour with Rory Storm. Pete's fans demonstrate angrily outside the Cavern Club, and Pete does not show up for the group's evening performance at the Riverpark Ballroom in Chester. Brian hires Johnny 'Hutch' Hutchinson of the Big Three (formerly Cass and the Cassanovas) to fill in on drums until Ringo is available.
August 18, 1962	Performance at the Cavern Club.

August 23, 1962	John and Cynthia are married at the Mount Pleasant Registry Office in Liverpool. Brian foots the bill for a lunchtime reception at Reece's Cafe, and the Lennons move into his Falkner Street flat.
	    Mersey Beat runs the story of the firing of Pete Best.
	    That evening, a performance at the Riverpark Ballroom in Chester.

August 27, 1962	Angry Pete Best fans gather around the entrance to the Cavern Club. In the scuffle which ensues, George's eye is blackened.
August 28, 1962	Ringo makes his first appearance as a Beatle in an evening performance at the Cavern Club with the Bluegenes and Gerry Levine and the Avengers. The final Beatle line-up of John, Paul, George and Ringo is now complete.
August 30, 1962	Performance at the Riverpark Ballroom, Chester.
September 3, 1962	Performance at the Queen's Hall, Widnes.
September 4, 1962	The Beatles travel to London and register at a hotel in Chelsea. Then, in EMI's Studio 2 in St John's Wood, the boys record their first single: *Love Me Do*. George Martin produces (assisted by Ron Richards), Norman Smith is the sound engineer, and session drummer Andy White sits in for Ringo, who is not yet used to playing with the group. During rehearsals, London photographer Dezo Hoffmann takes a series of publicity photos. It requires a total of 17 takes to get the number on tape. During the session, George Martin asks the boys: 'Anything you're not happy with about us?' George Harrison answers, 'Yes, I don't like your tie.'
September 6, 1962	Performance at the Riverside Ballroom, Chester.
September 8, 1962	Performance at the Majestic Ballroom, Birkenhead.
September 10, 1962	Performance at the Queen's Hall, Widnes. The same night, Pete Best debuts with his new band, the All Stars, at the Majestic Ballroom in Birkenhead.
September 17, 1962	Performance at the Queen's Hall, Widnes, with Billy Kramer.
September 22, 1962	Performance at the Majestic Ballroom, Birkenhead.
September 23, 1962	Evening performance at the Cavern Club with the Saints Jazz Band and the Dominoes.
September 26, 1962	Lunchtime and evening performances at the Cavern Club.

9 June

June

September

4 September

THE BEATLES
FIRST RECORD ON PARLOPHONE
LOVE ME DO
c/w
P.S. I LOVE YOU
RELEASED FRIDAY OCTOBER 5th
NEMS

5 October

October

November/December

September 28, 1962	Lunchtime performance at the Cavern Club.
September 30, 1962	Evening performance at the Cavern Club.
October 1, 1962	John, Paul, George and Ringo sign a five-year contract with Brian Epstein. This is their first legal contract, signed not only by the Beatles themselves, but also by the fathers of George and Paul, who are still minors.
October 3, 1962	Evening performance at the Cavern Club.
October 5, 1962	The Beatle's first single is released in England, on EMI's Parlophone label. The A side is *Love Me Do*, the B side is *P.S. I Love You*, the release number is R4949.
October 6, 1962	From 4.00 till 4.30 in the afternoon, the band signs copies of their new record at Dawson's Music Shop in Widnes.
October 7, 1962	Evening performance at the Cavern Club.
October 8, 1962	Lunchtime performance at the Cavern Club.
October 10, 1962	Lunchtime and evening performances at the Cavern Club.
October 11, 1962	*Love Me Do* becomes the first Beatles song to make the British charts, entering the *Record Retailer* Top Fifty at number 49.
October 12, 1962	Performance at the Tower Ballroom, New Brighton, with Little Richard, Billy Kramer, the Undertakers and Rory Storm.
October 13, 1962	Performance at the Cavern Club.
October 17, 1962	Lunchtime and evening performances at the Cavern Club.
October 22, 1962	Performance at the Queen's Hall, Widnes.
October 24, 1962	*Love Me Do* charts at No. 27 for a single week in the *New Musical Express* Top 30.
October 25, 1962	The boys sing *Love Me Do* in a recording session in Manchester for the BBC Light Programme's 'Teenagers' Turn', to be broadcast on October 26.
October 28, 1962	Performance at the Empire Theatre, Liverpool, with Little Richard, Craig Douglas and Jet Harris and the Jetblacks.
November 1–14, 1962	The Beatles' fifth trip to Hamburg, again for performances at the Star Club.
November 2, 1962	*Love Me Do* rises to No. 27 in the *New Musical Express* chart.
November 17, 1962	*Love Me Do* reaches No. 24 in the *Disc Weekly* chart.
November 18, 1962	Performance at the Cavern Club with the Mersey Beats.
November 19, 1962	A lunchtime performance at the Cavern Club, followed by an evening performance at the Majestic Ballroom, Birkenhead.
November 21, 1962	Lunchtime performance at the Cavern Club.
November 22, 1962	Performance at the Majestic Ballroom, Birkenhead.
November 23, 1962	Lunchtime performance at the Cavern Club. That evening, a performance at the Twelfth Annual Arts Ball, at the Tower Ballroom in New Brighton.
November 25, 1962	Evening performance at the Cavern Club.
November 26, 1962	*Please, Please Me, Ask Me Why* and *How Do You Do It* (by Mitch Murray) recorded at EMI's Number 2 Studio in London. The Beatles hate the Mitch Murray song and deliberately fluff it.
November 27, 1962	The Beatles record an appearance for BBC radio's Light Programme show, 'The Talent Spot', at the BBC Paris Studio in Regent Street. It is the Beatles' first London-based radio session. The programme is presented by Gary Marshal and features the Beatles playing *Love Me Do*, *P.S. I Love You* and *Twist And Shout*.
November 28, 1962	Evening performance at the Cavern Club.
November 29, 1962	Performance at the Majestic Ballroom, Birkenhead.
December 4, 1962	The Beatles appear on 'The Talent Spot'.
December 10, 1962	Performance at the Embassy Theatre, Peterborough, with Frank Ifield, Ted 'Kingsize' Taylor and Julie Grant.
December 12, 1962	George Martin attends performances by Gerry and the Pacemakers at the Majestic Ballroom in Birkenhead and by the Beatles at the Cavern Club.
December 17, 1962	The Beatles make their television debut on Granada TV's 'People and Places', broadcast from Manchester, produced by Johnny Hamp. They play *Some Other Guy* and other numbers, and receive £35 for the appearance.
December 18, 1962	The boys leave for their sixth and final trip to Hamburg, again to play at the Star Club; a banner hanging in the Grosse Freiheit on their arrival reads 'Welcome Beatles'. On Christmas Day, Kingsize Taylor tapes over 20 of their numbers: this early material is released 25 years later as a double album by Lingasong Limited.
December 20, 1962	*Love Me Do* peaks at No. 17 in *Record Retailer*. A total of 100,000 copies of the single are sold.
December 29, 1962	*Love Me Do* reaches No. 17 in *Record Mirror*.
December 31, 1962	The group returns from Hamburg.

THE BEATLES

Ringo received his first drum kit at the age of nineteen, a Christmas present from his parents. In old photos of Rory Storm and the Hurricanes, you sometimes catch a glimpse of this kit, with the name Ringo Starr proudly lettered on the front of the Premier bass drum.

When Ringo joined the Beatles in August 1962, he brought his drums with him. Although the name on the bass was covered over with a sheet of white paper from the EMI offices when the group's official publicity pictures were taken, snapshots made during the rehearsals for *Love Me Do* show the 'Ringo Starr' legend clearly.

When the British Beatles Fan Club designed an identifying logo for the group – the word 'Beatles' with the antennae of a beetle at the top of the 'B' – it was traced onto a large sheet of white paper and stretched over the front of Ringo's bass drum. And when the boys made their national television debut on 'Thank Your Lucky Stars' in January 1963, the 'beetle' logo was also on view. (For some reason, the logo was extremely popular in France, where in 1963 it appeared on posters which also carried a photo of each member of the group and the legend 'les Beatles'.)

Late in 1963, the band adopted a new logo 'THE' in small capital letters and, below it, 'BEATLES' in larger capitals, with the 'B' extending above the other letters and the 'T' extending below them. By this time Ringo had a new set of drums, the Ludwig Super Classic PC, model 980 in black mother-of-pearl, purchased from Ivor Arbiter, the British importer of Ludwig products. The legend on the front of the bass – 'Ludwig/THE BEATLES' – became known around the world, as perfect a symbol of the group as their mop-top haircuts and collarless suits.

And in 1970, the very first visual image to appear in the very last Beatle film, *Let It Be*, was – you've guessed it – 'Ludwig/THE BEATLES' from the front of Ringo's drum.

LK 4438-A

THE DECCA AUDITION

On the last day of 1961, John Lennon, Paul McCartney, George Harrison and Pete Best loaded their instruments, their sound equipment and themselves into Neil Aspinall's delivery van and took off for London, where talent scout Mike Smith had arranged an audition for them with Decca Records executives Dick Rowe and Beecher Stevens. It was freezing cold in the unheated van. Somewhere along the way Neil managed to get hopelessly lost, and the drive from Liverpool to London wound up taking over ten hours.

But on January 1, 1962, the boys arrived at the Decca studios in West Hampstead, London, on time. They played fifteen songs for Rowe and Stevens: originals (such as *Love Of The Loved*, *Like Dreamers Do* and *Hello Little Girl*), covers of rock'n'roll hits by other composers (like *Money*, *Searchin'* and *Memphis Tennessee*) and, on the advice of Brian Epstein, a few old standards (including *September In The Rain*, *Sheik Of Araby* and *Besame Mucho*).

The Beatles were nervous, tired and cold, and they felt they were playing badly, but Mike Smith kept egging them on and insisting that they sounded fine.

The Decca top brass did not agree. Two months later, they informed Brian that they were not interested in signing the group to a recording contract. In fact, they told him, bands featuring three guitars and a drummer were already on their way out. (Brian Poole and the Tremeloes, a London quintet who had auditioned for Decca on the same day as the

LK 4438-B

Beatles, *were* issued a contract. Their early releases attracted little attention, though, and it was not until June 1963 that they recorded their first hit: a cover of *Twist And Shout*, which had already been done successfully by the Beatles. Many fans of the Liverpool sound bought the record only because – hearing the name Brian *Poole* – they thought that the Tremeloes were a Liverpool group.)

At the end of 1976, the tapes of the Beatles' Decca audition were rediscovered, and eight of the songs were released on four bootleg singles. The sound quality was outstanding, and the discs rapidly became important collectors' items. In 1979, all fifteen of the numbers were made available together on a bootleg album, *The Decca Audition Tapes*. Finally, in 1982, Audio Fidelity released a legitimate album of twelve of the fifteen Decca audition tracks, excluding three Lennon-McCartney compositions, under the title *The Complete Silver Beatles*.

Listening to these songs more than two decades after they were recorded is an incredible experience. In spite of John's lack of interest in some of the tunes, Paul's unsteady voice (especially on the higher notes), George's too-careful guitar solos, the monotonous beat of Pete Best's drums, the quality of the early Beatles shines through. The Decca tapes provide a unique glimpse at an important event in the history of popular music in the making.

MERSEYSIDE'S OWN ENTERTAINMENTS PAPER

MERSEY BEAT

Vol. 1 No. 13   JANUARY 4-18, 1962   Price THREEPENCE

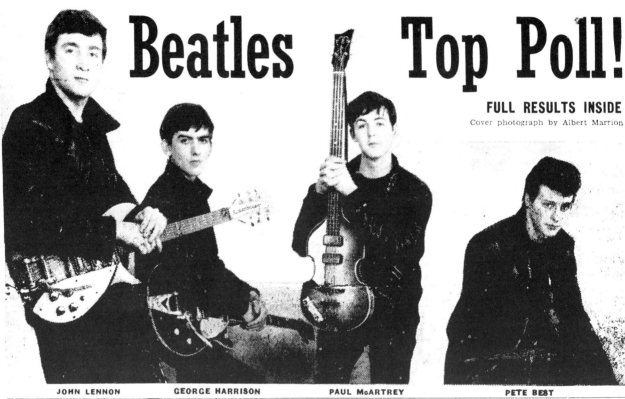

Beatles Top Poll!

FULL RESULTS INSIDE

Cover photograph by Albert Marrion

JOHN LENNON   GEORGE HARRISON   PAUL McCARTREY   PETE BEST

IN THIS ISSUE

POLL RESULTS

CLUBLAND

3   JACK O' CLUBS
3   N.U.R. No. 5 SOCIAL CLUB
7   ODD SPOT OPENS

PERSONALITIES

2   ALEX POWER
2   BERT DONN
2   TOM HARTLEY
7   JOHNNY SANDON

JAZZ

6   LEO RUTHERFORD
8   MERSEYSIDE JAZZ

FEATURES

2   EDITORIAL
5   NEMS TOP TEN

ALSO

2   ARTISTES DIRECTORY
3   CLASSIFIED
       ADVERTISEMENTS
5   MERSEY ROUNDABOUT

Beatles Top Poll!

The front page of the January 4, 1962 issue of *Mersey Beat* magazine is certainly one of the most frequently reproduced and imitated front pages in the history of journalism. On the cover of the Beatles' *Early Years* album, a pile of magazines featuring the famous front page can be seen. In the October 14, 1968 issue of *Life*, it peeks out from behind some plants. And so on. . . .

Mersey Beat was founded and edited by Bill Harry. Its first edition hit the stands on July 6, 1961: the 2000-copy print run was distributed around Liverpool by Harry himself. The issue included a humorous article by John Lennon, titled 'Being a Short Diversion on the Dubious Origin of Beatles'. In the article, John wrote that Paul 'is called McArtrey, son of Jim McArtrey, his father', which ex-

plains why Paul's last name often appeared in subsequent issues of *Mersey Beat* as either McArtrey or McArtney.

John continued to pen articles for the magazine, sometimes using his own name and sometimes hiding himself behind the pseudonym 'Beatcomber', a variant on the byline of the famous *Daily Express* columnist 'Beachcomber'.

Above: *the record cover.* Right: *the censored version from* Life *magazine.*

THE FIFTH BEATLE: PETE BEST

In the late fifties and early sixties it was always hard to find a decent drummer in Liverpool, where dozens of jazz combos and beat groups attempted to eke out meagre livings in the city's clubs and cellars. Drum kits were expensive and few Liverpudlians could afford them. If you had one, you were automatically in great demand – whether you were any *good* at playing the drums was a secondary consideration.

On August 16, 1960, the Beatles' search for a steady drummer seemed finally to have come to an end: on that day, shortly before their departure for their first trip to Hamburg, they asked Pete Best to join up with them and go along.

Pete agreed, but he never really seemed to fit in with the rest of the group. He was shy and soft-spoken, both onstage and off, while the other Beatles were outgoing and wild. There *were* fans who were attracted to Pete's sensitivity, though, and he built up a substantial following in Liverpool.

Two years later, the boys auditioned for Parlophone and George Martin informed Brian Epstein that he was interested in signing the Beatles to a recording contract, on condition that Pete was replaced by a studio drummer.

The contract was drawn up and signed, but neither Brian nor the other members of the group could bring themselves to break the news to Pete. Brian hoped to retain him in the concert formation, substituting another drummer for recording sessions. But John, Paul and George wanted Pete out; their preference was for Ringo Starr, a friend who was playing at the time with Rory Storm and the Hurricanes. They felt that once Ringo heard that the Beatles had a record contract he wouldn't be able to turn them down.

Brian was assigned to do the dirty work. In order to soften the blow a bit, he arranged a contract for Pete to play with Lee Curtis and the All Stars.

And then he fired him from the Beatles. Pete realized he had never *really* been a Beatle after all: like the various drummers who had preceded him in the group, he had been taken on more for the use of his drum kit than for his talent. The boys had not respected his playing, they had never even really become his friends.

Pete's tenure with the Beatles had lasted exactly two years: from August 16, 1960 until August 16, 1962. They were important, formative years for the group, years in

Pete Best paints his house (1965).

I NEED YOUR LOVIN' ☐ JUST WAIT AND SEE ☐ CASTING MY SPELL ☐ KEYS TO MY HEART
WHY DID YOU LEAVE ME BABY? ☐ SHIMMY LIKE MY SISTER KATE ☐ I CAN'T DO WITHOUT YOU NOW!
I'M BLUE ☐ SOME OTHER GUY ☐ SHE'S ALLRIGHT ☐ NOBODY BUT YOU ☐ LAST NIGHT

which the Beatles grew from a rag-tag collection of amateurs to a slick, professional act. And with Pete's departure and Ringo's arrival, the history of the Beatles truly began.

Pete Best himself kept on drumming. He formed a group of his own, the Pete Best Four, with Tony Waddington, Wayne Bickerton and Tommy McQuirk, but their sole single (*I'm Gonna Knock On Your Door/Fallin' In Love With You*) went nowhere and their album (interestingly titled *Best Of The Beatles*) shared the same fate. In April of 1965, with no future in sight, the band broke up.

A year later, the *Sunday Express* reported that Pete was working in a bakery for £18 a week. He refused to be interviewed, and dropped out of sight until August 1979, when he was hired as a technical adviser for the production of an American documentary titled *Birth Of The Beatles*. When filming for the programme was completed, he again dropped out of the public eye.

31

PHOTO SESSIONS: 1962

When Pete Best was fired in August 1962, all existing publicity pictures of the group became instantly useless. And since the boys were under contract to EMI and scheduled to record their first single on September 11, new photos were needed – and quickly!

Brian Epstein immediately called the Liverpool photographic studio 'Peter Kaye', run by Bill Connell, assisted by Les Chadwick. Connell arranged a photo session with the band in his studio the same day. But the Beatles were completely out of control throughout the session, rampaging around the studio and cracking endless jokes, and the photos which resulted were disastrous.

Several days later, Connell brought the group out on location and photographed them again, on the Mersey River ferry (with Pier Head visible in the background) and in a junk-filled vacant lot, where John, Paul, George and Ringo posed with their instruments in the middle of unkempt grass, garbage, an empty oildrum and a burned-out automobile. These pictures were deemed successful, and were the first publicity shots of the Beatles in their new lineup. One of them was later used on the cover of the *Please Please Me* sheet music.

Bill Connell also produced a

Two pictures from the Peter Kaye studio's first, rejected series.

PLEASE PLEASE ME

Recorded by **The Beatles** on PARLOPHONE

Paul
Ringo
John
George

Ringo were retouched, so that they fit the mood of Astrid's pictures of John and George.

Astrid's series of pictures of all four of the boys, each sitting on a wooden stool during their last trip to Hamburg, turned up a year later on posters which were distributed in France. And in 1968 she photographed George yet again, for the inner sleeve of his *Wonderwall Music* solo LP.

series of advertising photographs for Rushworth's, a Liverpool record store, showing the Beatles in the shop's display window holding the brand-new Gibson guitars which had just been imported for them from America.

The first publicity shots of the Beatles as recording artists were taken by Dezo Hoffmann, a show-business photographer, who was in EMI's Abbey Road studios when the group recorded *Love Me Do* and *P.S. I Love You* on September 11. Hoffmann remembers that George insisted on being photographed from the right side,

because his left eye was still blackened: a souvenir of the mob scene in front of the Cavern Club two weeks earlier, when angry Pete Best fans had attacked him.

But the photos finally selected by Parlophone for *Love Me Do* publicity were neither Kaye's nor Hoffmann's. Instead, Parlophone opted for a collage of four individual portraits of the boys: the pictures of John and George had been shot by Astrid Kirchherr in Hamburg, and the pictures of Paul and Ringo were taken by a photographer whose name had not been recorded. The shots of Paul and

Photos by Astrid Kirchherr

THE MAN BEHIND THE BEATLES

Brian Epstein died of a drug over-dose at his London flat on August 27, 1967. He had been known universally as the fifth Beatle, the well-dressed young businessman who accompanied the Fab Four around the world, booked their concerts, reserved their hotel rooms, arranged their publicity and shared their confidences. As famous as he was, though, Brian was also always something of a mystery figure. No one really knew why he had become the manager of the Beatles, nor what it was that made him such a phenomenal success.

Brian was born on September 19, 1934, in Rodney Street, Liverpool, the son of Harry and Queenie Epstein. He did not shine as a student – although his father sent him to several schools in an attempt to give him a decent education – and at the age of sixteen he was working full-time as an assistant furniture salesman in Harry Epstein's shop.

The next years were uneventful. He was called up for military service, but quickly rejected. He enrolled in an acting school, but dropped out after a few months.

In 1957, Harry Epstein opened a

new business venture: the North End Music Stores, or NEMS. Brian was put in charge of the record department, and he threw himself into his new job enthusiastically. Under his guidance, NEMS was soon the most important record store in Liverpool. Two years later, when a second branch was opened in Whitechapel (one of the foremost shopping streets in Liverpool), Brian was named its manager. By 1961, NEMS had the reputation of being the best-stocked record store in the north.

When Raymond Jones walked through its doors on October 28 of that year, looking for a single titled *My Bonnie* by a group called the Beatles, Brian's honour was at stake. He had never heard of the record or the group, but he promised Jones and the other customers who came asking for the single that he would locate it for them.

He quickly discovered that, although the disc had been released in West Germany, the Beatles themselves were a British

11 September 1962: Recording Love Me Do. *(photo: Dezo Hoffmann)*

group. Better still, they were actually from Liverpool. And best of all, they performed regularly at the Cavern Club, only a few streets away from Whitechapel. It was too much of a coincidence to ignore, and on November 9 Brian was in the audience for one of the Beatles' lunchtime concerts at the basement beat club.

The Cavern was the most informal of venues and Brian, in his suit and tie, felt completely out of place. Yet he stayed to be introduced to the Beatles and he visited them in their dressing room, where Paul played *My Bonnie* for him and told him that the single had been released on the Polydor label.

He ordered 12 dozen (144) copies; they sold out almost immediately. Even for a poor student, the numbers were easy to add up: popularity in Liverpool plus popularity in Hamburg plus strong sales of a single on which they appeared only as a backing group clearly equalled something very special. Brian invited the Beatles to meet with him at his office on December 3, and at that meeting he offered to become their manager.

The reasons behind that offer

have remained a riddle to this day. Brian had virtually nothing at all in common with the Beatles: their backgrounds, their personalities, their interests were worlds apart. Brian didn't even much care for the boys' music.

Was he acting purely as a businessman, who instinctively recognized the group's potential for success? Was he an altruist, wanting simply to help some local boys make good? Was he a dedicated record salesman, looking to generate goodwill for his store? Or was he nothing more than a homosexual, who had fallen for four rough and sensual youths?

Whatever the reason, ten days later the Beatles signed a contract naming Brian as their manager. Brian himself did not sign: he was later to explain that he hadn't wanted to tie the boys down.

For the time being, Brian's management didn't change things much: the group's performances in Liverpool and Hamburg went on much as before. Brian was able to negotiate higher wages for them, though. He had publicity pictures shot, and he began informing his contacts throughout the recording industry that he had taken over the

management of 'a top group' from Liverpool. His contacts' first reaction was to hoot with laughter.

Selling the Beatles

With his reputation as manager of the most important record store in northern England, Brian thought it would be easy for him to arrange an audition for the Beatles. He was right: within a month he had persuaded Mike Smith, a talent scout for Decca Records, to come to Liverpool especially to attend one of the boys' performances. Smith came, heard, and was conquered, and on the first day of 1962 the Beatles auditioned for Decca executives Dick Rowe and Beecher Stevens in London. But Rowe and Stevens did not share Mike Smith's enthusiasm, and they decided against offering the group a recording contract.

Brian was not discouraged. He approached and was rejected by the Columbia and HMV labels (both owned by EMI). And still he went on. 'Someday they'll be bigger than Elvis Presley,' he promised.

The tide turned in April 1962, when Brian met music publisher Syd Coleman and played him a tape of a Beatles performance. Coleman thought the material was interesting and introduced Brian to George Martin, who managed the Parlophone label (which was also owned by EMI) and was also impressed by the tapes. An audition was scheduled for June 6. Brian was so confident of a positive outcome that, even before the audition, he sent a telegram to *Mersey Beat* announcing that the Beatles had signed a contract with Parlophone.

He turned out to be right again: the contract was signed in July. There was one condition, though. George Martin insisted that Pete Best be replaced by a better drummer, and when the group's first recording session took place, on September 11, 1962, Ringo Starr had taken over for Pete in the line-up.

On that day Brian's dreams became reality as the very first Beatle single – *Love Me Do* and *P.S. I Love You*, both Lennon/McCartney compositions – was recorded.

The rest, of course, is history.

The first publicity shots of the Beatles as recording artists. A sheet of white paper covers the front of Ringo's bass drum. (photos: Dezo Hoffmann)

Late in 1962, just before their departure for their final trip to Hamburg, the Beatles recorded their second single. Publicity pictures were taken during the session by an EMI staff photographer named Angus McBean.

Still a bit uncomfortable before the cameras, the boys posed in a variety of far-fetched settings. The best-known of these photos was McBean's shot of the group looking down from a balcony inside EMI's headquarters at 20 Manchester Square in London: it was this picture which was used on the covers of the *Please Please Me* LP and the *Beatles No. 1* EP.

In 1969, after the group had recorded an album to be titled *The Beatles Get Back*, John came up with the idea of using an updated version of the *Please Please Me* photo on its cover. Angus McBean was called in, and the Beatles returned six years older, to Manchester Square. But the *Get Back* project was ultimately cancelled, and the new photo disappeared

PHOTO SESSIONS: 1962

ON PARLOPHONE

RECORDS

THE BEATLES

Three different shots of the Beatles in a stairwell at 20 Manchester Square, London, the location of EMI headquarters. (photos: Angus McBean)

from sight. It turned up again four years later on the cover of a double album titled *The Beatles/1967–1970*, with the matching *Please Please Me* shot on a companion double album titled *The Beatles/1962–1966*.

George Martin listens to the Beatles rehearsing Please Please Me. *(photo: Dezo Hoffmann)*

PLEASE PLEASE ME

In the early sixties, it was still unusual for recording artists to select their own material – and it was even more unusual for them to *write* it as well. Producer George Martin's decision to allow the Beatles to record one of their own compositions *Love Me Do*, for their very first single was, needless to say, practically unheard of.

Love Me Do was reasonably successful, peaking at the No. 17 spot in two British charts, *Record Retailer* and *Record Mirror*. But Martin still wasn't convinced that Lennon and McCartney should continue penning their own songs. For the second Beatle single he selected a tune by Mitch Murray, *How Do You Do It*, which he had come across via a friend, music publisher Dick James.

When the Beatles arrived at EMI's recording studios in St John's Wood at six in the afternoon on Monday, November 26, 1962, and George Martin suggested *How Do You Do It* for their next disc, the boys refused. They had already

made their choice, they said, and were going to record two more of their own songs: *Please Please Me* and *Ask Me Why*.

As their producer, Martin held all the trump cards. Diplomatically, he suggested a compromise: if the boys would first record *How Do You Do It*, he would agree to let them put the other two songs on tape as well. As a result, John, Paul, George and Ringo, determined to have it their own way, moped unenthusiastically through *How Do You Do It*, then pulled out all the stops for *Please Please Me*. Even George Martin was sold: as soon as the final chord had faded away, he was on the studio intercom saying, 'Congratulations, boys, you've just recorded a hit!' After a break for tea, *Ask Me Why* was also laid down.

Dick James was disappointed that his suggestion for the second Beatle single had been rejected, but as soon as he heard *Please Please Me* he was also convinced that the right decision had been made.

With Brian Epstein at his side, he telephoned his friend Philip Jones, producer of the influential British television programme 'Thank Your Lucky Stars', played the tape over the phone, and within five minutes had arranged the Beatles' first important TV appearance. (He also arranged a brilliant future for himself by asking Brian to allow him to become the group's music publisher.)

By February 16, *Please Please Me* was the number one single in the *New Musical Express* chart, although it peaked at No. 2 in *Record Retailer*, *Record Mirror* and the BBC's own chart. It seemed as though the only loser was Mitch Murray, who had written *How Do You Do It*.

But there is a postscript: a month earlier, on January 22, another one of Brian Epstein's Liverpool groups had recorded the song, and on April 6 *How Do You Do It* made it to the top of the British charts after all, the first hit single by Gerry and the Pacemakers.

January 1, 1963	A five-day concert tour of Scotland begins.
January 7, 1963	Performance at the Majestic Ballroom, Birkenhead. The hall is completely sold out, and an additional 500 fans are turned away at the door.
January 10, 1963	Performance at the Grafton Ballroom, Liverpool.
January 11, 1963	Taping session for ABC-TV's 'Thank Your Lucky Stars'; the boys sing *Please Please Me* and *Ask Me Why*. The programme will be broadcast on February 2. The Beatles record their contribution to Radio Luxembourg's 'The Friday Spectacular' before an audience of 120 at EMI's studio. The songs played are *Carol, Lend Me Your Comb* and, of course, *Please, Please Me*.
January 12, 1963	Although George Martin wants to use a Mitch Murray composition titled *How Do You Do It* as a follow-up to *Love Me Do*, the Beatles insist on releasing another Lennon/McCartney song instead; today *Please Please Me* is issued as the band's second single, with *Ask Me Why* on the flip side. George Martin puts Brian in contact with Dick James, who will become the group's music publisher, and Brian suggests that Martin gets Gerry and the Pacemakers to record *How Do You Do It*.
January 18, 1963	The boys appear on Radio Luxembourg's 'The Friday Spectacular' in a session recorded on January 11.
January 22, 1963	Under George Martin's supervision, Gerry and the Pacemakers record *How Do You Do It*, their first single. Meanwhile, the Beatles record appearances on the Light Programme's 'The Talent Spot' and 'Saturday Club', as well as being interviewed on that day's edition of 'Pop In'.
January 25, 1963	Brian signs a contract with Vee-Jay Records, who will release Beatle material in America.
January 31, 1963	Performance at the Majestic Ballroom, Birkenhead. Because of the enormous demand for tickets, the Beatles wind up playing two complete shows.

31 January

February

February 2, 1963	The Beatles make their national television debut on ABC-TV's 'Thank Your Lucky Stars', an appearance arranged by Dick James. The same evening, a performance at the Gaumont Theatre in Bradford launches a four-week concert tour through England, with Helen Shapiro (who receives top billing), Danny Williams, Kenny Lynch, the Honeys, the Kestrels, Dave Allen and the Red Price Orchestra. Part of the show is taped by ABC-TV for 'Thank Your Lucky Stars'.
February 4, 1963	Capitol Records releases *Love Me Do* in Canada.
February 5, 1963	Performance at the Gaumont Theatre, Doncaster.
February 6, 1963	Performance at the Granada Theatre, Bedford.
February 7, 1963	Performance at the Odeon Theatre, Wakefield.
February 8, 1963	Performance at the ABC Theatre, Carlisle. Afterwards, a party is held at the Midlands Hotel, but the Beatles are not admitted because of their leather jackets.
February 9, 1963	Performance at the Odeon Theatre, Sunderland.
February 10, 1963	Performance at the Embassy Theatre, Peterborough.

11 February

February 11, 1963	In London, the Beatles spend a total of twelve hours recording their first LP: *Please Please Me*. Also recorded, but not used on the album, are *Bad To Me, I'm In Love, Hold Me Tight, Keep Your Hands Off My Baby* and *I'll Keep You Satisfied*.
February 14, 1963	Valentine's Day concert at the Locarno Ballroom, Liverpool.
February 16, 1963	The *Please Please Me* single reaches No. 1 in the *New Musical Express* Top 30, and peaks at No. 2 in *Record Retailer, Record Mirror* and the BBC chart.
February 18, 1963	Jay Livingstone (of Capitol Records in the United States) informs George Martin that *Please Please Me* is not suited for the American market, and will not be released by Capitol
February 23, 1963	Performance at the Granada Theatre, Mansfield. By now the Beatles' popularity has grown so great that the tour promoters decide to make them the programme's top attraction, moving Helen Shapiro to second billing.

11 February

February

22 March

February 24, 1963	Performance at the Coventry Theatre, Coventry. Northern Songs Limited is founded, with John, Paul, Brian and Dick James as its directors. The first Northern Song to be published will be *From Me To You*.
February 26, 1963	Performance at the Odeon Theatre, Taunton.
February 27, 1963	Performance at the Rialto Theatre, York.
February 28, 1963	In the bus from York to Shrewsbury, John and Paul write *From Me To You*. The title is based on the *New Musical Express'* letters column, which is called 'From You To Us'. Performance at the Granada Theatre, Shrewsbury.
March 1, 1963	Performance at the Odeon Theatre, Southport.
March 2, 1963	Performance at the City Hall, Sheffield.
March 3, 1963	Performance at the Gaumont Theatre, Hanley.
March 4, 1963	In London, the Beatles record their third single: *From Me To You* and, as the B side, *Thank You Girl*.
March 6, 1963	The Beatles record an interview and three songs – *Misery, Do You Want To Know A Secret* and *Please Please Me* – at the Playhouse Theatre, Manchester, for the radio programme 'Here We Go', broadcast on March 12.
March 9, 1963	A performance at the Granada Theatre in East Ham opens a new British concert tour with American artists Tommy Roe and Chris Montez. There are four warm-up acts: the Viscounts, Debbie Lee, Tony Marsh and the Terry Young Six.
March 10, 1963	Performance at the Hippodrome Theatre, Birmingham.
March 12, 1963	Performance at the Granada Theatre, Bedford. The Beatles appear for the fifth and last time on the radio programme 'Here We Go', previously recorded on March 6.
March 13, 1963	Performance at the Rialto Theatre, York.
March 14, 1963	Performance at the Gaumont Theatre, Wolverhampton.
March 15, 1963	Performance at the Colston Hall, Bristol.
March 16, 1963	Performance at the City Hall, Sheffield.
March 17, 1963	Performance at the Embassy Theatre, Peterborough.
March 18, 1963	Performance at the ABC Theatre, Gloucester.
March 19, 1963	Performance at the ABC Theatre, Cambridge.
March 20, 1963	Performance at the Ritz, Romford.
March 21, 1963	The boys record an interview and three songs – *Misery, Do You Want To Know A Secret* and *Please Please Me* – for 'On the Scene', to be broadcast on March 28. Performance at the ABC Theatre, Croydon.
March 22, 1963	*Please Please Me*, the first Beatle LP, is released. That evening, the band performs at the Gaumont Theatre, Doncaster.
March 23, 1963	Performance at the City Hall, Newcastle.
March 24, 1963	Performance at the Empire Ballroom, Liverpool.
March 26, 1963	Performance at the Granada Theatre, Mansfield.
March 27, 1963	Performance at the ABC Theatre, Northampton.
March 28, 1963	Performance at the ABC Theatre, Exeter. Appearance on the radio programme 'On The Scene' is broadcast.
March 29, 1963	Performance at the Odeon Theatre, Lewisham.
March 30, 1963	Performance at the Guildhall Theatre, Portsmouth.
March 31, 1963	Performance at the De Montfort Hall, Leicester.
April 1, 1963	The Beatles, in the category 'Promising Newcomers', play at the *New Musical Express'* poll winners' concert at the Empire Pool, Wembley.
April 2–11, 1963	John and Brian vacation together in Spain, where John writes *Bad To Me* for Billy Kramer.
April 8, 1963	While John is in Spain, Cynthia gives birth to their first child, John Charles Julian Lennon, in the Sefton General Hospital, Liverpool.
April 11, 1963	Tony Barrow goes to work as the Beatles' press agent.
April 12, 1963	*From Me To You*, the third Beatles single, is released, as *Please Please Me*, the first Beatles LP, reaches the top of the hit parade, where it will remain for 30 weeks, eventually being replaced by *With The Beatles* on December 5. That evening, a performance at the Cavern Club.
April 16, 1963	Appearance on BBC-TV's 'The 625 Show'. The Beatles perform three songs, including *Please Please Me*; the rest of the cast includes Jimmy Young, Rolf and Tino, Bobbi Carrol, Hank Locklin, Woot Steenhuis, the Micky Greeve Orchestra and Johnny Pearson.
April 26, 1963	Billy Kramer, under contract to Brian Epstein and with a new middle initial and a new band, releases his first single. The label reads Billy J. Kramer and the Dakotas,

	and also carries the names Lennon and McCartney, who have composed both of the single's sides: *Do You Want To Know A Secret* and *I'll Be On My Way*.
April 29, 1963	John, Paul, George and Ringo leave England for a twelve-day vacation in Tenerife, in the Canary Islands.
May 9, 1963	The Beatles perform in a concert entitled 'Swinging Sound '62' at the Royal Albert Hall in London. The concert is broadcast live between 9.10 and 10.15 pm, with the Beatles appearing from 10.03 to 10.08. After the concert, Paul meets actress Jane Asher who had been posing, screaming, for a *Radio Times* photographer. Jane accompanies the Beatles to Chris Hutchins' flat in King's Road, Chelsea. Jane and Paul quickly become close friends.
May 11, 1963	Performance at the Imperial Ballroom, Nelson.
May 14, 1963	Performance at the Rank Theatre, Sunderland.
May 15, 1963	Performance at the Royalty Theatre, Chester.
May 17, 1963	In Dezo Hoffmann's Wardour Street studio, the Beatles pose in grey suits for their best-known publicity pictures. Performance in the BBC-TV programme 'Pops and Lennie'.
May 18, 1963	A performance at the Adelphi Theatre in Slough opens the Beatles' third concert tour through the United Kingdom. They share top billing with Roy Orbison and Gerry and the Pacemakers, and there are six warm-up acts: David Macbeth, Louise Cordet, Erkey Grant, Ian Crawford, the Terry Young Six and Tony Marsh.
May 19, 1963	Performance at the Gaumont Theatre, Henley.
May 20, 1963	Performance at the Gaumont Theatre, Southampton.
May 21, 1963	At the Playhouse Theatre, Manchester, the Beatles record six songs for BBC radio's 'Saturday Club', to be broadcast on May 25. The songs are *I Saw Her Standing There, Do You Want To Know A Secret, Boys, Long Tall Sally, From Me To You* and *Money (That's What I Want)*.
May 22, 1963	Performance at the Gaumont Theatre, Ipswich.
May 23, 1963	Performance at the Odeon Theatre, Nottingham.
May 24, 1963	Performance at the Granada Theatre, Walthamstow.
May 25, 1963	Performance on 'Saturday Club' (BBC Radio Light Programme), previously recorded on May 21. Two concerts at the City Hall, Sheffield.
May 26, 1963	Performance at the Empire Theatre, Liverpool.
May 27, 1963	Performance at the Capitol Theatre in Cardiff, Wales. In America, Vee-Jay Records releases the *From Me To You/Thank You Girl* single.
May 28, 1963	Performance at the Gaumont Theatre, Worcester.
May 29, 1963	Performance at the Rialto Theatre, York.
May 30, 1963	Performance at the ABC Theatre, Manchester.
May 31, 1963	Performance at the Odeon Theatre, Southend.
June 1, 1963	Performance at the Granada Theatre, Tooting.
June 2, 1963	Performance at the Hippodrome Theatre, Brighton.
June 3, 1963	Performance at the Granada Theatre, Woolwich.
June 4, 1963	BBC Radio begins a 15-week series of programmes entitled 'Pop Go the Beatles'. Performance at the Town Hall, Birmingham.
June 5, 1963	Performance at the Odeon Theatre, Leeds.
June 7, 1963	Performance at the Odeon Theatre, Glasgow.
June 8, 1963	Performance at the City Hall, Newcastle.
June 9, 1963	Performance at the King George Hall in Blackburn ends the Beatles' third tour of the UK.
June 12, 1963	Charity concert in aid of the NSPCC (National Society for the Prevention of Cruelty to Children) at the Grafton Ballroom, West Derby Road, Liverpool 6.
June 14, 1963	Performance at the Tower Ballroom, New Brighton.
June 16, 1963	Performance at the Odeon Theatre, Romford, with Gerry and the Pacemakers and Billy J. Kramer and the Dakotas.
June 18, 1963	In celebration of his 21st birthday, Paul is escorted to the street outside the EMI studios and ceremoniously 'bumped' on the pavement. Later in the day, there is a birthday party at his Aunt Jinny's house in Birkenhead.
June 22, 1963	John tapes an appearance as a member of BBC-TV's 'Juke Box Jury', then flies by helicopter to Abergavenny for a performance at the Town Hall.
June 23, 1963	Appearance in the BBC Radio Light Programme's 'Easy Beat'.
June 26, 1963	The EP ('extended-play' 45 rpm record, including four songs as opposed to the two songs of a single) *Twist And Shout* is released.
June 28, 1963	Performance at the Queen's Hall, Leeds.

17 May

18 May

June

26 June

1 July

22 July

22–27 July

June 29, 1963	The Beatles record an appearance for ABC-TV's 'Thank Your Lucky Stars', as part of a programme devoted entirely to Liverpool musicians. The show will be aired on October 9 and rerun on November 13. John's pre-recorded appearance on 'Juke Box Jury' is broadcast by BBC Television.
June 30, 1963	Performance at the Regal Theatre, Yarmouth.
July 1, 1963	In the studio to record a new single: *She Loves You* and *I'll Get You*. Dezo Hoffmann photographs the boys in the studio, in a park, in their hotel room, buying bananas at the Berwick Street market, and in a narrow alley called Rupert Court.
July 3, 1963	John, Paul, George and Ringo are in Manchester to tape a radio appearance on the BBC Light Programme's 'The Beat Show'. It is recorded at the Playhouse Theatre and features *From Me To You*, *A Taste Of Honey* and *Twist And Shout*. The programme is broadcast the next day, July 4.
July 5, 1963	Performance at the Plaza Ballroom, Oldhill.
July 7, 1963	Performance at the ABC Theatre, Blackpool.
July 8–13, 1963	A week of concerts, two shows per evening, at the Winter Gardens Theatre in Margate. Also on the bill are Billy J. Kramer and the Dakotas.
July 15, 1963	*All My Loving* is recorded for the new LP.
July 21, 1963	Performance at the Queen's Theatre, Blackpool, where the first signs of Beatlemania are visible: 4000 ticketless fans form such an impenetrable crowd outside the sold-out theatre that the Beatles are forced to enter via the roof.
July 22, 1963	Vee-Jay Records release the first American Beatle LP: *Introducing The Beatles*. On the album's cover the boys are billed as 'England's No. 1 vocal group'.
July 22–27, 1963	A week of concerts at the Odeon Theatre in Weston-Super-Mare. Also on the bill are Gerry and the Pacemakers and Tommy Quickly. During the week, photographer Dezo Hoffmann takes pictures of the Beatles on the beach in Victorian swimming costumes.
July 26, 1963	Billy J. Kramer and the Dakotas release their new single, *Bad To Me*, again a Lennon and McCartney composition.
July 28, 1963	Performance at the ABC Theatre, Great Yarmouth.
July 29–30, 1963	In the studio to record *She Loves You* and *I'll Get You* for the new single, plus additional tracks for the new LP.
July 30, 1963	Liverpool singer Tommy Quickly releases his first single: *Tip Of My Tongue*, a Lennon/McCartney composition. The same day, Decca Records issues a single by Pete Best: *I'm Gonna Knock On Your Door* and, on the flip side, *I Fall In Love With You*.
July 31, 1963	Performance at the Imperial Ballroom, Nelson.
August 1, 1963	The first issue of *The Beatles Monthly Book*, 28 pages of news, facts and photos, appears. That night, the band plays in Southport.
August 2, 1963	Performance at the Grafton Ballroom in Liverpool, with the Undertakers, the Dennisons and the Cascades.
August 3, 1963	The Beatles perform for the 292nd and final time at the Cavern Club. The Escorts and the Mersey Beats also appear.
August 4, 1963	Performance at the Queen's Theatre, Blackpool.
August 6, 1963	Performance in Abbotsfield Park, Ormston, Manchester, with Brian Poole and the Tremeloes and other groups. The show is called 'A Twist and Shout Dance'.
August 6–9, 1963	Nightly performances at the Springfield Ballroom, St Helier, Jersey.
August 11, 1963	Performance at the ABC Theatre, Blackpool.
August 12–17, 1963	A week of concerts at the Odeon Theatre in Llandudno, Wales, with Billy J. Kramer and the Dakotas and Tommy Quickly.
August 18, 1963	Performance at the Princess Theatre, Torquay.
August 19, 1963	Performance on Granada TV's 'Scene at 6.30'. The boys sing *Twist And Shout, This Boy* and *I Want To Hold Your Hand*.
August 19–24, 1963	A week of concerts at the Gaumont Theatre in Bournemouth, with Billy J. Kramer and the Dakotas.
August 20, 1963	*Glad All Over* and *I Just Don't Understand*, two songs never recorded by the Beatles in the studio, are sung by the band on 'Pop Go the Beatles'.
August 23, 1963	*She Loves You/I'll Get You*, the fourth Beatle single, is released. Although the record has not yet been played on the radio, EMI has already received orders for 500,000 copies.
August 24, 1963	Appearance in ABC-TV's 'Thank Your Lucky Stars – Summer Spin'.
August 25, 1963	Performance at the Queen's Theatre, Blackpool.
August 26–31, 1963	A week of concerts at the Odeon Theatre in Southport, with Gerry and the Pacemakers and Tommy Quickly.
August 30, 1963	The Fourmost, a new Liverpool band under contract to Brian Epstein, releases a

1 August

	single titled *Hello Little Girl*, a Lennon and McCartney composition.
September 1, 1963	Performance at the Regal Theatre, Yarmouth. The show is filmed for later broadcast on ABC-TV's 'Big Night Out'.
September 3, 1963	Performance at the Queen's Theatre, Blackpool.
September 4, 1963	*She Loves You* reaches No. 1 in the *New Musical Express* chart and stays there for four weeks. A performance at the Gaumont Theatre in Worcester begins a short tour with Mike Berry and Freddie Starr and the Midnighters.
September 5, 1963	Performance at the Gaumont Theatre, Taunton.
September 6, 1963	Performance at the Odeon Theatre, Luton. Earlier in the day, in Liverpool, Brian signs a contract with Priscilla White, Ringo's mother's hairdresser and cloakroom girl at the Cavern Club. Priscilla will use the stage name Cilla Black.
September 7, 1963	ABC broadcasts 'Big Night Out' and the band performs live at the Fairfields Theatre in Croydon.
September 8, 1963	Performance at the ABC Theatre, Blackpool.
September 10, 1963	This week's edition of the BBC Radio series 'Pop Go the Beatles' includes renditions of *The Hippy Hippy Shake, Too Much Monkey Business* and other numbers.
September 12, 1963	*She Loves You* reaches No. 1 in *Record Retailer*'s chart where it will remain for four weeks.
September 13, 1963	Performance at the Public Hall, Preston.
September 14, 1963	Third time lucky: *She Loves You* reaches No. 1 in the *Record Mirror* chart, where it also remains for four weeks. Performance at the Memorial Hall, Nantwich.
September 15, 1963	Performance at the Royal Albert Hall, London.
September 17, 1963	On 'Pop Go the Beatles' this week: *Lucille* and other numbers. That evening, a performance at the Queen's Theatre, Blackpool.
September 19, 1963	The Beatles take three-week vacations: Paul and Ringo leave for Athens, John and Cynthia head for the George V Hotel in Paris (where they meet Astrid Kirchherr), and George and his brother Peter fly to America to visit their sister Louise in Benton, Illinois.
October 1963	Following Brian's example, all four Beatles decide to move to London. Brian himself finds houses for John and Cynthia at 13 Emperor's Gate, Kensington, and for George and Ringo at Whaddon House, Williams Mews, Knightsbridge. (They will not actually move in till early 1964.) Paul moves in with Jane Asher at her parents' home, 57 Wimpole Street, London, W1.
October 5, 1963	A performance at the Concert Hall in Glasgow begins a short tour through Scotland.
October 6, 1963	Performance at the Regal Theatre, Kirkcaldy.
October 7, 1963	Performance at the Caird Hall, Dundee.
October 9, 1963	BBC-TV broadcasts 'The Mersey Sound', a documentary film about the Liverpool sound.
October 10, 1963	The press finally gets around to announcing that John is married and a father.
October 11, 1963	The Beatles receive their first gold record, for the sale of over a million copies of *She Loves You*. That evening, they perform in Trentham Gardens, Stoke-on-Trent.
October 13, 1963	In a live performance on ATV's 'Sunday Night at the London Palladium', the band sings *I Want To Hold Your Hand*, *This Boy*, *All My Loving*, *Money* and *Twist And Shout*. Thousands of fans beleaguer the Palladium, screaming so loudly that the noise can be heard inside the theatre and, via the television microphones, in living rooms throughout Britain.
October 14, 1963	For the first time, the word 'Beatlemania' appears in the British press.
October 15, 1963	Performance at the Floral Pavilion, Southport.
October 17, 1963	Beatle fans block traffic outside a Bond Street restaurant in London, as, inside, Paul lunches with the winner of a 'Why I Like the Beatles' contest.
October 18, 1963	Performance at the Shrewsbury Music Hall, Shrewsbury.
October 19, 1963	Recording session for the next single: *I Want To Hold Your Hand* and *This Boy*. While in the studio the Beatles also record a special single, which will be sent as a Christmas present to all members of their British fan club.
October 20, 1963	An ABC-TV camera crew films the boys in Birmingham for 'Thank Your Lucky Stars'. During the session, the studio is stormed by 3000 fans. The show will be broadcast on October 26.
October 24, 1963	A performance at the Karlaplan Theater in Stockholm kicks off a week-long tour of Sweden. The show is taped for subsequent broadcast on Swedish radio.
October 25, 1963	In England, the annual Ivor Novello Awards are announced. The Ivor Novello awards are sponsored by BASCA (the British Association of Songwriters, Composers and Authors) and are restricted to Britons. Some are determined by

6 September

11 October

13 October

1 November

4 November

16 November

22 November

29 November

quantifying sales; others are decided by a panel of judges. In 1963 the Beatles win five awards: the Top Selling Record in Britain (*She Loves You*); the Second Top Selling Record (*I Want To Hold Your Hand*); the Most Broadcast Song on British Radio (*She Loves You*); the Second Most Outstanding Song (*All My Loving*); and the Most Outstanding Contribution to British Music.
Performance in Karlstadt, Sweden.

October 26, 1963	'Thank Your Lucky Stars' is broadcast by ABC-TV and Brian Epstein is a member of BBC-TV's 'Juke Box Jury'. Two performances at the Kungliga Tennishallen, Stockholm, Sweden.
October 27, 1963	Two performances in Gothenburg, Sweden.
October 28, 1963	Performance in Boras, Sweden.
October 29, 1963	Performance in Eskilstuna, Sweden.
October 30, 1963	After a taping session for the Swedish television programme 'Drop In', which will be broadcast on November 3, the boys fly back to England, where thousands of fans greet them at the airport.
November 1, 1963	Release date of the EP *Beatles No. 1*, plus two new singles by other artists but featuring Lennon/McCartney compositions: Billy J. Kramer and the Dakotas' *I'll Keep You Satisfied*, and the Rolling Stones' *I Wanna Be Your Man*. A performance at the Odeon Theatre in Cheltenham begins a new tour of England. On the bill with the Beatles are the Brook Brothers, Peter Jay and the Jaywalkers, the Kestrels and the Vernon Girls.
November 2, 1963	Performance at the City Hall, Sheffield.
November 3, 1963	Performance at the Odeon Theatre, Leeds.
November 4, 1963	The Royal Family is in the audience and the Beatles are on the bill with Marlene Dietrich, Maurice Chevalier and Vera Lynn; the occasion is the Royal Variety Performance at the Prince of Wales Theatre in London. During the show, John speaks these unforgettable words: 'During the next number, would those in the cheap seats clap their hands. The rest of you just rattle your jewellery.'
November 5, 1963	Brian and Billy J. Kramer leave for America, where Brian will meet Ed Sullivan and sign a contract for three appearances by the Beatles and two by Gerry and the Pacemakers on Sullivan's television variety show. In order to impress the Americans he has dealings with, Brian takes rooms in the most expensive hotels everywhere he goes in America: the trip winds up costing some £2000. Meanwhile, the Beatles perform at the Adelphi Theatre in Slough.
November 6, 1963	Performance at the ABC Theatre, Northampton.
November 7, 1963	Over to Ireland for a performance at the Ritz in Dublin.
November 8, 1963	Performance at the Adelphi Theatre, Belfast.
November 9, 1963	Back to England for a performance at the Granada Theatre in East Ham.
November 10, 1963	Performance at the Hippodrome Theatre, Birmingham. In Holland, the Dutch Beatles Fan Club is founded by Har van Fulpen, who has received official permission to do so from the original fan club in England.
November 12, 1963	Paul has gastric flu, so a scheduled appearance at the Guildhall Theatre in Portsmouth is postponed. It will be held three weeks later, on December 3.
November 13, 1963	Performance at the ABC Theatre, Plymouth. The same night, the BBC reruns the documentary 'The Mersey Beat', in response to many requests by viewers.
November 14, 1963	Performance at the ABC Theatre, Exeter.
November 15, 1963	Performance at the Colston Hall, Bristol. The Fourmost's second single is released. Titled *I'm In Love*, it is another Lennon/McCartney composition.
November 16, 1963	Performance at the Winter Gardens, Bournemouth, filmed by three American television crews for future broadcast.
November 17, 1963	A performance at the Coventry Theatre in Coventry is photographed for a spread in *Life* magazine.
November 18, 1963	Sir Joseph Lockwood of EMI presents the Beatles with a silver record marking the sale of over 250,000 copies of the *Please Please Me* LP.
November 19, 1963	Performance at the Gaumont Theatre, Wolverhampton.
November 20, 1963	*She Loves You* returns to the No. 1 position in the *NME* chart, where it will stay for a further two weeks. Performance at the Ardwick Apollo Theatre, Manchester. A camera crew from Pathé British News records several numbers for an eight-minute documentary film about the group.
November 21, 1963	Performance at the ABC Theatre, Carlisle.
November 22, 1963	The new album, *With The Beatles*, is released; it features vocal spots by all four members of the group, and includes George's first composition, *Don't Bother Me*. A quarter of a million copies of the disc have already been ordered, so for the first time in British musical history an LP goes silver *before* its release. The same evening, the band performs at the Globe Theatre in Stockton.
November 23, 1963	Performance at the City Hall, Newcastle.

November 24, 1963	Performance at the ABC Theatre, Hull.
November 25, 1963	In Canada, Capitol Records release an album titled *Beatlemania With The Beatles*.
November 26, 1963	Performance at the ABC Theatre, Cambridge. Afterwards, the boys stay in Cambridge at the University Arms Hotel.
November 27, 1963	Performance at the Rialto Cinema, York.
November 28, 1963	*She Loves You* returns to No. 1 in *Record Retailer*'s chart, where it remains for another two weeks. Performance at the ABC Theatre, Lincoln. Ringo has earache and is brought, in disguise, to a local hospital.
November 29, 1963	A new record sets a new record: prior to today's release of the fifth Beatles single, *I Want To Hold Your Hand/This Boy*, music stores have already ordered over a million copies of the disc, which thus goes 'platinum' before its release. The same evening, the band performs at the ABC Theatre in Huddersfield.
November 30, 1963	*She Loves You* returns to *Record Mirror*'s No. 1 spot, but only stays on top for one week. Performance at the Empire Theatre, Sunderland. The crowds outside the theatre are so thick that the Beatles must leave via the fire station next door.
December 1, 1963	Performance at the De Montfort Hall, Leicester.
December 3, 1963	In ATV's Studio C in Elstree, the Beatles wear straw hats and sing *On Moonlight Bay* in a taping session for the 'Morecambe and Wise Show'. The same evening, a charity performance in the Grand Ballroom of the Grosvenor House Hotel in London, to benefit spastic children.
December 2, 1963	Performance at the Guildhall Theatre in Portsmouth, rescheduled from November 12.
December 5, 1963	Dora Bryan's novelty Christmas single, *All I Want For Christmas Is A Beatle*, enters the charts.
December 6, 1963	Members of the British Beatles Fan Club receive their first Christmas present from the group: *The Beatles Christmas Record*. It is a spoken thank-you note to the fans, and includes Beatle-ized versions of several Christmas carols.
December 7, 1963	In the afternoon, the Beatles give a special performance for the Northern Area Fan Club Convention at the Liverpool Empire. Part of the show is recorded by BBC-TV for a programme called 'It's the Beatles!', which will also include other material filmed at the convention. The Beatles perform 12 songs. An hour later, the boys tape an appearance as the jury members on BBC-TV's 'Juke Box Jury'. And the same evening, the group gives two performances at the Odeon Cinema in Liverpool.
December 8, 1963	Performance at the Odeon Theatre, Lewisham.
December 9, 1963	Performance at the Odeon Theatre, Southend.
December 10, 1963	After running out of petrol, John, Paul, George and Ringo have to hitchhike to reach their performance at the Gaumont Theatre in Doncaster.
December 11, 1963	Performance at the Futurist Theatre, Scarborough.
December 12, 1963	Performance at the Odeon Theatre, Nottingham.
December 13, 1963	Performance at the Gaumont Theatre, Southampton.
December 14, 1963	Performance at the Wimbledon Palais for the Southern England Fan Club Convention. All 3000 of the fans present get to shake hands with a Beatle.
December 21, 1963	The first preview of 'The Beatles' Christmas Show', with Rolf Harris, Billy J. Kramer and the Dakotas, the Fourmost, Cilla Black, Tommy Quickly and the Barron Knights, is held at the Gaumont Theatre in Bradford.
December 22, 1963	A second preview of the Christmas show is held, this time at the Empire Hall in Liverpool.
December 23, 1963	Radio Luxembourg broadcasts the first programme of a weekly series titled 'It's the Beatles'.
December 24, 1963	'The Beatles' Christmas Show' premieres at the Finsbury Park Astoria Theatre in London (now the Rainbow). After the performance, a helicopter chartered by Brian Epstein flies John, Paul, George and Ringo to Liverpool to celebrate Christmas with their families.
December 25, 1963	A special Christmas edition of 'Thank Your Lucky Stars' is broadcast, featuring the Beatles, Cilla Black, the Searchers, Billy J. Kramer and the Dakotas, Gerry and the Pacemakers and other acts.
December 26, 1963	The Beatles have their own two-hour radio special on the BBC Light Programme. Among ten numbers, they twice sing an altered version of *From Me To You* called *From Us To You*, which is also the name of the programme. The programme is presented by Rolf Harris and consists of a montage of previously broadcast interviews with additional chat between Rolf and the boys.
December 26–31, 1963	The band closes out the year with two performances of 'The Beatles' Christmas Show' per night at the Finsbury Park Astoria. The show will continue running through to January 11, 1964.

2 December

6 December

7 December

14 December

22 December

JUMP FOR JOY!

John films the other three in Sefton Park.

The best-known publicity shots of the Beatles from 1963 and 1964 were taken by Dezo Hoffmann, a freelance photographer who was born in Czechoslovakia and trained as a movie cameraman. Hoffmann fought in the Spanish Civil War during the 1930s, then found himself in England in 1940 and decided to make London his home.

In 1963, he travelled to Liverpool to take pictures of the Beatles for *Record Mirror*, a London music weekly, and met the boys at Brian Epstein's NEMS. Whatever it is that clicks between people clicked immediately between Hoffmann and the group. He so enjoyed their enthusiasm and their humour that he wound up staying longer in Liverpool than he had planned: he photographed the boys at their homes, at a barbershop and in Liverpool's Sefton Park, near Penny Lane. Paul drove them all from location to location in his old dark green Ford Classic.

At Sefton Park, the Beatles took home movies of each other with Hoffmann's 8 mm camera. And the photographer himself took a series of 'flying Beatles' pictures, using a technique borrowed from film animation: he made the boys jump up into the air, and, shooting from below, snapped his shutter as they reached the high point of each jump.

After several days of picture-taking all over Liverpool, the Beatles went off on a concert tour through England with Tommy Roe and Chris Montez, and Dezo Hoffmann returned to London. Over the coming months, whenever the Beatles were in town for concerts and appearances on BBC Radio, they always found time for a visit to Hoffmann's studio and a session in front of his cameras.

Before the Royal Variety Show, 4 November 1963.

Paul McCartney

PYX

THE BEATLES

Dezo Hoffmann

52

Dezo Hoffmann renewed his friendship with the Beatles when the boys took part in the BBC's 'Swinging Sound, '63' concert at the Royal Albert Hall in London on May 9, 1963. When the group returned to London a week later for a television appearance, Hoffmann had lunch with them at the Budapest Restaurant in Greek Street, snapped pictures of them buying bananas in Berwick Street Market, took them to the Westminster Photographic Shop to see the home movies they had shot of each other months before in Liverpool, and strolled with them through Rupert Court to his studio on the second and third floors of a house in Wardour Street, Soho.

In the studio, Hoffmann took a new series of pictures, with the boys wearing their famous grey suits and seated on barstools, gathered around a chair, standing, sitting, pointing. Brian Epstein titled the series 'Nempics' and numbered them 'Nempose No. 1' and so on. Thousands of prints were distributed to fan clubs and press agencies around the world by the British Beatles Fan Club in Monmouth Street, and the poses eventually became the best-known publicity shots of the Beatles ever made. They appeared on magazine covers, posters, T-shirts, curtains, nylon stockings . . . the list is practically endless. When the *Hello*

Goodbye promotional film was made on November 10, 1967, John, Paul, George and Ringo referred fondly back to these Hoffmann photos by donning their old grey suits and reassuming the appropriate poses, to recreate the image which had swept the world only a few years earlier.

Hoffmann himself remembers an experiment he performed in Paris, when the pictures were still relatively new: 'We had five different photos, one of the group and one of each Beatle. When we went to Paris in January 1964, we had reprints made and we offered them for sale in the lobby of the Olympia Theatre. I decided to conduct a sort of 'Gallup Poll', and see which of the five pictures sold the best. So I asked the saleswoman to set out exactly 100 copies of each picture, and after the first performance I went out to the lobby and counted up how many of each shot

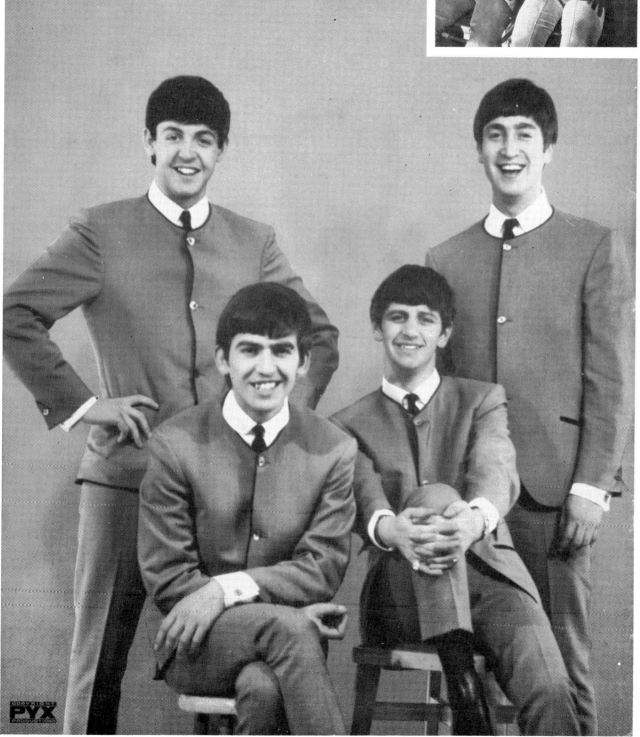

'Pyx Productions' was established by Dezo Hoffmann.

yeah! yeah! yeah!

were left. She'd sold no pictures of Paul, one of John, two of George, four of Ringo and about fourteen of the group together. I didn't know what to do – this was crazy! But the audience was full of boys, and I thought maybe they're less interested in pictures than girls are. The next day I did the whole thing again, and this time they sold two pictures of John, two of George,

five of Paul, 20 of the group and 40 of Ringo. The third day, only a few pictures of John and Paul were sold, but the shots of Ringo and the group sold out completely. It was clear that the French went for Ringo in a big way, with his long nose and his working-class image. The other boys were all jealous, because like an idiot I told them.'

Hoffmann's photographs of the Beatles, taken between September 1962 and spring 1963, were collected in a book titled *The Beatles*, with text by Patrick Maugham and published by the photographer's own Pyx Productions Ltd. The volume sold 100,000 copies in England, and an American edition of a million copies (arranged by New York disc jockey Murray Kaufman during the group's first visit to New York) sold out within three weeks of publication.

In the film *A Hard Day's Night*,

Yeah! YEAH! YEAH!

Paul's grandfather (played by Wilfrid Brambell) tries to pick up some extra income by forging the Beatles' signatures on publicity photos and selling them as genuinely-autographed pictures. In real life, the boys' signatures were either printed directly onto the photos or signed by road manager Neil Aspinall – when the

Beatles occasionally autographed photos themselves, they had to be careful that their real signatures were not too different from Aspinall's forgeries!

After accompanying the Beatles to Paris and America, Dezo Hoffmann began seeing less of the

Beatles

group, because, as he says, 'They got into drugs'. However, as early as December 1963, Paul McCartney said of him, 'He's all right for a pop photographer I suppose, but at the beginning of the year we thought Hoffmann was the greatest photographer in the world.' This suggests that the Beatles themselves were already looking for someone with a more adventurous style, long before they began to experiment with drugs.

Today, Dezo Hoffmann is in his middle seventies and still active as a publicity photographer, with a studio not far from the building in which he photographed the Beatles in 1963. He has taken pictures of the Rolling Stones, Jimi Hendrix, Rod Stewart, Eric Clapton, David Bowie, Cliff Richard, Manfred Mann and many, many other top artists.

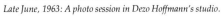
Late June, 1963: A photo session in Dezo Hoffmann's studio.

60

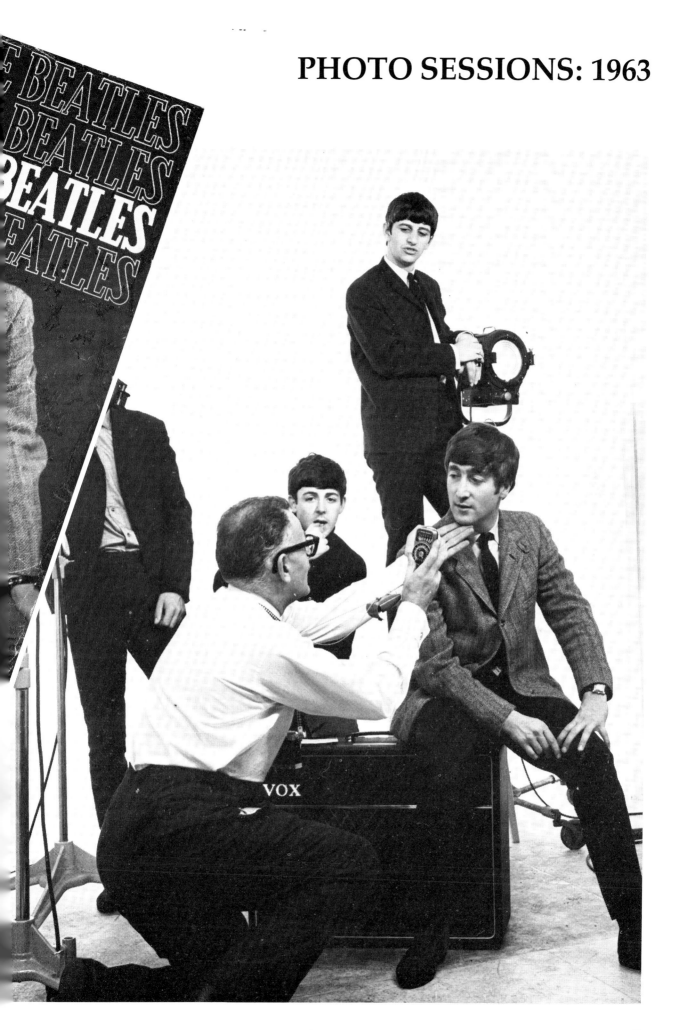

From July 22–27, 1963, the Beatles performed nightly at the Odeon Theatre in the west country resort of Weston-super-Mare. Dezo Hoffmann came down from London to photograph the boys on the roof of their hotel and sunbathing on its terrace. He also had them pose on the beach in Victorian bathing costumes which he'd brought along for them to wear: playing leap-frog, flying kites, standing on a car, riding a donkey. . . .

The rooftop pictures were later used in an advertising campaign for Ty-Phoo tea, and also turned up as part of a series of Beatle bubblegum cards. True Beatle maniacs were interested in *every thing* to do with the group, no matter how trivial.

WITH THE BEATLES

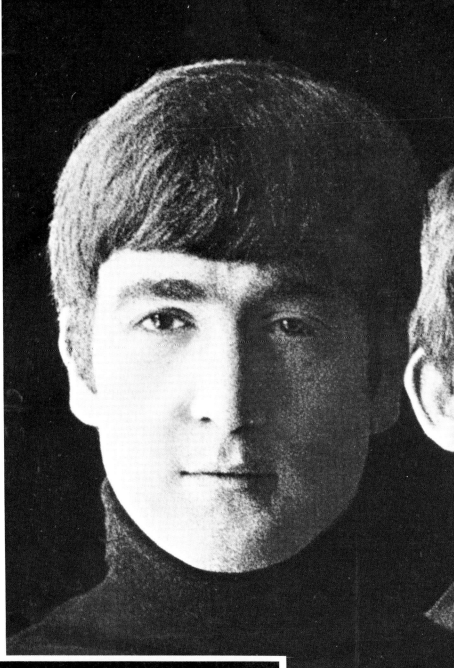

The second Beatle LP was released in the autumn of 1963. Its cover photo was to become world-famous: John, Paul, George and Ringo looked like French intellectuals in their black turtlenecks, shot against a black background and lit from the side in the popular Richard Avedon style.

But in 1963 the Beatles were not yet famous enough to be photographed by the great Avedon himself. The *With the Beatles* cover assignment went instead to Robert Freeman, an important London fashion photographer and a friend of John and Cynthia Lennon who had moved to a flat above Freeman's in Emperor's Gate, Kensington, at around the same time.

The picture which resulted was so successful that Freeman was immediately named 'Special Beatles Photographer'. In that capacity he joined the group on their whistle-stop tour of America and shot hundreds of pictures of them in New York's Central Park, in Carnegie Hall, in Washington, D.C., on Miami Beach, and with Cassius Clay.

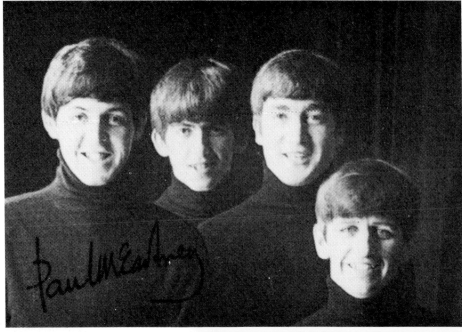

1964

January 1–11, 1964	'The Beatles' Christmas Show' continues filling the 3000-seat Finsbury Park Astoria Theatre twice nightly. By the end of its run, over 100,000 people have seen the show.
January 1, 1964	In America, a $50,000 campaign to promote the Beatles is launched by Capitol Records.
January 3, 1964	'The Jack Paar Show' (NBC–TV) includes scenes from the Beatles' November 16, 1963 performance at the Winter Gardens in Bournemouth. This is the group's first appearance on American television.
January 4, 1964	*I Want To Hold Your Hand* reaches the top of the Australian hit parade.
January 12, 1964	The Beatles make their second live appearance on ATV's 'Saturday Night at the London Palladium'.
January 13, 1964	In America, Capitol Records officially releases their first Beatles single: *I Want To Hold Your Hand* and *I Saw Her Standing There*.
January 14, 1964	John, Paul and George leave for a series of concerts in Paris; Ringo, held up by a thick Liverpool mist, misses the plane from London. Forty journalists are at Le Bourget Airport to meet the flight, but no fans show up.
January 15, 1964	Photo sessions along the Champs Elysées. Ringo arrives in Paris late in the afternoon, and a tryout concert is held at the Cyrano Theatre in Versailles in the evening.
January 16, 1964	The first of a series of performances at the Olympia Theatre in Paris, with Trini Lopez and Sylvie Vartan as the headliners and the Beatles appearing as a warm-up band. During the Beatles' set, the electricity goes out three times. The evening is filmed by a French television crew. There are empty seats in the theatre.
January 17, 1964	In their rooms at the George V Hotel in Paris, the band hears the news that, after selling half a million copies in eight days, *I Want To Hold Your Hand* has hit the top of the American hit parade.
January 18, 1964	*I Want To Hold Your Hand* enters the *Billboard* chart in America at No. 45. It will be up to No. 3 within a week. In the Pathé-Marconi recording studio in Paris, the Beatles record German versions of *She Loves You* and *I Want To Hold Your Hand*: *Sie Liebt Dich* and *Komm' Gib' Mir Deine Hand*. They also record the instrumental track for *You Can't Do That*, a new song.
January 20, 1964	In America, Capitol Records releases their first Beatle LP: *Meet The Beatles!*
January 23, 1964	The band's Olympia Theatre performances are attracting more and more attention: the house is sold out every night, and it is clear that the audiences are coming, not to see the headliners, but to see the Beatles.
January 29, 1964	The *Sie Liebt Dich/Komm' Gib' Mir Deine Hand* single is released in Germany.
January 31, 1964	Pete Best signs a contract with Decca Records, the label which turned down an opportunity to sign the Beatles a year earlier. Pete's band includes Tony Waddington on lead guitar, Tommy McQuirk on rhythm guitar and Wayne Bickerton on bass.
February 1, 1964	*I Want To Hold Your Hand* reaches No. 1 on the American *Billboard* chart.
February 5, 1964	The boys return from Paris.
February 7, 1964	The Beatles take off for their first concert tour of America. John, Paul, George, Ringo, Cynthia, Brian, Maureen Cleave (of the London *Evening Standard*), George Harrison (of the *Liverpool Echo*), Harry Benson (a photographer for the *Daily Express*) and producer Phil Spector fly first class, while Mal Evans, Neil Aspinall and photographers Dezo Hoffmann and Robert Freeman are in the plane's economy section. On arrival at New York's Kennedy Airport, the boys are greeted by 3000 fans and 100 journalists. They hold a press conference, then head for downtown Manhattan in four Cadillac limousines, with one Beatle and one reporter to a car. The Plaza Hotel has booked suites 1209 through 1216 for 'four English businessmen', but as hundreds of fans beleaguer the hotel the Plaza's management realize that the 'businessmen' they are expecting are, in fact, the Beatles. A hundred of New York's Finest are called in to protect the hotel from the swarm of fans; inside security is provided by the Burns Detective Agency. The release of four appropriate singles celebrates the group's first trip to

15 January

18 January

DIE BEATLES

29 January

7 February

America: the Swans' *The Boy With The Beatle Hair*, Sonny Curtis' *A Beatle I Want To Be*, the Liverpools' *Beatlemania In The USA* and the Buddies' *The Beatles*, an instrumental.

Meanwhile, in England, the *All My Loving* EP is released.

February 8, 1964	Murray Kaufman – who as Murray the K is a popular disc jockey on New York radio station WINS-AM and who has already begun referring to himself as the fifth Beatle – takes John, Paul and Ringo on a guided tour of New York. George, who has a sore throat, is visited by his sister Louise and treated by the Plaza's Dr Gordon: in spite of the trouble with his throat, he is interviewed via long-distance telephone by Brian Matthew for BBC Radio's 'Saturday Club'. The other three Beatles hold a press conference in Central Park, take a bus ride through Harlem and attend a camera rehearsal for 'The Ed Sullivan Show' at CBS-TV's 53rd Street studios, with Neil Aspinall standing in for George. (The 'arrow' set, designed by Bill Bohnert, is meant to emphasize the fact that the Beatles are *here*.) George rejoins John, Paul and Ringo in time for dinner at Club 21; afterwards, Paul goes onto the Playboy Club and George, John and Ringo return to the Plaza.

8 February

February 9, 1964 — The Beatles perform live on 'The Ed Sullivan Show' (CBS-TV) and record several additional numbers to be aired on the February 23 programme. There are 728 audience seats available in the studio, for which Sullivan has received some 50,000 requests for tickets; at home, 73 million viewers watch the Fab Four sing three numbers: *All My Loving*, *She Loves You* and *This Boy*. After the broadcast, Murray the K takes the Beatles to New York's Playboy Club, where Ringo dances the Twist.

10 February

February 10, 1964 — The day is given over to interviews, photo sessions and a press conference in the Plaza Hotel's Baroque Room, the evening to relaxation at two of New York's best-known nightspots, the Headliner and the Improvisation.

February 11, 1964 — New York's airports are snowed in so a special train brings the Beatles to Washington, D.C. Hundreds of fans and reporters throng every station the train passes. In America's capital city, the Beatles check into rooms on the seventh floor of the exclusive Shoreham Hotel. The 8600-seat Coliseum Theater is completely sold out for the band's evening performance; they appear on a revolving stage, and a camera crew from CBS-TV records two numbers: *Till There Was You* and *I Want To Hold Your Hand*. After the show, Ambassador David Ormsby-Gore (Lord Harlech) throws a reception in honour of the group at the British embassy: an over-enthusiastic guest snips off a lock of Ringo's hair, though, and the Beatles leave the party angrily. They decide to avoid this sort of official reception in the future.

11 February

February 12, 1964 — The Beatles return to New York by train. They are greeted at Penn Station by 10,000 fans, and 10,000 more await them outside the Plaza Hotel. In the evening they play two sold-out shows at Carnegie Hall, for which they earn $10,000 per show; promoter Sid Bernstein manages to squeeze an extra 50 seats onto the stage. Outside the theatre, scalpers have no trouble selling tickets for $100 each.

February 13, 1964 — The Beatles fly to Miami, Florida. Thousands of fans gather outside their hotel, the Deauville, in Miami Beach.

12 February

February 14, 1964 — The boys pose around the swimming pool of a large Florida villa, for a photo spread in *Life* magazine. Afterwards they go sailing on Bernard Castro's luxurious yacht (where John and Paul write *Can't Buy Me Love*), then dine at the home of police sergeant Buddy Bresner.

February 15, 1964 — Rehearsals for the Ed Sullivan show are held at the Deauville, and attended by 2600 fans.

14 February

February 16, 1964 — 'The Ed Sullivan Show', broadcast live from the Deauville Hotel, features the Beatles performing *I Saw Her Standing There*, *I Want To Hold Your Hand*, *From Me To You*, *Twist And Shout*, *Please Please Me* and *She Loves You*. The Deauville's auditorium seats 2600, but CBS-TV has mistakenly sold 3500 tickets; during the show, fights break out among the 900 ticketholders turned away at the door. After the broadcast, a party for the Beatles and 40 other guests is thrown by Maurice Lansberg, owner of the Deauville.

February 17, 1964 — A day off for waterskiing and fishing.

February 18, 1964 — The Beatles meet Cassius Clay at the boxer's training camp. In the evening, the band sees Elvis Presley's *Fun In Acapulco* at a drive-in and sends postcards of Miami to journalists in England.

February 19–21, 1964 — A mini-vacation: three days of sun and sand in Miami Beach.

February 22, 1964 — The Beatles return to England, and thousands of fans come out to greet them at London Airport.

February 23, 1964 — At the Teddington Studios, the group is filmed for an appearance on ABC-TV's 'Big Night Out', which will be broadcast on February 29 (it's a Leap Year).

14 February

February 25, 1964 — George, the last Beatle to turn 21, receives 60 postal sacks containing some 30,000 birthday cards and presents. He spends the day with the other Beatles, recording tracks for *A Hard Day's Night* and vocals for *Can't Buy Me Love* and *You Can't Do That*.

February 26, 1964 — In America, Vee-Jay Records releases an album titled *Jolly What! The Beatles And Frank Ifield On Stage*. Fans who buy the album expecting live material from the Beatles are disappointed: one side of the disc was recorded at a Frank Ifield concert, and the other side is a collection of previously-released Beatles singles.

23 February

67

26 February

13 March

March

23 March

April

18 April

27 April

Technically speaking, the album's title is accurate (it *does* contain songs by the Beatles, and it *does* contain songs by Frank Ifield on stage), but it is clearly an exploitative cash-in on the popularity of the Beatles.

February 28, 1964	In England, a single titled *World Without Love* is released, performed by Peter and Gordon. Peter is Peter Asher, Jane's brother, and the song is a Lennon/McCartney composition. Gordon is Gordon Waller, who met Peter Asher at boarding school in 1959. Polydor puts out a single titled *Cry For A Shadow*, a Beatles instrumental, with *Why* on the flip side. The numbers were recorded in Germany in 1961 during a session where Tony Sheridan sang and the Beatles served as his backing band. Now, of course, they are credited as being by 'The Beatles With Tony Sheridan'. *Cry For A Shadow* is the only song John and George ever wrote together.
February 29, 1964	On ABC-TV, the Beatles perform in short skits on 'Big Night Out', while Brian is again a member of BBC-TV's 'Juke Box Jury'.
March 2, 1964	Filming begins on the first Beatles movie, *A Hard Day's Night*, titled accidentally by Ringo. The picture is directed by Richard Lester and produced by Walter Shenson on a shoestring budget. The first week's shooting takes place on a train riding back and forth between Paddington and Minehead stations: in total, 2500 miles of railway track are covered. During the course of the filming, George meets Patti Boyd, who is playing the part of a schoolgirl in the film, having worked with Dick Lester on Smith's Crisps TV commercials in the early sixties.
March 13, 1964	Filming for *A Hard Day's Night* at London's Gatwick Airport.
March 20, 1964	The *Can't Buy Me Love* single is released; on the flip side, *You Can't Do That*, George plays a twelve-string guitar for the first time. To promote the new single, the Beatles tape an appearance for the April 27 edition of Rediffusion-TV's 'Ready, Steady, Go!'
March 23, 1964	John's first book, *In His Own Write*, is issued by British publisher Jonathan Cape; the title was suggested by Paul. In its first year in print the book will sell 400,000 copies in England and America.
March 25, 1964	Taping session for an appearance on BBC-TV's 'Top of the Pops'.
March 30, 1964	Beginning of a week-long series of concerts at the Empire Theatre in Liverpool. BBC-TV broadcasts a documentary about Brian Epstein in 'Panorama'. Pete Best appears in 'I've Got A Secret' on American television.
March 31, 1964	The Beatles again make musical history: in America, the top five singles in this week's *Billboard* 'Hot 100' are *Can't Buy Me Love*, *Twist and Shout*, *She Loves You*, *I Want To Hold Your Hand* and *Please Please Me*, with seven more Beatle singles occupying positions 16, 44, 49, 68, 78, 84 and 88!
April 2, 1964	Derek Taylor, formerly a reporter for the *Daily Express* newspaper, goes to work for NEMS as Brian's personal assistant.
April 4, 1964	This week's edition of the BBC Light Programme's 'Saturday Club' includes the Beatles singing *I Got A Woman*, *Sure To Fall* (In Love With You).
April 10, 1964	In America, *The Beatles' Second Album* is released.
April 12, 1964	Scenes for *A Hard Day's Night* are filmed at the Marylebone Station in London.
April 16, 1964	The group is in the studio to record the title song for *A Hard Day's Night*. While there, they are visited and interviewed by Ed Sullivan.
April 18, 1964	Live appearance on ATV's 'Morecambe and Wise Show'.
April 23, 1964	Foyle's, a London bookshop, holds its annual Christina Foyle Literary Luncheon at the Dorchester Hotel and presents an award to John for *In His Own Write*. John's acceptance speech, in full, is: 'Thank you very much; you've got a lucky face.'
April 24, 1964	The filming of *A Hard Day's Night* is completed.
April 26, 1964	An ATV camera crew films the Beatles' performance at the *New Musical Express'* poll winners' concert, held as usual at the Empire Pool in Wembley.
April 27–28, 1964	Taping sessions for Rediffusion-TV's 'Around the Beatles', with guest stars Millie, Cilla Black, Long John Baldry and P. J. Proby, and presented by Murray the K. Jack Good produces the programme. In an unusual version of *Shout*, each Beatle takes a turn as lead vocalist.
April 29, 1964	Performance in Edinburgh, Scotland.
April 30, 1964	Performance at the Odeon Theatre, Glasgow, Scotland.
May 6, 1964	'Around the Beatles' is broadcast by Rediffusion-TV.
May 8, 1964	The Strangers release a single titled *One And One Is Two*, a Lennon/McCartney composition.
May 10, 1964	Radio Luxembourg broadcasts the first segment of a Beatle documentary titled 'This Is Their Life'.
May 10–11, 1964	In the studio to record *You Like Me Too Much*, *Bad Boy*, *Dizzy Miss Lizzy* and *Tell Me What You See*.
May 12, 1964	In two groups, the Beatles and their ladies leave for three-week vacations: Paul, Jane, Ringo and Maureen head for the Virgin Islands via Paris, Lisbon and San Juan, while John, Cynthia, George and Patti are off to Papeete and Polynesia via

	Amsterdam, Vancouver and Honolulu. Aboard a yacht called 'Happy Days' in the Virgin Islands, Paul will write *Things We Said Today* and *Always, And Only*.
May 15, 1964	*Love Me Do*, which peaked at number seventeen in the British charts, reaches the number one spot in America.
May 17, 1964	The second segment of 'This Is Their Life' is broadcast on Radio Luxembourg.
May 18, 1964	BBC Radio broadcasts a special Whit Monday show featuring the Beatles, once more using the title, 'From Us To You'.
May 24, 1964	In America, 'The Ed Sullivan Show' features a previously-recorded clip of the Beatles singing *You Can't Do That*.
May 29, 1964	Polydor rereleases an old Beatle cover of *Ain't She Sweet*, with *If You Love Me, Baby* on the flip side.
May 31, 1964	Back from vacation, the Beatles do two shows titled 'Pops Alive!' at the Prince of Wales Theatre in London.
June 1–3, 1964	At the Olympic Studios in Barnes, the boys record several numbers for Side Two of the upcoming *A Hard Day's Night* LP: *Anytime At All*, *Things We Said Today*, *When I Get Home* and *I'll Be Back*.
June 3, 1964	In the studio in Barnes, Ringo suddenly collapses. He is admitted to a hospital and diagnosed as suffering from exhaustion.
June 4, 1964	Jimmy Nicol replaces Ringo on drums as the band begins a month-long international tour. The first stop is Denmark, where 6000 fans greet them at the airport outside Copenhagen. They stay at the Royal Hotel, across from Tivoli Gardens, and do two sold-out performances at the 4400-seat KB Hall.
June 5, 1964	John, Paul, George and Jimmy fly to Schiphol Airport in the Netherlands, where 3000 fans and an army of reporters await them. After a press conference, they travel to Treslong in Hillegom for a television taping. In England, the Applejacks release a single title *Like Dreamers Do*, a Lennon/McCartney composition.
June 6, 1964	The day begins with a boat trip through the Amsterdam canals. Tens of thousands of fans line the route; many of them jump into the water and try to swim up to the tour boat, but are held back by the city's water police. The enthusiastic crowds cause lengthy delays, and the Beatles wind up arriving two hours late for their concerts at the auction hall in Blokker, 'Op Hoop van Zegen'. The hall is only half-full for the afternoon show, which was added to the schedule by Radio Veronica, a Dutch pirate station, at the very last minute.
June 7, 1964	The group flies to London and is joined by Cynthia and John's Aunt Mimi for a connecting flight to Hong Kong, where they play two concerts at the Princess Theatre. Although the local promoter charges double the normal prices for events at the Princess, both shows are completely sold out.
June 8, 1964	In England, Rediffusion-TV reruns 'Around the Beatles'.
June 9, 1964	In spite of a heavy downpour, 2000 fans gather at the airport outside Sydney, New South Wales, to welcome the Beatles to Australia. In Sydney, the boys check into the Sheraton Hotel and do two sold-out shows. In America, an interview album titled *American Tour with Ed Rudy* is released.
June 11, 1964	Ringo is discharged from hospital.
June 12, 1964	300,000 fans await the Beatles' arrival at the airport in Adelaide, South Australia: the largest welcoming committee the band has ever had. In the evening, a performance at the Centennial Hall.
June 13, 1964	Tonight's performance in Adelaide is the end of the tour for substitute drummer Jimmy Nicol, who returns to England and his regular spot as a member of Georgie Fame and the Blue Flames.
June 14, 1964	John, Paul and George leave for Melbourne, Victoria, Australia.
June 15–17, 1964	With Ringo back behind the drums, the reunited Beatles give three performances at the Festival Hall, Melbourne.
June 18, 1964	Performance in Sydney. The *Daily Mirror*, an Australian newspaper, throws a party to celebrate Paul's 22nd birthday.
June 19, 1964	Performance in Sydney. In England, the *Long Tall Sally* EP is released.
June 20, 1964	Performance in Sydney. Polydor releases an album titled *The Beatles' First*, containing songs recorded in 1961 with Tony Sheridan.
June 21, 1964	Departure by plane for New Zealand.
June 22–27, 1964	Performances in Christchurch, Dunedin and Auckland.
June 27, 1964	After their last performance in Christchurch, the Beatles fly back to Australia for a brief vacation.
June 29, 1964	A performance in Brisbane, Queensland concludes the international tour. In America, the soundtrack of *A Hard Day's Night* is released. It features songs by the Beatles and additional music by George Martin.
July 2, 1964	A triumphant return to England, with more than 12,000 fans gathered to greet the

5 June

9 June

18 June

69

22 June

2 July

6 July

8 July

SOMETHING NEW
THE BEATLES

20 July

	band at Heathrow Airport. George is charged £30 import duty on the Pentax camera he bought in Hong Kong.
July 3, 1964	Decca Records releases a single by the Pete Best Four: *I'm Gonna Knock On Your Door* and *Why Did I Fall In Love With You*.
July 5, 1964	As a present for his father, Paul spends £1200 on a racehorse called Drake's Drum.
July 6, 1964	Thousands of fans disrupt London traffic in Piccadilly Circus, where *A Hard Day's Night* is having its Royal Premiere.
July 7, 1964	Ringo, the oldest Beatle, turns 24. He receives a pair of diamond cufflinks from Brian and, after a television taping session with John, Paul and George, celebrates quietly at home with his parents.
July 8, 1964	Two new Beatle records are released: a single (*A Hard Day's Night/Things We Said Today*) and an LP (*A Hard Day's Night*). In BBC-TV's 'Top of the Pops', the Beatles sing *A Hard Day's Night*.
July 9, 1964	John buys a house in Weybridge for £20,000.
July 10, 1964	The Beatles fly to Liverpool for the 'northern' premiere of *A Hard Day's Night*. There are thousands of fans at the airport and more than 100,000 lining the route to City Hall, where they are welcomed by the Mayor of Liverpool and officially received by the City Council. An album titled *Off The Beatle Track* is released: it consists of instrumental versions of Beatle songs, performed by George Martin and his orchestra.
July 11, 1964	The boys prerecord an appearance on ABC-TV's 'Thank Your Lucky Stars'.
July 12, 1964	Performance at the Hippodrome Theatre in Brighton, with the Fourmost and Jimmy Nicol. Returning from the concert in his Jaguar, George is involved in an accident and receives minor injuries.
July 14, 1964	The Beatles record seven songs to be broadcast on 'Top Gear' two days later.
July 15, 1964	ATV broadcasts a documentary titled 'The Road to Beatlemania'.
July 16, 1964	The Beatles are heard on 'Top Gear', in a programme recorded two days earlier and presented by Brian Matthew.
July 17, 1964	George buys a house in Esher, Surrey, for £20,000. There are rumours that Frank Sinatra, Sammy Davis, Dean Martin and Bing Crosby, calling themselves 'the Bumbles', have made a record parodying the Beatles. The disc, however, is never released.
July 18, 1964	Billy J. Kramer and the Dakotas release their new single. It is again a Lennon/McCartney composition: *From a Window*.
July 19, 1964	Performance at the ABC Theatre, Blackpool. Part of the show is filmed by ABC-TV for later broadcast on 'Big Night Out'.
July 20, 1964	In America, Capitol Records releases the *Something New* album.
July 23, 1964	The Beatles appear as waiters in the 'Night of 100 Stars' charity show at the Palladium Theatre in London.
July 25, 1964	George is a jury member on the BBC's 'Juke Box Jury', broadcast live from the White City Studios. Afterwards, next week's programme is taped: this time with Ringo sitting on the jury.
July 26, 1964	Performance at the Opera House, Blackpool.
July 28, 1964	At Stockholm Airport, 3000 fans welcome the Beatles to Sweden. That evening, John and Paul receive mild electrical shocks from their equipment during two performances at Johanneshov's Isstadium in Stockholm.
July 29, 1964	Two more performances at Johanneshov's Isstadium, Stockholm.
July 30, 1964	The group flies back to England.
July 31, 1964	Cilla Black releases her new single, *It's For You*, a Lennon/McCartney composition.
August 1, 1964	Ringo's previously-recorded appearance on 'Juke Box Jury' is broadcast by BBC-TV.
August 2, 1964	Performance at the Gaumont Theatre, Bournemouth.
August 3, 1964	The Beatles star in their own programme, 'From Us to You', on the BBC Light Programme, while, the same day, BBC-TV broadcasts a documentary titled 'Follow the Beatles', about the filming of *A Hard Day's Night*.
August 9, 1964	Performance at the Futurist Theatre, Scarborough.
August 11, 1964	In the studio for a recording session.
August 12, 1964	In America, *A Hard Day's Night* has simultaneous premieres in 500 theatres.
August 16, 1964	Performance at the Opera House, Blackpool.
August 18, 1964	The Beatles fly out of London Airport bound for a major concert tour of the United States. On their arrival in San Francisco, they are welcomed with a gigantic tickertape parade. The manager of the Hilton Hotel, where they will be staying, tries to keep the hordes of fans around the building well-behaved by promising to distribute, free, all of John, Paul, George and Ringo's used towels and sheets. Inside the Hilton, a woman guest is murdered by a burglar: members of the hotel

	staff hear screams around the time of the crime, but pay no attention, putting the noise down to over-excited Beatle fans.
August 19, 1964	The kick-off concert of the band's second American tour, held at the San Francisco Cow Palace, is attended by 17,000 fans. Warming up the crowd are Jackie DeShannon, the Righteous Brothers, the Bill Black Combo and the Exciters.
August 20, 1964	Performance at the Convention Hall, Las Vegas.
August 21, 1964	Performance at the Municipal Stadium, Seattle. Afterwards, the boys spend the night at the Edgewater Inn. When they hear that the motel's management plans to sell their used bed linen to fans, they destroy their sheets with a vile mixture of milk, orange juice and liquor.
August 22, 1964	Performance at the Empire Stadium in Vancouver, Canada.
August 23, 1964	Two performances at the Hollywood Bowl in Los Angeles, both taped by Capital Records. The shows are so completely sold out that not even Frank Sinatra and Dean Martin can get hold of tickets.
August 24, 1964	*Slow Down* is released as the new American Beatle single, with *Matchbox* on the flip side.
August 24–25, 1964	The group takes two days off.
August 26, 1964	Performance at the Red Rock Stadium, Denver.
August 27, 1964	Performance at the Cincinnati Gardens, Cincinnati. During a press conference at the city airport, the Beatles sing *Hello Dolly* to the assembled reporters.
August 28–29, 1964	Two performances at the Forest Hills Stadium, New York.
August 30, 1964	Performance at the Convention Hall, Atlantic City.
September 1, 1964	*The Beatles Monthly Book* makes its first appearance in America, where a double issue will be published every two months.
September 2, 1964	Performance at the Convention Hall, Philadelphia.
September 3, 1964	Performance at the State Fair Coliseum, Indianapolis.
September 4, 1964	Performance at the Auditorium, Milwaukee.
September 5, 1964	Performance at the International Amphitheater, Chicago.
September 6, 1964	Performance at the Olympic Stadium, Detroit.
September 7, 1964	Performance at the Maple Leaf Gardens, Toronto, Canada.
September 8–10, 1964	Three days of rest and relaxation.
September 11, 1964	George founds Harrisongs Ltd, a publishing company for his own songs. Performance at the Gator Bowl in Jacksonville, Alabama. The Beatles only consent to play this date after the promoters agree to admit non-whites to the show. Meanwhile, a new Peter and Gordon single is released in England. It is titled *I Don't Want To See You Again*, and is a Lennon/McCartney composition.
September 12, 1964	Performance at the Boston Gardens, Boston.
September 13, 1964	Performance at the Civil Center, Baltimore.
September 14, 1964	Performance at the Civic Arena, Pittsburgh.
September 15, 1964	Performance at the Public Auditorium, Cleveland. During the show, over-enthusiastic fans storm the stage and police officers bring events to a halt in order to remove them. After 15 minutes, the performance resumes.
September 16, 1964	Performance at the City Park Stadium, New Orleans.
September 17, 1964	This was originally scheduled as a day of rest after six days of performances and travel, but during the course of the tour Charles O. Finley has persuaded Brian and the band to accept $150,000 for making it seven in a row with a performance at the Municipal Stadium in Kansas City, Missouri.
September 18, 1964	Tonight's performance at the Memorial Coliseum in Dallas is the 25th and last of the tour. In one month, the Beatles have travelled some 15,000 miles back and forth across America.
September 19, 1964	Brian turns 30, and he and the Beatles enjoy a well-earned rest on a ranch in the Ozark Hills of Missouri. Brian's birthday present from the band is an antique telephone.
September 20, 1964	One final performance in America: a charity concert at New York's Forest Hills Stadium which raises $25,000 for the United Cerebral Palsy Association. Derek Taylor, who has found it impossible to work with Brian, quits his job at NEMS.
September 21, 1964	The Beatles fly back to England.
September 22, 1964	From now till October 8, the boys are in the recording studio almost every day to work on their new album, *Beatles For Sale*. Two of the songs recorded during these sessions, *You'll Know What To Do* and *Always And Only*, are not used on the album.
October 4, 1964	The Souvenir Press publishes Brian's autobiographical *A Cellarful of Noise*, written in collaboration with Derek Taylor. Brian has paid Derek £600 plus 2½% of all

21 August

15 September

4 October

9 October

9 October

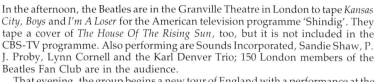

23 November

	royalties for his assistance, but later, when the book turns out to be surprisingly successful, he gives Derek a £600 bonus. Ringo receives his first driver's licence and buys a Facel Vega sports car.
October 9, 1964	In the afternoon, the Beatles are in the Granville Theatre in London to tape *Kansas City*, *Boys* and *I'm A Loser* for the American television programme 'Shindig'. They tape a cover of *The House Of The Rising Sun*, too, but it is not included in the CBS-TV programme. Also performing are Sounds Incorporated, Sandie Shaw, P. J. Proby, Lynn Cornell and the Karl Denver Trio; 150 London members of the Beatles Fan Club are in the audience. That evening, the group begins a new tour of England with a performance at the Gaumont Theatre in Bradford. Mary Wells, Tommy Quickly, Sounds Incorporated, Michael Haslam, the Remo Four, the Rustics and Bob Bain are also on the bill. A fan throws a life-size teddy bear up onto the stage: it is a birthday present for John, who is 24 today.
October 10, 1964	Performance at the De Montfort Hall, Leicester.
October 11, 1964	Performance at the Odeon Theatre, Birmingham.
October 13, 1964	Performance at the ABC Theatre, Wigan.
October 14, 1964	Performance at the Ardwick Apollo in Ardwick, a suburb of Manchester. A camera crew from ABC-TV films the show.
October 15, 1964	Performance at the Globe Theatre, Stockton.
October 16, 1964	An afternoon taping for Rediffusion-TV's 'Ready, Steady, Go!' and an evening performance at the ABC Theatre, Hull. Outside England, *If I Fell* and *Tell Me Why* are released as a single.
October 19, 1964	Performance at the ABC Theatre, Edinburgh.
October 20, 1964	Performance at the Caird Hall, Dundee.
October 21, 1964	Performance at the Odeon Theatre, Glasgow.
October 22, 1964	Performance at the Odeon Theatre, Leeds.
October 23, 1964	Performance at the Gaumont State Theatre, Kilburn.
October 24, 1964	Performance at the Granada Theatre, Walthamstow.
October 25, 1964	Performance at the Hippodrome Theatre, Brighton. The annual Ivor Novello Awards are announced, and five of them go to the Beatles.
October 26–27, 1964	In the studio to record a Christmas present for British fan club members: *Another Beatles Christmas Record*.
October 28, 1964	Performance at the ABC Theatre, Exeter.
October 29, 1964	Performance at the ABC Theatre, Plymouth.
October 30, 1964	Performance at the Gaumont Theatre, Bournemouth.
October 31, 1964	Performance at the Gaumont Theatre, Ipswich.
November 1, 1964	Performance at the Finsbury Park Astoria, London.
November 2, 1964	Performance at the Ritz, Belfast.
November 3, 1964	Two EPs are released: *A Hard Day's Night* and *A Hard Day's Night (No. 2)*.
November 4, 1964	Penguin Books publishes a collection of interviews with the Beatles, written by Michael Braun and titled *Love Me Do*. Ten years later, John will refer back to it as the best book ever written about the Beatles. That evening, a performance at the Ritz in Luton.
November 5, 1964	Performance at the Odeon Theatre, Nottingham.
November 6, 1964	Performance at the Gaumont Theatre, Southampton.
November 7, 1964	Performance at the Capitol Theatre, Cardiff.
November 8, 1964	Performance at the Empire Theatre, Liverpool.
November 9, 1964	Performance at the City Hall, Sheffield.
November 10, 1964	Interview with Brian Matthew on BBC-TV's 'Top of the Pops'; that evening, a performance at the Colston Hall in Bristol brings the band's month-long tour of England to a close.
November 13, 1964	Rory Storm and the Hurricanes, the group Ringo left to join the Beatles, release their first single. It is on the Parlophone label and the songs are titled *America* and *Since You Broke My Heart*.
November 17, 1964	Taping session at the Playhouse Theatre, Manchester, for the BBC Light Programme's 'Top Gear'.
November 21, 1964	Taping session for ABC-TV's 'Thank Your Lucky Stars'.
November 23, 1964	In America, Capitol Records releases an album of interviews: *The Beatles' Story*.
November 24, 1964	Paul's father, James McCartney, remarries. His bride is Angela Williams.
November 25, 1964	The Beatles tape a session for the Boxing Day edition of 'Saturday Club'.

November 26, 1964	'Top Gear', featuring the Beatles, is broadcast; previously recorded on November 17.
November 27, 1964	The eighth Beatle single, *I Feel Fine* and *She's A Woman* is released, and the songs make their television debut on Rediffusion-TV's 'Ready, Steady, Go!'
December 1, 1964	Ringo's tonsils are removed at the University College Hospital in London. The hospital's telephone lines are completely blocked by fans calling to ask about his condition; finally, a 24-hour Ringo-line is opened, which can be called for the latest progress report.
December 3, 1964	Broadcast of part one of some standard BBC Beatles footage to back *I Feel Fine* on BBC-TV's 'Top of the Pops'.
December 4, 1964	In time for the Christmas rush, a new LP hits the market: *Beatles For Sale*.
December 5, 1964	The British Beatles Fan Club announces that its membership has now reached 65,000.
December 9, 1964	Broadcast of part two of the Beatles film to back *I Feel Fine* on BBC-TV's 'Top of the Pops'.
December 10, 1964	Ringo, in the pink of health, is discharged from University College Hospital.
December 15, 1964	With nine shopping days left before Christmas, Capitol Records releases the *Beatles '65* LP in America.
December 18, 1964	George leaves England for a vacation in the Bahamas.
December 19, 1964	*Another Beatles Christmas Record*, the band's Christmas present for British members of their fan club, is released.
December 21–23, 1964	Rehearsals for 'Another Beatles' Christmas Show'.
December 24, 1964	'Another Beatles' Christmas Show' premieres at the Hammersmith Odeon Theatre in London, with Freddie and the Dreamers, the Mike Cotton Sound, Jimmy Saville, Sounds Incorporated, the Yardbirds, Elkie Brooks and Ray Fell on the programme. There will be two performances per day, every day except Sunday, through January 16, 1965.
December 26, 1964	As wax Beatles go on display at Madame Tussaud's, the real Beatles are guests in the BBC Radio Light Programme's 'Saturday Club'. Road manager Neil Aspinall receives a belated Christmas present from his four bosses: a Jaguar sports car.

4 December

15 December

19 December

BEATLES IN PARIS

After taking England by storm in 1963 – with a triumphant series of national TV appearances, a string of silver and gold records, a spot in the Royal Variety Show, a phenomenally successful Christmas show, and a movie in the works – the next step for the Beatles seemed clear: conquer the rest of the world.

A contract for a short tour of the United States had already been signed. American camera crews were filming the group's performances for US broadcast. In the first week of the year, *I Want To Hold Your Hand* hit the top of the singles charts in Australia; a week later it entered the American hit parade.

On the late afternoon of Tuesday, January 14, 1964 London was blanketed in mist. John, Paul, George, Brian, Mal Evans, publicity chief Brian Sommerville and several journalists waited nervously at London Airport. Would the fog lift long enough for their Comet 4B to take off? And where in the world was Ringo?

Ringo was still in Liverpool, himself delayed by the impenetrable mist. But in London it finally began to clear, and the drummerless Beatles lifted off for the City of Light.

A three-week stay in Paris had been planned, to be followed by the departure for America. The boys were to be part of a variety show featuring Sylvie Vartan and Trini Lopez at the Olympia Theatre, the most important music hall in France.

The Beatles were not yet very well known in that country, and no one knew what kind of a reception to expect. The short flight seemed endless. Around six, the plane touched down at Le Bourget Airport. A mob of photographers and journalists shouted questions in French, but there was not a fan to be seen.

The boys were driven into Paris, to the exclusive George V Hotel near the Champs Elysées, where Brian had reserved the most expensive rooms for the party.

John and Paul spent the evening in their suite, talking over the songs they were writing for their upcoming film.

After a late English breakfast, the boys left the George V at three in the afternoon to pose for pictures along the Champs Elysées. They had excellent cameras of their own

The Beatles in front of a poster showing pictures taken by Astrid Kirchherr back in 1962.

The Beatles

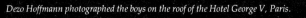

Dezo Hoffmann photographed the boys on the roof of the Hotel George V, Paris.

press.

That evening, the reunited Beatles held a try-out concert at the Cyrano Theatre in Versailles. The audience was very different from the sort of crowd they were used to: there were more boys than girls for one thing, and much less screaming. One youngster who jumped onto the stage and started dancing with John was removed by Mal Evans.

The next morning's newspapers featured photos of the group and a number of lengthy articles. Little was said about their music,

with them, and photographed each other at the usual tourist spots. Their presence occasioned an assortment of traffic jams and detours, and before things got too out of hand they returned to their hotel to await the arrival of Ringo, who landed at Le Bourget at 5 pm.

Brian had made an arrangement with BEA (British European Airways), whereby the boys and their entourage would be given three weeks' worth of free air travel back and forth between Paris and London, in exchange for publicity photographs of the Beatles holding up a sign bearing the letters TLES next to the BEA logo painted on the side of their aeroplane.

With that deal in operation, BEA helped make sure that there was another crowd of photographers stationed at Le Bourget on Ringo's

arrival, and the drive into Paris (in a British car driven by Stuart Turner and registered for the Monte Carlo Rally) was also well covered by the

Performance in Versailles: more boys than girls.

though: the emphasis was on their mod clothing, especially John's spectacles, leather cap and black jacket.

The first two performances at the Olympia Theatre took place that day, January 16. Neither show was sold out: the two o'clock matinee was attended mostly by young boys, while it was the upper elements of Parisian society who turned out for the evening concert (as well as Petula Clark, Johnny Halliday, Françoise Hardy, Richard Anthony, Brian Epstein and George Martin with his fiancée Judy).

The reviews in the morning papers were not promising: *Paris Libéré* passed over the Beatles' sound as nothing more than old-fashioned rock'n'roll; *l'Aurore* was more impressed by Trini Lopez. Only *France Soir* reacted positively, pointing out that no artists had ever been as loudly applauded at the Olympia as the Beatles were.

In the hotel, the boys received some better news: *I Want To Hold Your Hand* had leapt to the top of the American charts and was

The Beatles at the Cafe Boheme, photographed with salesgirl Mirabelle.

breaking sales records across the States. The celebration lasted until the following morning.

And in spite of the weak reviews, the French started flocking to the Olympia Theatre in greater and greater numbers. Soon every show was a sell-out – and it was clear that the crowds were coming to see the Beatles, not Trini Lopez and Sylvie Vartan. Music stores loaded their display windows with Beatles records, and giant posters around the city advertised the group's performances.

At a Pathé-Marconi recording studio, the instrumental tracks for You Can't Do That were laid down, with George Martin producing and Norman Smith as the sound engineer. The boys also recorded German-language versions of She Loves You and I Want To Hold Your Hand: the single was available in Germany eleven days later.

The Beatles' days in Paris followed a standard pattern: sleep in until the middle of the afternoon, meet with journalists, play two shows at the Olympia, go out for a late supper, then back to the George V to talk and write new songs until 5 am.

It was, all things considered, a monotonous life. And it was not even profitable: after three weeks in Paris, the Beatles' earnings amounted to barely enough to pay their enormous hotel bill!

79

THE BEATLES IN HOLLAND

The Beatles first visited Holland on August 17, 1960. They were just passing through on their way to West Germany to begin the first of six concert engagements in Hamburg, but were in the country long enough to have themselves photographed in front of an Arnhem war memorial bearing the inscription 'Their name liveth for evermore' and to steal a harmonica from a music shop in the same city.

The boys went through the Netherlands several more times while travelling back and forth between England and Hamburg, but their first performances in the land of Hans Brinker and the Silver Skates did not take place until 1964.

On June 4 of that year, they began an international concert tour which would eventually take them as far away as Hong Kong, Australia and New Zealand. Their first stop was Denmark, where they played two sell-out shows at the KB Hall in Copenhagen. The next day, June 5, an SAS Caravelle brought them from Scandinavia to the Lowlands, touching down at Amsterdam's Schiphol Airport at one o'clock on a brisk Friday afternoon.

As John, Paul, George and Jimmy Nicol (who was filling in on drums for an ailing Ringo) disembarked, some 4000 eager fans screamed a welcome from behind the airport's heavy iron fences. Hundreds of photographers and reporters stormed towards the lads, and angry fistfights broke out between the press, KLM personnel and the Koninklijke Marechaussee (National Guard). Police threw a protective cordon around the Beatles, who were meanwhile being greeted by four girls in typical Dutch folk costume and presented with the famous Volendam fishing caps. John was later to remark: 'That was the first time I ever saw the police fighting with photographers instead of fans. It's an interesting custom, probably typically Dutch.'

After a short but heavily-attended press conference in Schiphol's VIP lounge, four cars drove the boys to their hotel, the Doelen, situated beside the Amstel River in the heart of Amsterdam. The Doelenstraat had been fenced off to keep other traffic away, and mounted police were on guard. As they strolled into the hotel, a shower of ticker tape enveloped them and a horde of waiting fans chanted 'Beatles, Beatles, Beatles....'

They were received by Maup Caransa, owner of the Doelen, who brought them to their quarters: the luxurious Empire Suite. Outside the building, the fans moved across to the Kloveniersburgwal and the chorus of chanting began anew. One man sailed by in a small boat and screamed up at the group through a megaphone, but he was quickly removed by the police.

At about three o'clock, the boys left Amsterdam for Studio Treslong in Hillegom, where they were to rehearse for a television appearance scheduled for taping that evening. Most of the small town was fenced off and guarded by an 80-man police force, but to mislead the thousands of fans hoping for a glimpse of their idols, the cars transporting the Beatles drove in through the *un*protected side of Hillegom.

Work began at 4 pm, under the direction of Ben de Jong. Journalists and photographers were present as the rehearsals began, but impresario Dick van Gelder soon sent them away. Dutch singer Rudi Carrell was allowed to stay, and happily found himself sitting in briefly on drums.

Brian Epstein kept the press away even during the boys' dinner break. Only Beatlemaniac Trudy Benninck, a fifteen-year-old who had flown all the way from Bangkok just to see her heroes, was allowed behind the studio's double set of curtains for a long conversation with Paul.

The taping session began at 8 pm, with 500 youngsters in attendance. Host Herman Stok called for questions from the crowd, and television reporter Berend Boudewijn translated the questions into English and the Beatles' replies back into Dutch.

And then the group took to the stage. To everyone's surprise, they did not really sing: a pre-recorded tape was played, and the Beatles merely mouthed the words. Paul explained: 'Our sound has to be perfect. And that only happens in the recording studio; to be honest, I don't trust any other engineer anywhere in the world.'

Press conference in the VIP room, Schiphol Airport.

The presidents pass.

She Loves You and *All My Loving* received only lukewarm response, but the audience finally decided to make the best of it and began to dance. Cabaret star Wim Kan came in quietly after the programme had already begun, with strict instructions that he was not to be shown on camera: 'Just wonderful,' was his enthusiastic reaction, 'as wonderful as Christmas.'

As the boys mimed to *Roll Over Beethoven* and *Long Tall Sally*, the

Television director Ben de Jong with his stars.

dense crowd eventually blocked them off from the TV cameras. From time to time they even stopped 'singing' and 'playing', but the taped music rolled merrily on. 'Horrible,' commented impresario Lou van Rees.

The next morning, back in Amsterdam, the four lads ate a late breakfast at their hotel. At 11.30 they stepped abroad a tour boat with Trudy Benninck, Berend Boudewijn and his video camera and several other journalists, for a 90-minute ride through the city's canals organized by their Dutch record company. They laughed disparagingly at the mobs of buz-

Left: *Wim Kan in the TV studio.* Below: *the fans greet their heroes.*

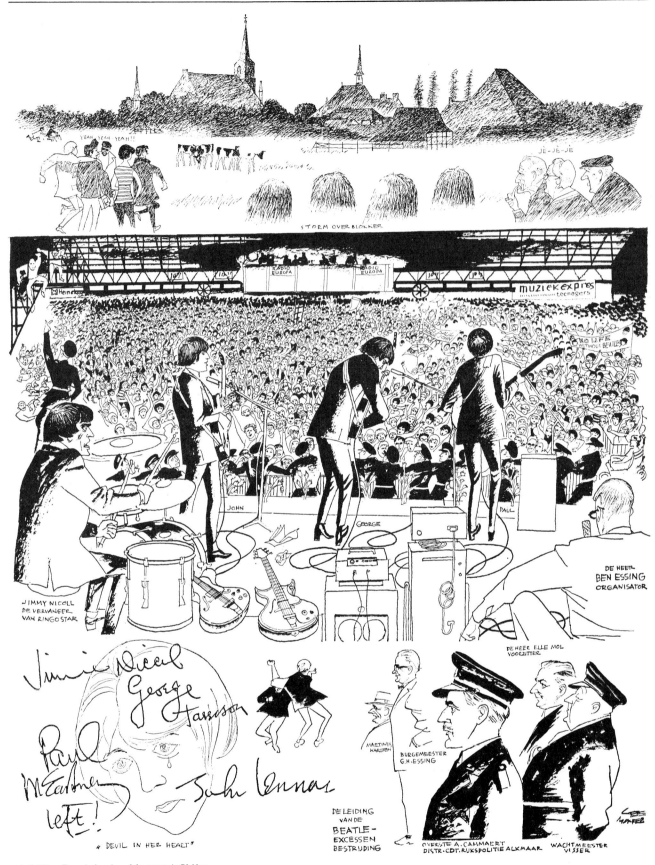

Artist Eppo Doeve's drawing of the events in Blokker.

zing teenagers lined along the route, many of whom wound up in the water. One boy fell or jumped in three times before he was finally able to reach the boat and shake hands with a couple of Beatles.

The boys were expected at the Blokker auction hall at three in the afternoon, to play a concert which had been added onto their schedule at the last moment when their evening show sold out. But by 3.30, they had not yet turned up. The numerous warm-up acts – the Toreros, the Hot Jumpers, the

Fancy Five, Jack and Bill, the Candy Kids, John Rasell and his Clan, 'Twist Queen' Wanda, Karin Kent, the Dominique Quintet, and, finally, popular Dutch singer Ciska Peters – stretched as much as possible. Finally the Beatles arrived. The hall was not even half-full, and John, Paul, George and Jimmy played for 25 minutes before only 2500 fans. Just before their final number, *Long Tall Sally*, Paul thanked the audience in Dutch for being there.

That evening, however, the auction hall was packed – 7500 strong. Two rows of police barricades kept the crowd away from the stage, and firemen, police and dogs were at the ready. Promoter Ben Essing had repeatedly to call for silence and order.

The Beatles played eight songs, then took off again for Amsterdam. For their two 25-minute perform-

Rescued by the police!

ances, they had earned 90,000 Dutch guilders. Wim Kan, who was in the audience for the evening show, was no longer enthusiastic: 'It was worse than the French Revolution,' he complained.

Afterwards, reporters asked Jimmy Nicol how he had felt. 'Overwhelmed,' he answered. 'I felt like a kid in the stands at an important football match, who all of a sudden gets asked to come out on the field and play.' Although he announced plans to form his own band and return to Holland, Jimmy's days with the Beatles were the highpoint and the finish of his career.

And what did the other Beatles think of the Netherlands? 'We can't say anything special about Holland,' John admitted, 'except we want to get some wooden shoes, but everyone knows that. Otherwise, Holland's about the same to us as every other country.'

'Yeah, wooden shoes,' Paul agreed. 'Otherwise we're just tired.'

The Beatles during their performance in the Blokker auction hall.

25 February 1964: George opens his birthday post, with Bettina Rose on his left and Anne Collingham on his right.

18 June 1963: Paul gets the bumps for his birthday in a London street. (photos: Dezo Hoffmann)

It's Your BIRTHDAY!

7 July 1964: Ringo's birthday.

Until very recently, a person's 21st birthday is a major event in his life: it was at 21 that he became, legally, an adult. (Nowadays eighteen is the more realistic age of legal adulthood.) An obvious symbol for the young man or woman first entering adulthood is the key, and it's also important to ensure that the new 21-year-old truly gets into the 'swing' of things by giving him the bumps. (How John passed *his* 21st birthday is not known, although he may well have been in Paris with Paul.)

As early as 1962, a Beatle fan with money to spend found more to spend it on than merely singles and albums. The standard array of posters, T-shirts and key chains came first, and were quickly followed up by Beatle pens, schoolbags, bubblegum cards, puzzles, plates, cups and hats. Next came Beatle wigs to wear under or instead of the Beatle hats, and as the boys' popularity continued to soar a wide range of new – and often very strange! – items appeared: Beatle dresses, Beatle nylons, Beatle sheets, Beatle towels, Beatle diaries, Beatle breadbins, Beatle talcum powder ... there were even inflatable Beatles!

In order to maintain control of this enormous merchandizing empire, Brian Epstein established a separate corporation called Stramsact Ltd. A Stramsact franchise was opened in every country where Beatle items were manufactured (the American branch was called Seltaeb, which is Beatles spelled backwards), and before the Beatle name or a picture of the group could be placed on any product, an appropriate royalty had to be agreed on. A percentage of all royalties collected in this manner was paid out to Stramsact's London headquarters, the idea being that John, Paul, George, Ringo and Brian would eventually share the wealth. For various complicated reasons, however, the Beatles themselves never did receive any of the profits from the commercialization of their name and image.

Today, these old Beatle objects have become sought-after collectors' items. A Beatle dress can be

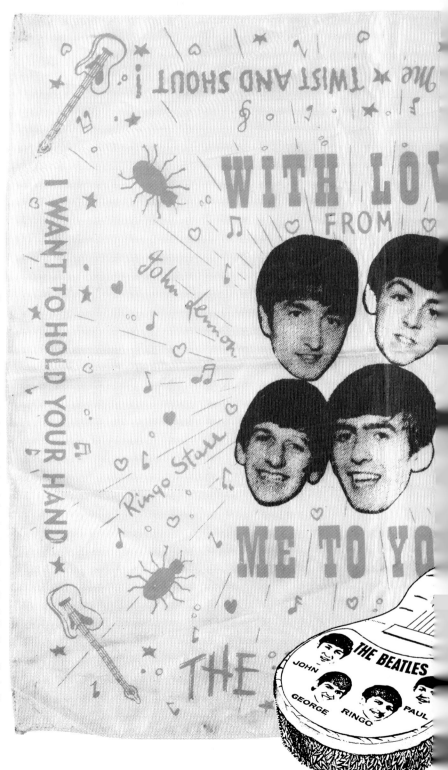

auctioned off for a small fortune at most Beatle conventions. The owner of a Beatle curtain is even better off, since a curtain is big enough to cut into pieces, which can be sold or traded to many collectors instead of only one.

The truly fanatic Beatlemaniac will buy just about anything with the name of the group tacked on to it, from Beatle coins to the wrappers from packages of Beatle bubblegum, from Beatle postcards to Beatle suspender belts.

Handkerchief from the collection of Lydia Pachter-Boeken.

PHOTO SESSIONS: 1964

Robert Freeman was the Beatles' official photographer in 1964 and 1965, and he
shot the pictures which appeared on the covers of the *Beatles for Sale*, *Beatles '65*,
Help! and *Rubber Soul* albums as well as the cover picture for the EP *Beatles For Sale
No. 2*. *Beatles '65* was an American album, released in December 1964, and the
photos on this page were taken during Freeman's camera session for its cover.

The *Rubber Soul* cover was probably Freeman's best shot of the Beatles: he
photographed the boys from below with a wide-angle lens, resulting in a strange
but vividly memorable image. Some fans felt that the Beatles looked 'like corpses'
on *Rubber Soul*, but Freeman shrugged such complaints off with the explanation
that he was only doing his best to come up with a new approach for every cover,

IN

with original solutions for what was becoming a tricky problem: how to keep presenting the Beatles in fresh ways to a public which had by then seen the group in almost every costume, post and setting imaginable.

(P.S. When Ringo married Maureen Cox in February 1965, it was Bob Freeman who took their wedding pictures!)

THE BEATLES

1965

11 February

Late February

Late March

The Early BEATLES

22 March

9 April

January 9, 1965	John reads several of his poems in the BBC's satirical radio programme 'Not Only . . . But Also'.
January 16, 1965	Two final performances of 'Another Beatles' Christmas Show' at the Hammersmith Odeon Theatre, London.
January 20, 1965	Broadcast of a clip from 'Shindig' on BBC-TV. 'Shindig' was an American ABC-TV show. The Beatles performed *Kansas City*, *I'm A Loser* and *Boys* which were pre-recorded at the Granville Theatre, Walham Road, Fulham, London.
January 27, 1965	George is a witness at the wedding of his brother Peter in the Maghull district of Liverpool; John and Cynthia Lennon and George and Judy Martin leave for a skiing vacation in St Moritz, and Paul heads for a holiday in Tunisia.
February 9, 1965	In the studio to record *Ticket To Ride* and *Yes It Is*, which will be released as a single in exactly two months.
February 10, 1965	A Cynthia Lennon fan club, complete with its own monthly magazine, is set up in England.
February 11, 1965	Ringo marries Maureen Cox at Caxton Hall in London. George is there, making it his second wedding in sixteen days, and John and Cynthia are back from Switzerland in time to be present, but Paul is still in Africa and misses the ceremony.
February 15, 1965	John receives his driver's licence, and the Beatles enter the studio for a week's recording of songs for their forthcoming second film.
February 18, 1965	Northern Songs Ltd, goes public. A thriving concern, its shares are immediately in great demand.
February 22, 1965	The Beatles fly to the Bahamas, where Richard Lester will direct them in their new film. While there, George will write a song called *I Need You* for Patti.
March 10. 1965	Back in England for additional shooting at the Twickenham Studios in London.
March 13, 1965	To Austria for more filming. Cast and crew stay at the Marietta Hotel in Obertauern.
March 20, 1965	The Beatles are interviewed by telephone from Austria on BBC Radio's 'Saturday Club'.
March 22, 1965	In America, Capitol Records releases the LP *The Early Beatles*.
April 1, 1965	Although it is in financial difficulties, Brian buys the Saville Theatre in London.
April 3, 1965	To promote the *Ticket To Ride* single, Paul and Ringo appear live in the ITV programme 'Thank Your Lucky Stars' and are interviewed by Brian Matthew. They also perform *Ticket to Ride* which is to be released the following Friday, April 9. The magazine *Mersey Beat* reports that Pete Best has given up his musical career.
April 4, 1965	John and Paul write the title song for their new film, *Help!*
April 6, 1965	Parlophone releases the EP *Beatles For Sale*.
April 9, 1965	Release date of the *Ticket To Ride/Yes It Is* single, the band's ninth.
April 11, 1965	Performance at the annual *New Musical Express* poll winners' concert at the Empire Pool in Wembley. This year, the Beatles are the number one group in the poll. On ABC-TV's 'The Eamonn Andrews Show', which is broadcast live, the Beatles appear in the panel and sing two songs.
April 13, 1965	In the studio to record *Help!*
April 14, 1965	Paul pays £40,000 for a large Victorian house at 7 Cavendish, in St John's Wood, London. He also sends the following telegram to the Campaign for Nuclear Disarmament: 'I agree with CND. They should ban all bombs. Bombs are no good to anyone. We might as well ban the bomb as be blown up by it.'
April 15, 1965	An appearance on BBC-TV's 'Top of the Pops' to promote the new single.
April 16, 1965	John and Paul are interviewed on Rediffusion-TV's 'Ready Steady Goes Live'.
April 18, 1965	ABC-TV broadcasts last week's *New Musical Express* poll winners' concert.
May 4, 1965	During a filming session on Salisbury Plain, someone breaks into John's car and steals his clothing.

May 12, 1965	Shooting on *Help!*, the second Beatle film, is completed.
May 26, 1965	Recording session for BBC radio special Whit Monday show takes place at No. 1 Studio, Piccadilly Theatre, London.
June 2, 1965	Paul and Jane leave for a brief vacation in Albufeira, Portugal.
June 4, 1965	The EP *Beatles for Sale (No. 2)* is released.
June 7, 1965	The Beatles have their own two-hour Whit Monday show entitled 'The Beatles (Invite You To Take A Ticket to Ride)' on BBC radio. The programme is produced by Keith Bateson, introduced by Denny Piercy and featured nine songs and lots of interviews. It was pre-recorded on May 26.
June 12, 1965	John, Paul, George and Ringo are officially notified that they have been named Members of the Order of the British Empire (MBE). John's comment: 'I thought you had to drive tanks and win wars to get one . . . When my envelope arrived marked OHMS, I thought I was being called up.' And Paul's: 'I'm going to wear it in the garden.'
June 13, 1965	Northern Songs announces that, to date, 1337 cover versions of Beatle songs have been recorded. In America, Capitol Records releases the LP *Beatles VI*.
June 14, 1965	To protest at the decoration of the Beatles, Paul Pearson, Hector Dupuis, Jack Berg, David Evan Rees and Cyril Hearns send their own MBEs back to the Queen.
June 17, 1965	Lieutenant-General Sir William Oliver states that, in his opinion, the Beatles have earned their MBEs. Lord Netherthorpe disagrees, though, and Colonel Frederick Wragg carries his own disapproval a step further, returning all twelve of his decorations to the Queen and announcing that he is cancelling a bequest of £11,000 to the Labour Party on the grounds that, as the party in power at the time, they had sanctioned the awards to the Beatles. 'Is he leaving us the money instead?' John quips in an interview, on hearing about the cancellation.
June 18, 1965	Stanley Ellis, Douglas Moffit and Richard Pape return their MBEs. John, a guest on BBC-TV's current affairs programme, 'Tonight', discusses his forthcoming second book, *A Spaniard In The Works*.
June 20, 1965	A short tour through southern Europe begins with a performance at the Palais des Sports in Paris. A French television crew from ORTF films the concert.
June 22, 1965	Performance at the Palais d'Hiver, Lyon, France.
June 24, 1965	*A Spaniard in the Works* is published by Jonathan Cape. Performance at the Velodromo Vigonelli, Milan, Italy.
June 26, 1965	Performance at the Palazzo degli Sport, Genoa, Italy.
June 27, 1965	Performance at the Adriana Hotel, Rome. EMI makes a stereo recording of the show.
June 28, 1965	In order to see Rome without being swamped by fans, the Beatles begin a sightseeing tour at 5 am. Afterwards, they travel to France and hold a press conference at the Hotel Negresco in Nice.
June 29, 1965	A free day, spent on the yacht of tour promoter Felix Marouani.
June 30, 1965	Performance at the Palais des Fêtes, Nice.
July 1, 1965	Performance in Jerez, Spain.
July 2, 1965	Performance at the Plaza de Toros Monumental, Madrid. In front of 10,000 fans, Paul introduces each number in Spanish.
July 3, 1965	A performance at the Plaza de Toros in Barcelona, before 18,000 fans, brings the two-week tour of southern Europe to a close. In its 'World of Books' programme, BBC Radio broadcasts an interview with John.
July 4, 1965	The usual swarm of fans turns out at London Airport to welcome the Beatles back to England.
July 17, 1965	Film clips from *Help!* are featured on the 200th episode of ABC-TV's 'Thank Your Lucky Stars'.
July 19, 1965	The tenth Beatle single, *Help!/I'm Down*, is released in the US.
July 23, 1965	The *Help!/I'm Down* single is released in the UK.
July 24, 1965	Ringo buys a £37,000 house in Weybridge.
July 29, 1965	*Help!* has its world premiere at the Pavilion Theatre in London, with Princess Margaret and Lord Snowdon in the audience. The evening's proceeds will be donated to charity.
August 1, 1965	To promote the new single, part of the Beatles' performance at the ABC Theatre in Blackpool is broadcast live in ABC-TV's 'Blackpool Night Out'. Just before the show begins, the boys receive a present from the Moody Blues: four baked fish. During the show, they use an organ for the first time on stage and sing *I Do Like to Be Beside the Seaside* and other numbers.

15 April

4 June

13 June

1 July

4 July

	August 6, 1965	The *Help!* LP is released. On the cover, John, Paul, George and Ringo are semaphore signalling a message to their fans: the photograph has been reverse-printed, though making the coded message unreadable. Holding the album up to a mirror allows anyone with a knowledge of semaphore to read the letters LPUS, or 'Help us!'
	August 7, 1965	John buys his Aunt Mimi a bungalow in Bournemouth.

6 August

August 8, 1965 — John and George are at the Richmond Jazz Festival to see the Animals in concert. The festival is filmed for American television by Brian's production company, Subafilms. Also performing on stage and in the movie are the Who, the Yardbirds, the Moody Blues, Georgie Fame, Manfred Mann, Spencer Davis and Rod Stewart.

August 12, 1965 — Brian takes out a £1 million insurance policy on each Beatle for the forthcoming American tour. He also signs a contract with the trio Paddy, Klaus and Gibson: Klaus is Klaus Voormann, and Gibson Kemp is married to Klaus' former fiancée and Stuart Sutcliffe's former girlfriend, Astrid Kirchherr.

August 13, 1965 — The Beatles fly to New York, where they check into the Warwick Hotel at 54th Street and Sixth Avenue and are visited by Bob Dylan. Coinciding with their return to the US, Capitol Records releases an American version of the *Help!* LP, on which Side One features songs from the movie performed by the band and Side Two consists of additional film music composed by George Martin and performed by the George Martin Orchestra.

13 August

August 14, 1965 — Rehearsals and taping for 'The Ed Sullivan Show' in CBS-TV's Studio 50. The set includes *I Feel Fine*, *I'm Down*, *Ticket To Ride*, *Yesterday*, *Act Naturally* and *Help!* During rehearsals, Paul accompanies himself on a Hammond organ and jokingly sings his original version of *Yesterday: Scrambled Eggs*. Also appearing in the show is Cilla Black.

14 August

August 15, 1965 — The Beatles travel from the roof of their hotel in downtown Manhattan to Shea Stadium on Long Island via helicopter; an armoured car from the Wells Fargo Bank carries them from their helicopter to the stage, where Ed Sullivan introduces them to 56,000 screaming fans (who have been warmed up by the King Curtis Band, Cannibal and the Headhunters, Brenda Holloway and Sounds Incorporated), and the band's third tour of America begins. In 30 minutes onstage, they play twelve songs.

August 16, 1965 — Today has been kept open on the schedule, just in case last night's open-air concert had been rained off. Since yesterday's weather was fine, today becomes a day off, and the Beatles are visited by journalists, disc jockeys, the Supremes, the Exciters, the Ronettes, Del Shannon and Bob Dylan. Meanwhile, Brian Epstein also pays a call: during a visit with attorney Nat Weiss, Brian establishes Nemperor Artists to represent American groups. Nemperor's first release will be the Cyrkle's *Red Rubber Ball*, an immediate million seller.

August 17, 1965 — The Beatles fly to Canada for two performances at the Maple Leaf Gardens in Toronto. Total audience for the pair of concerts: 35,000.

August 18, 1965 — The band again plays to 35,000 people, this time with a single performance at the Atlanta Stadium in Atlanta. After the show they fly to Houston, where hundreds of fans await them at the airport – at 2 am!

August 19, 1965 — Performance at the Sam Houston Coliseum, Houston.

August 20, 1965 — Two performances at Comiskey Park, Chicago.

August 21, 1965 — Performance at the Metropolitan Stadium, Minneapolis. The boys leave the stadium in a laundry truck and spend the night at the Lemington Motor Inn.

August 22, 1965 — Before their performance at the Portland Coliseum in Portland, Oregon, the Beatles are visited in their dressing room by Carl Wilson and Mike Love of the Beach Boys.

August 23, 1965 — While airborne, one engine of the plane carrying the Beatles to Los Angeles catches fire. Although there is no real danger, the press treats the incident as if the band has barely escaped a flaming death. In order to provide John, Paul, George and Ringo with at least a measure of privacy during their stay in California Brian has rented them a villa and kept its location completely secret. Within ten hours of the group's arrival in LA, however, the address – 2850 Benedict Canyon Drive – leaks out.

15 August

August 24, 1965 — Alan Livingstone of Capital Records throws a party for the group; the guest list includes Tony Bennett, Jane Fonda, Rock Hudson, Groucho Marx, Dean Martin, Hayley Mills and Jimmy Stewart. During the course of the evening, Paul and George sneak away to meet the Byrds in a Los Angeles recording studio.

August 25, 1965 — The Beatles spend their days off swimming and seeing films; during this period they experiment with LSD (along with several friends, including Roger McGuinn and Peter Fonda). Tripping, Fonda says at one point, 'I know what it's like to be dead,' a line which John will later use in the song *She Said, She Said*. Meanwhile, hundreds of letters and packages are delivered to their 'secret' address in Benedict Canyon.

17 August

August 27, 1965 — A meeting of the giants: the Beatles spend three hours with Elvis Presley at Presley's Bel-Air home. They pass the time playing and singing dozens of songs from the Presley repertoire.

18 August

August 28, 1965	The band travels by bus to San Diego and performs in front of 20,000 fans at Balboa Stadium. On the return trip the bus, a luxury model, breaks down.
August 29, 1965	At a press conference, the Beatles receive a gold record for the *Help!* LP. That evening, during their performance at the Hollywood Bowl in Los Angeles, one of the 18,000 fans in attendance gives birth to a healthy and happy baby. The show is recorded in stereo by EMI.
August 30, 1965	Another performance at the Hollywood Bowl, again recorded in stereo by EMI.
August 31, 1965	Two performances at the Cow Palace in San Francisco conclude the American tour.
September 1, 1965	Although the Beatles' flight gets into London at 4 am, hundreds of fans are waiting at the airport to greet them.
September 2, 1965	John and Cynthia leave for a vacation in the south of Europe.
September 7, 1965	Brian signs a managerial contract with the Moody Blues.
September 9, 1965	In America, 'The Ed Sullivan Show' features an appearance by the Beatles, pre-recorded on August 14.
September 13, 1965	In Queen Charlotte's Maternity Hospital, Hammersmith, London, Maureen Starkey gives birth to a son, Zak, at 8 am.
September 17, 1965	*That Means A Lot*, a Lennon/McCartney composition, is released as the new P. J. Proby single.
September 20, 1965	If at first you don't succeed. . . . In America, Cameo Records releases *Kansas City* and *Boys*, while Mr Maestro Records releases *I Can't Do Without You Now* and *Key To My Heart*. Both singles have been recorded by Pete Best, who 'retired' from his musical career less than six months earlier.
September 25, 1965	American children tuning in to Saturday morning television get to see the first episode of a weekly series of Beatle cartoons, designed by Peter Sander.
October 1, 1965	Not released as a single in England until a decade later, *Yesterday* today reaches the number one slot on America's hit parades.
October 3, 1965	The Beatles consider a script titled *A Kind of Loving*, which has been proposed for their next film project.
October 4, 1965	Paul is in Liverpool to visit old friends.
October 12, 1965	At the EMI studios in Abbey Road, London, the Beatles begin recording tracks for their new album, which will be called *Rubber Soul*. Recorded during the *Rubber Soul* sessions but not released on the album: *Maisy Jones*, *Baby Jane I'm Sorry*, *If You've Got Troubles*, *That Means A Lot* and *Rubber Soul*.
October 19, 1965	For the third consecutive year, the band records a Christmas single for their British fans.
October 26, 1965	In the Great Throne Room at Buckingham Palace, Queen Elizabeth II presents John, Paul, George and Ringo with their MBEs. A military band plays *Can't Buy Me Love* – as a march! – to celebrate the occasion. Before the ceremony, John smokes pot while sitting on the toilet in a palace bathroom. Afterwards the Beatles hold a press conference at the Saville Theatre and a private party at Les Ambassadeurs.
November 1965	The Beatles spend much of the month in the studio, recording material for the *Rubber Soul* album and the new single.
November 1, 1965	Granada-TV tapes a programme called 'The Music of Lennon and McCartney', which will be broadcast on December 17.
November 7, 1965	In America, Capitol Records releases *Boys* and *Kansas City* as a single (not to be confused with the Cameo Records single featuring the same songs performed by Pete Best and issued six weeks earlier). The disc is only on the market for a week: Brian quickly has it recalled, as he feels that it does not represent the group's current style.
November 25, 1965	Harrod's, the most famous department store in London, is closed to the public for two hours so that the Beatles can do their Christmas shopping. Included on the boys' shopping lists are gifts for the leaders of every officially-recognized Beatle fan club in the world.
December 1, 1965	The *Rubber Soul* LP is released.
December 2, 1965	An appearance on BBC-TV's 'Top of the Pops' to promote the new single and the new album.
December 3, 1965	The new single, *Day Tripper* and *We Can Work It Out*, is released. On the way to begin a new tour of the United Kingdom with a performance at the Odeon Theatre in Glasgow, George's £300 Gretsch 'Countryman' guitar falls out of the car and is run over and destroyed by a truck. Warming up the Glasgow audience for the Beatles are the Moody Blues, Steve Aldo, Beryl Marsden, the Koobas and the Paramounts.
December 4, 1965	Performance at the City Hall, Newcastle.
December 5, 1965	Release date of the EP *The Beatles' Million Sellers*. Performance at the Empire Theatre, Liverpool.

24 August

20 September

26 October

October/November

1 November

1 December

93

8 December

20 December

31 December

December 7, 1965	Producer Walter Shenson meets with the boys to discuss their next film, *A Kind Of Loving* (based on the book *A Talent for Loving*). The project will later be dropped.
	Performance at the Ardwick Apollo Theatre, Manchester.
December 8, 1965	Performance at the City Hall, Sheffield.
December 9, 1965	Performance at the Odeon Theatre, Birmingham.
December 10, 1965	Performance at the Hammersmith Odeon Theatre, London.
December 11, 1965	Performance at the Finsbury Park Astoria Theatre, London.
December 12, 1965	The tour closes with a performance at the Capitol Theatre in Cardiff, Wales.
December 17, 1965	Granada-TV broadcasts the previously-recorded programme, 'The Music of Lennon and McCartney'. In addition to the Beatles, the show also features appearances by Marianne Faithfull, Cilla Black, Peter and Gordon, Billy J. Kramer, Lulu, Peter Sellers and the George Martin Orchestra, all performing Lennon/McCartney compositions.
December 20, 1965	British fan club members receive their annual gift from the Beatles: *The Third Christmas Record*.
December 25, 1965	BBC Radio broadcasts a special Christmas edition of 'Saturday Club', starring the Beatles.
	George proposes to Patti Boyd.
December 30, 1965	*Paul's Christmas Album*, recorded earlier in the month and pressed as an edition of only four copies, is presented to John, George, Ringo and Jane.
	Brian signs a managerial contract with a cabaret act called the Scaffold. One member of the group is Paul's brother Michael, who uses the stage name Mike McGear. The Scaffold's first single will be a song titled *Two Days Monday*.
December 31, 1965	Piccadilly Records, a subsidiary of Pye Records, releases a single: *That's My Life* and *The Next Time You Feel Important*. The artist is Freddie Lennon, John's father!

The historic Shea Stadium

'Normal' Norman: The Beatles' Engineer

Nowadays, making a record involves an enormous amount of teamwork. But back when the Beatles first began their recording career, the process was considerably simpler and the complete studio staff consisted of a producer, George Martin, and an engineer, Norman Smith.

This legendary figure – quickly dubbed 'Normal' Norman by John Lennon – began his career at EMI in 1958. He was among those present on June 6, 1962, when the Beatles had their Parlophone audition. 'Their sound didn't impress me much,' he remembers. 'Actually, they were pretty bad. We even had to adjust their amplifiers for them! They played for about 20 minutes, songs like *Besame Mucho*. But afterwards they came into the control booth and we got to talking with them – and really, *that* was fascinating. I really think the Beatles got their recording contract because of that conversation. Let's be honest: they got that contract because of their enthusiasm, their presence, not because of their music. During that one conversation, we realized that they were something special.'

Normal Norman was also behind the controls when the group recorded their first single, *Love Me Do*, on September 11, 1962. 'That was some job. I don't think I'll be giving away any secrets when I say that Ringo never even played on that number. We had to replace him with a studio drummer – not because he wasn't good enough, but more because he hadn't been playing with the other boys for very long, and he just wasn't used to them yet. After the first take we

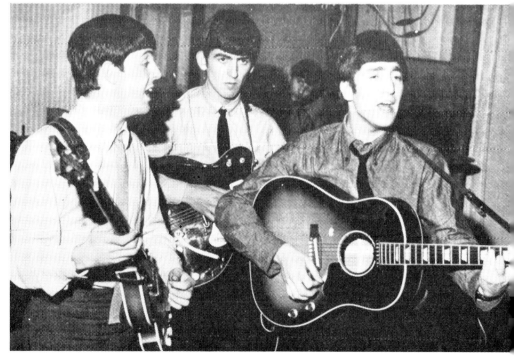

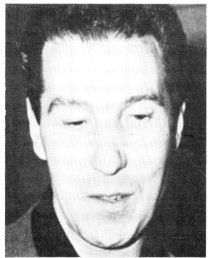

Norman Smith in 1965.

1 July 1963: Rehearsing She Loves You.

July 1963. Left: *Ringo sings* I Wanna Be Your Man; *Right: George sings* Don't Bother Me. *(photos: Norman Parkinson)*

9 February 1965: *John, Paul and George sing* Yes It Is.

listened to the tape. It was horrible. Their equipment wasn't good enough. We hooked Paul's guitar up to our own bass amplifier, and we had to tie John's amplifier together because it was rattling so loud.'

Smith made an important contribution to the development of the Beatles' 'Mersey' sound. 'I kept the sound relatively "dry",' he explains. 'I hated all that echo that everyone was using back then. And I placed the singers' microphones right there with the rest of the band, although singers were usually hidden away in a separate recording booth. I thought that was a bad idea, because you lost the live feel of the session.'

To the Beatlemaniacs, Norman Smith's anecdotes are fascinating: 'When we recorded their first album, there was something wrong with John's voice – he had a big jar of throat tablets standing next to him. But he made it through well enough. We did the whole LP in one day; that was normal then. At the end of the afternoon we took a break, and then we decided to record *Twist And Shout* as the final number. We got it in only one take. We *had* to get it in only one take, because John's voice was really going to pieces.'

Smith's engineering was considered so essential to the Beatles's recording work that, when the boys went into the Pathé-Marconi studios in Paris to record *Sie Liebt Dich*, *Komm, Gib' Mir Deine Hand* and the instrumental tracks for *You Can't Do That* in January of 1964, George Martin flew him to France for the session. 'We were a real team in those days,' Norman recalled fondly, 'the four boys, George Martin and I. It all started quietly enough, but when Beatlemania broke loose I used to wonder why the other residents of St John's Wood didn't just kick us out. There were *always* girls around, on the roof, in the halls, everywhere. Once I had to drag a girl out of the studio bathroom: when I opened the door she ran out screaming. I almost died of shock. I was just in time to grab her by the hair. Another time there was a girl following Paul through the halls. I threw her to the ground with a rugby tackle. I *had* to. We always had a lot of fun together. We recorded a lot of strange remarks,

13 April 1965: Paul and John during the recording of Help.

13 April 1966: Talking over Paperback Writer.

April 1965: Paul, Norman Smith and George Martin in the control booth.

and *Who Was It* – charted. A third change of persona was less successful: calling himself Curtiss Mason, he released a cover of *Monkberry Moon Delight*, a McCartney tune, and it went nowhere. Not one to press his luck, he chose to abandon his career as a singer.

1 February 1968: Singing Lady Madonna.

jokes, imitations and craziness. It's all still in the EMI archives; someday they'll use it as a piece of pop history.'

Smith left the Beatles team in 1965. George Martin had quit his job as full-time producer for EMI in order to start his own independent production company, Air (although he was to continue working for EMI on a freelance basis, especially on Beatle projects), and after the end of the *Rubber Soul* sessions he offered Normal Norman a position as producer. Smith accepted, even though it meant the end of his reign as the Beatles' engineer.

One final piece of pop history was written by Norman Smith himself; he made several singles under the name of Hurricane Smith, three of which – *Don't Let It Die, Oh Babe What Would You Say*

November 1965: In the studio during a Rubber Soul session.

Liverpool belongs to the working classes. Its inhabitants used to work mainly at the docks, living mainly in terraces of old unpretentious housing. All four Beatles grew up in this working-class milieu; when the rest of Britain first began to notice them, they were all still living in their simple family homes. But that aspect of the boys' lives – like so much else – was soon to change dramatically.

THE BEATLES' HOMES

JOHN

PAUL

GEORGE

RINGO

Freddie Lennon, John's father, was a sailor who was almost never home; eighteen months after his son's birth, he announced to his wife Julia that he was leaving England for good, never to return. Julia divorced him and, planning to remarry, farmed her son out to her sister, Mimi Smith. John grew up in Aunt Mimi's house at 251 Menlove Avenue, Woolton, Liverpool.

After their marriage in August 1962, John and Cynthia moved into Brian Epstein's flat in Falkner Street, but they soon found themselves back at Aunt Mimi's. The following autumn they left Liverpool for London, but Mimi stayed behind until, several years later, John bought her a bungalow in the south coast seaside resort of Bournemouth.

When Paul McCartney was born, his parents lived in Anfield, a suburb of Liverpool. His father, a cotton salesman who had been put to work in a machine shop during the Second World War, was a jazz musician in his spare time; after the war, he became an inspector for the city's sanitation department. The family moved several times during Paul's childhood: to Knowsley Estate in Wallasey, to Speke, to Ardwick, and finally (when Paul was thirteen) to 20 Forthlin Road, Allerton. When the Beatles began to build up a local following, Paul was still living in Forthlin Road with his father and his brother Michael; his mother, Mary, had died in 1956.

George Harrison's first home was 12 Arnold Grove, Wavertree, Liverpool, where he lived with his parents (his father was a bus driver), his brothers Peter and Harry, and his sister Louise. In 1949 the Harrisons moved to a modern council house at 25 Upton Green in Speke, and it was there that George spent most of his youth. Peter, Harry and Louise married and moved away (Louise to America), but George was still living with his parents when Love Me Do was released in 1962.

By 1963, George was able to buy the family a new home, at 174 Mackets Lane, where he had a bedroom and a sitting room for himself. Both rooms were soon overflowing with gifts and letters from ardent Beatle fans.

Ringo Starr was born Richard Starkey, and spent the first few years of his life at 9 Madryn Street in Dingle, a poor area of Liverpool. At the age of three, Ringo's parents divorced: the weekly rent of fifteen shillings was too high for Mrs Starkey alone, so she and her son moved to 10 Admiral Grove, where the rent was only ten shillings.

Mrs Starkey eventually remarried; her second husband was a housepainter named Harry Graves. The three of them were still living in Admiral Grove when the Beatles' fame began to spread.

Like the other Beatles, Ringo moved to London in 1963. And like the other Beatles, he was soon in a position to buy a larger house for his mother. But Mrs Graves chose to stay where she was, until finally, in 1965, she allowed Ringo to give her a bungalow in Gateacre Park, still in Liverpool (left).

Artist's impression of John's house in Weybridge, 'Kenwood'.

JOHN

PAUL

GEORGE

RINGO

As their popularity grew, the Beatles found it necessary to spend more and more time in London's recording studios, radio and television stations. And London was more than 200 miles from Liverpool. Brian Epstein was the first to make the move to the capital; he lived at 13, Chapel Street, Belgravia from 1963 to the time of his death. In the autumn of 1963, the boys followed their manager's example: John and Cynthia took a flat in Emperor's Gate, Kensington; Brian found a house for George and Ringo in King William's Mews, Knightsbridge; Paul moved into Jane Asher's parents' house in Wimpole Street. But the Beatles' London addresses quickly leaked out, and in order to protect themselves from the constant demands of their fans they began to look for more isolated and private residences outside the City. Dr Walter Strach, the group's accountant, was given the assignment of locating suitable quarters for them; because he lived in Esher, Surrey, which was within easy reach of central London, he began his search in that area. He came up with a house for George in Esher itself, and houses for John and Ringo in nearby Weybridge; Paul, more cosmopolitan than his fellow Beatles, decided to stay on in London.

John's house in Weybridge, outside London, was a Tudor-style villa called Kenwood, located on an exclusive private estate called St George's Hill, now the home of several international stars. The house had a large number of rooms, a huge garden and a swimming pool; John added on a private recording studio, his 'music room', where he could experiment with electronic instruments and professional sound equipment.

After his divorce from Cynthia, John left Kenwood and paid over £145,000 for Tittenhurst Park, near Ascot, Berkshire, a Georgian mansion set in 72 acres of parkland. The park itself was closed off to the public.

In 1971, John and Yoko Ono moved to New York City. At first they set up house in Greenwich Village, but when an apartment in the exclusive Dakota building became available, they bought it. As more apartments opened up in the Dakota, the Lennons kept buying them, and they also purchased houses and farms in the countryside around New York.

Late in 1963, when all four Beatles moved to London, Paul moved in with his girlfriend, Jane Asher, at her family home in the Harley Street area, north of Oxford Street, W.1. The address was 57 Wimpole Street. In 1965 he bought a 140-year-old, three-storey house at 7 Cavendish, St John's Wood (right), near EMI's Abbey Road studios. It was within a five-minute car ride of Savile Row in Mayfair, which would later house the offices of Apple. The house was hidden from view behind a high wall; its iron gate could be opened and closed from inside by remote control. After buying the house, Paul had it carefully and expensively restored to its original appearance; like John, he added in a private recording studio. Paul still uses his London house on occasions. In June 1966 he also acquired a farm in Campbeltown, Scotland. In the mid-seventies he purchased a converted windmill at Peasmarsh, 2½ miles north of Rye in East Sussex. He divides his time between all three homes.

George and Patti Harrison's large house, Kinfawn, was located in the centre of a large park at Claremont, Esher, Surrey, and was built around a swimming pool. In 1967, the outside walls were painted in psychedelic colours (designed by George himself), and a mosaic wall next to the swimming pool was also added (designed by John). On January 14, 1970, George bought Friar Park, an enormous mansion with extensive grounds near Henley-on-Thames, Oxfordshire. It was built in the 1870s by Sir Francis Crisp and used to be a Roman Catholic convent until 1969. The mansion has 30 rooms, including a ballroom which George converted into a recording studio called F.P.S.H.O.T. (Friar Park Studios, Henley on Thames). It was here that he recorded the albums Dark Horse, 33⅓ and George Harrison. For those interested in a look at the Friar Park, it appears on the front cover of All Things Must Pass and the inside cover of Living In The Material World (far right), while the grounds can be seen on the inside covers of Dark Horse and 33⅓.

Ringo did not stay in London for long: the house Dr Strach found for him in Weybridge, called Sunny Heights, was only a few hundred yards away from John and Cynthia's Kenwood. Ringo immediately added a bar, a swimming pool, and his own movie theatre, and in September 1966 he decided it was time to do some extensive renovation. For that purpose, he started his own construction company, Bricky Builders. Ringo was fond of asking the journalists he often showed around Sunny Heights, 'What's a scruff like me doing in a place like this?'

Ringo's ex-wife Maureen still lives at Sunny Heights, but Starr himself has become a citizen of the world. In 1969 he purchased Peter Seller's estate Brookfield (far right), then sold it a few months later and returned to London. Since then, he has lived in George's Esher home, at Tittenhurst Park, in Amsterdam, in Monaco and elsewhere. He is now a permanent UK resident once more, back at John's former home Tittenhurst Park, London Road, Ascot, where his application for a council grant of £500 to modernize the stables has recently been turned down.

101

PARIS REVISITED!
PHOTO SESSIONS: 1965

After the shooting for *Help!* was finished, the Beatles did a brief concert tour of Europe while post-production work on the film was underway. There were shows in Paris, Lyons, Milan, Genoa, Rome, Nice, Jerez, Madrid and Barcelona. On the first day of the tour – June 20, 1965 – the boys were photographed on the roof of their hotel by Parisian journalists. This picture appeared in *Salut les Copains*, a French magazine.

BEATLES CARTOONS

Two successful tours of America, record sales in the millions, countless souvenirs flooding the marketplace.... How else could the Beatles be merchandized?

In 1965, artist Peter Sander was assigned to design the character models for a series of animated cartoons about the group, aimed at the Saturday morning television audience, mainly juvenile. His drawings were based on the boys' first film – 'I saw A Hard Day's Night 'til I knew it by heart,' he later recalled – in which they wore tight silver-grey suits, were constantly being chased by hordes of young girls, and tossed off dryly comical comments in their Liverpudlian accents.

The animated Beatles were given identifying personality traits: 'John has a rather mocking expression ... Paul is the stylish Beatle ... George never looks at you when

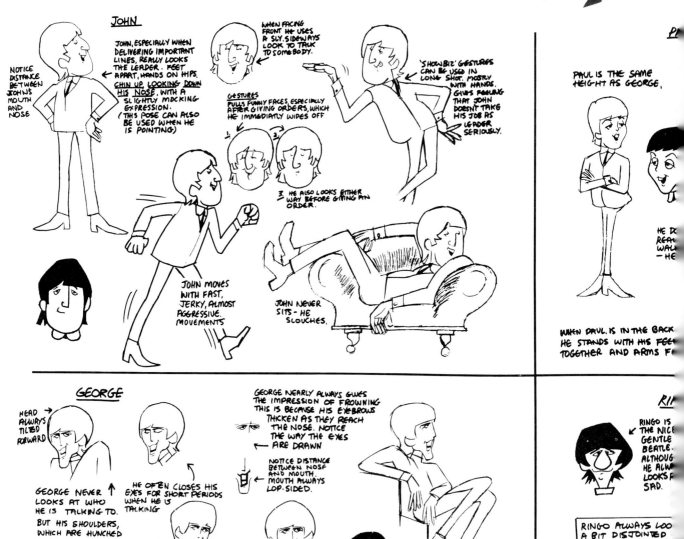

104

he's talking ... Ringo is the friendly Beatle, although he always seems sad. ...'

Each cartoon was based on an existing Beatle song, and 70 animators brought the 39 episodes to life, with Al Brodax producing.

The King Features Syndicate released the series in the United States, and as a tie-in marketed inflatable versions of the four main characters. Although the Beatles themselves were not satisfied with the finished product and were able to prevent the cartoons from being broadcast in England, by the end of the sixties they had been shown around most of the rest of the world.

Where are the Beatle cartoons today? No one seems to know. All that's left is Peter Sander's original model sheet, and the storyboard for one of the 39 episodes.

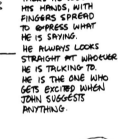

PAUL IS THE MOST POISED AND STYLISH BEATLE. WHEN HE TALKS HE USES HIS HANDS, WITH FINGERS SPREAD TO EXPRESS WHAT HE IS SAYING.
HE ALWAYS LOOKS STRAIGHT AT WHOEVER HE IS TALKING TO. HE IS THE ONE WHO GETS EXCITED WHEN JOHN SUGGESTS ANYTHING.

PAUL SITS AS THOUGH HE WAS READY TO JUMP UP AND GET ON WITH WHATEVER IS HAPPENING.

WHEN HE IS MAKING HIS OWN SUGGESTIONS AND COMMENTS, ESPECIALLY ONES SUGGESTING MISCHIEF. HE COVERS UP BY ASSUMING A MOCK INNOCENT LOOK, EYES WIDE AND HEAD TILTED TO ONE SIDE.

HE TENDS TO PUT HIS HAND TO HIS MOUTH WHEN HE IS EXCITED

KEEP UPPER LIP PROTRUDING

KEEP RINGO'S NECK THIN TO HELP THE DISJOINTED LOOK.

HAIR ...CK ...AND SHAGGY

NORMALLY, RINGO IS ALWAYS DEADPAN BUT SHOULD AN EXPRESSION BE REQUIRED THE MAIN MOVEMENT IS ARCHING THE EYEBROWS. KEEP MOUTH IN A WAVY LINE.

...RINGO ...S, HAVING ...A FUNNY ...K, HE ...S HIS

RINGO IS ½ HEAD SMALLER THAN GEORGE AND PAUL

...RINGO ...OS HE ...AYS ...PS ...ARD. ...OTHES ...TO LOOK ...OUGH ...ARE A ...O BIG.

RINGO SITS NORMALLY, SLIGHTLY HUNCHED.

105

1966

21 January

Late January

1 April

13 April

5 May

January 1, 1966	Parlophone releases a disc titled *Sing A Song Of Beatles*, on which music publisher Dick James warbles a medley of Beatle tunes.
January 14, 1966	Ringo and Maureen leave for a vacation in Malaga, on the south coast of Spain.
January 21, 1966	George marries Patricia Anne Boyd at the Registry Office in Epsom, Surrey, with Paul among those present. For their honeymoon, the Harrisons fly to Barbados.
January 28, 1966	Brian takes over the Vic Lewis Organization, making him the manager of Matt Monro and Donovan, and the European agent for Tony Bennett, Herb Alpert, Pat Boone, Trini Lopez, the Supremes, Johnny Mathis and other America-based acts.
February 11, 1966	Peter and Gordon release a new single, *Woman*, with music and lyrics by Bernard Webb. Not until the record becomes a hit is it revealed that Bernard Webb is really Paul McCartney, who has chosen this way of proving that the song is good enough to make it on its own merits, even without the McCartney name attached to it.
February 28, 1966	As a result of current owner Ray McFall's unpaid £10,000 tax bill, the Cavern Club is closed.
March 1, 1966	BBC-TV broadcasts the world premiere of a film titled *The Beatles At Shea Stadium*.
March 4, 1966	Release date of the *Yesterday* EP. The London *Evening Standard* publishes Maureen Cleave's interview with John, in which the most outspoken Beatle says: 'Christianity will go, it will vanish and shrink. I needn't argue about that. I'm right and I will be proved right. We're more popular than Jesus now. I don't know which will go first – rock and roll or Christianity.'
March 22, 1966	Paul and Jane leave for a skiing vacation in Klosters, Switzerland.
April 1, 1966	John, Cynthia, Ringo and Maureen leave for a vacation on Tobago, a British island in the Caribbean.
April 5, 1966	Jane turns 20, and her birthday present from Paul is 20 dresses. John and Paul sell off a portion of their shares in Northern Songs, each receiving £146,000. Their remaining shares are worth some £1,000,000.
April 6, 1966	The Beatles begin recording sessions for their next album. The first song taped is tentatively titled *The Void*, later changed to *Tomorrow Never Knows*.
April 13, 1966	*Paperback Writer* is recorded; backing vocalists include the French harmony group Les Frères Jacques.
April 18, 1966	The Cavern Club is sold to café proprietor Joe Davey.
April 20, 1966	The vocal tracks for *Eleanor Rigby* are recorded. Its original title, *Daisy Hawkins*, is changed after Paul notices the name 'Rigby' on a Bristol clothing shop.
April 25, 1966	*Rain* is recorded.
April 27, 1966	The string tracks for *Eleanor Rigby* are recorded.
May 1, 1966	The Beatles perform at the annual *New Musical Express* poll winners' concert at the Empire Pool in Wembley, after appearances by the Small Faces, Spencer Davis, Roy Orbison, the Yardbirds, Cliff Richard, the Who and the Rolling Stones. Although the event is not planned as the Beatles' final British concert, they are never to play before a paying audience in England again.
May 4, 1966	A live appearance on BBC Radio's 'Saturday Club'.
May 5, 1966	Following a taping for 'The Ed Sullivan Show', John, Paul, George and Ringo attend a Bob Dylan concert at the Royal Albert Hall in London. Afterwards, Paul, Dylan, Keith Richard and Brian Jones spend some time together at Dolly's Club, also in London, then go up to Dylan's room at the Mayfair Hotel.
May 15, 1966	In the studio to work on the *Revolver* album.
May 20, 1966	Michael Lindsay-Hogg directs the shooting of a promotional film, made to plug the new single, *Paperback Writer* and *Rain*, on BBC-TV's 'Top of the Pops'. Shooting takes place at Chiswick House in London.
June 4, 1966	The Beatles are interviewed on BBC Radio's 'Saturday Club'.
June 9, 1966	The promotional film for the new single is broadcast on 'Top of the Pops'.

June 10, 1966	The *Paperback Writer/Rain* single is released.
June 15, 1966	In America, Capitol Records releases the *Yesterday And Today* album. On the cover, John, Paul, George and Ringo are wearing butchers' smocks and holding bits and pieces of children's dolls, liberally drenched with ketchup. The photograph immediately causes a major controversy: it is considered tasteless and disgusting. A few days later, the album is withdrawn from circulation, and later rereleased with a less offensive cover. The original cover, known as the 'butcher cover', quickly becomes an important collectors' item and fetches high prices.
June 16, 1966	A big surprise: the Beatles live on BBC-TV's 'Top of the Pops', their first live television appearance since August 1965.
June 17, 1966	Paul buys a farm in Mackrihanish, Kintyre, Scotland.
June 18, 1966	Appearance on ABC-TV's 'Thank Your Lucky Stars'.
June 22, 1966	Sibylla's, a new disco, opens its doors in London; the owners are George Harrison and Sir William Pigott-Brown. Among the opening-night guests are the Beatles and the Rolling Stones.
June 23, 1966	The boys leave for a short series of concerts in West Germany; on their arrival in Munich, they check into the Hotel Bayerischer Hof.
June 24, 1966	Two performances at the Circus Krone in Munich, one of which is videotaped by ZDR for German television. Also on the bill are Cliff Bennett and the Rebel Rousers and Peter and Gordon. After midnight, when the second show is finished, the Beatles travel by train to Essen.
June 25, 1966	Afternoon performance at the Gruga Halle, Essen.
June 26, 1966	Performance at the Ernst Merck Halle, Hamburg. During the course of the evening, Astrid Kirchherr visits the Beatles in their dressing rooms. Outside the building, the police use water cannons to keep the crowd under control. After their show, the boys spend the night at the Schloss Hotel in nearby Tremsbuttel.
June 27, 1966	Departure for Tokyo. In order to avoid a typhoon over Japan, the plane makes an unscheduled stop in Anchorage, Alaska.
June 30–July 2, 1966	Performances at the Budo Kan Hall, Tokyo. Only half of the 200,000 requests for tickets can be filled, in spite of the addition of three afternoon shows. One concert is filmed for broadcast on Japanese television.
July 3, 1966	The Beatles fly to the Philippines, where all approach roads to Manila Airport are blocked by some 50,000 fans.
July 4, 1966	John, Paul, George and Ringo play for their largest audience: 100,000 fans at the Araneta Coliseum in Manila. It is not altogether a happy day for the Beatles, though; they turn down an invitation from Imelda Marcos, wife of the president of the Philippines, to attend a party at the presidential palace, and this refusal is considered an insult to the head of state. As a result, members of the national police force 'escort' them forcibly back to their aeroplane.
July 5–7, 1966	Three days off, in and around the Intercontinental Hotel in New Delhi, India. John and Paul each buy a sitar, while George picks up a whole collection of Indian instruments.
July 8, 1966	After two weeks in Germany, Japan, the Philippines and India, the Beatles return to Heathrow Airport and the *Nowhere Man* EP is released.
July 12, 1966	John and Paul receive three Ivor Novello Awards, for *We Can Work It Out*, *Yesterday* and *Help!*
July 23, 1966	Prime Minister Harold Wilson and the mayor of Liverpool officiate at the reopening of the Cavern Club. Although the Beatles are not present at the festivities, they send a good-luck telegram.
July 29, 1966	The band refuses to sign a contract for a series of concerts in South Africa, a rejection of the apartheid policy which would have banned blacks from attending the shows.
July 31, 1966	After John's claim that the Beatles are more popular than Jesus is published in *Datebook* magazine, an enormous amount of anti-Beatle sentiment erupts in America. Today, under the leadership of the Ku Klux Klan, giant piles of Beatles albums, Beatle scrapbooks and Beatle photographs are incinerated on Beatle bonfires across the United States. The first fire is lit in Birmingham, Alabama.
August 4, 1966	Several American radio stations announce that they will no longer broadcast Beatle records (because of John's comment about Jesus), and the South African government officially bans the playing of Beatle music within South Africa's borders (probably because of the band's refusal to play there).
August 5, 1966	Release dates of the *Revolver* LP and the first cover version of a song from that album (Cliff Bennett and the Rebel Rousers' cover of *Got To Get You Into My Life*). Many more covers of tunes from *Revolver* will follow.
August 6, 1966	The number of American radio stations boycotting the Beatles passes 30. Meanwhile, Paul is interviewed by David Frost on BBC Radio's 'David Frost at the Phonograph'.
August 7, 1966	Brian Epstein is prepared to pay one million dollars to cancel the band's forthcoming tour of America: the safety of his artists is, for him, the most important consideration. However, after a quick visit to the United States and a consultation

20 May

15 June

26 June

31 July

5 August

23 August

29 August

17 September

20 September

25 November

9 December

	with the group, the final decision is to go ahead with the tour.
August 8, 1966	The new single, *Eleanor Rigby* and *Yellow Submarine*, is released.
August 9, 1966	British fans circulate a petition requesting the Beatles not to go to America. The trip, the fans feel, may be hazardous to their heroes' health.
August 11, 1966	Nervously, the Beatles leave for America.
August 12, 1966	In the luxurious Astor Park Hotel in Chicago, John apologizes for his comparison of the Beatles' popularity with that of Jesus Christ. He closes the press conference by announcing, 'I wish I'd kept me big mouth shut.'
	That evening, the group's fourth (and last) concert tour of America begins with a performance at Chicago's International Amphitheater. There are, happily, no anti-Beatle incidents.
August 13, 1966	Performance at the Olympic Stadium, Detroit.
August 14, 1966	Performance at the Municipal Stadium, Cleveland.
August 15, 1966	Performance at the Washington Stadium, Washington, D.C.
August 16, 1966	Performance at the Philadelphia Stadium, Philadelphia.
August 17, 1966	Performance at the Maple Leaf Gardens, Toronto, Canada.
August 18, 1966	Performance at the Suffolk Down Racetrack, Boston.
August 19, 1966	Performance at the Memphis Coliseum, Memphis, the first and only time during the tour when the Ku Klux Klan attempts to disrupt the Beatles' show.
August 20, 1966	Performance at Crosley Field, Cincinnati.
August 21, 1966	Performance at the Bush Stadium, St Louis.
August 23–24, 1966	Two performances at Shea Stadium, New York.
August 25, 1966	Performance at the Seattle Coliseum, Seattle. The boys again stay at the Edgewater Inn, which after their last visit picked up some extra dollars by selling their bedlinen to fans. This time, Ringo has to hide in a cleaning closet to escape the hordes of Beatlemaniacs who storm the motel's hallways.
August 28, 1966	Performance at Dodger Stadium, Los Angeles.
August 29, 1966	At the Beatles' request, Tony Barrow films and records all of tonight's performance at Candlestick Park in San Francisco. It is the final concert of the American tour; although John, Paul, George and Ringo probably all know by now that it is to be their last appearance together before a paying audience anywhere, they have not yet discussed the matter. Brian does not attent the show – he spends the evening with Nat Weiss at their hotel. During the flight back to England, George tells Tony Barrow: 'Well, I guess that's it. I'm not a Beatle anymore.'
August 31, 1966	To the great relief of the thousands of fans awaiting their arrival at Heathrow Airport, the Beatles make it back from America safe and sound.
September 3, 1966	John leaves for Celle, in northern West Germany, where Richard Lester is shooting an anti-war-film titled *How I Won The War*, in which John has an acting part. John has his hair cut short for his role in the picture; director Lester wields the scissors.
September 15, 1966	John travels by train to Paris, where he spends several days with Paul and Brian. Paul and Brian then return by air to London, while John flies onto Almería, Spain, for further shooting of *How I Won The War*. While in Almería, John writes *Strawberry Fields Forever*.
September 16, 1966	George and Patti leave for India, where George takes sitar lessons from Ravi Shankar.
September 19, 1966	Ringo sets up his own construction company, Bricky Builders, to handle the renovation of his house.
September 20, 1966	Ringo flies to Spain, where he stays with John for several days.
October 8, 1966	Ringo and Maureen leave for a vacation in Malaga.
October 13, 1966	Denny Laine leaves the Moody Blues. He will later become one of the original members of Paul McCartney's post-Beatles group, Wings.
October 14, 1966	Paul begins writing the music for a film titled *The Family Way*; soon after, he leaves for a vacation in Kenya.
November 8, 1966	John meets Yoko Ono during a preview of her exhibition, 'Unfinished Paintings and Objects', at the Indica Art Gallery in London, where it will officially run from November 9 through November 12.
November 9, 1966	Paul is involved in an automobile accident. Several years later, during the 'Paul is dead' uproar, rumour will have it that he was fatally injured in this collision.
November 10, 1966	Newly-released publicity photographs show the boys with beards and moustaches. Razor blade sales to male Beatle fans immediately take a turn for the worse.
November 19, 1966	Paul returns from Kenya.
November 24, 1966	In the studio to begin recording the new album.
November 25, 1966	*Everywhere It's Christmas*, the fourth Christmas single for British fans, is recorded.

| November 28, 1966 | The George Martin Orchestra releases an album titled *The Beatle Girls*, featuring instrumental versions of *Anna, Michelle, Eleanor Rigby, Girl* and other Beatles numbers. |

| December 9, 1966 | Since EMI doesn't have a new Beatles LP ready for Christmas-season release, they issue an anthology album titled *A Collection Of Beatles Oldies ... But Goodies* instead. The disc's only 'new' song is *Bad Boy*, which, although it appeared on the American *Beatles VI* album in June 1965, is now made available to the British public for the first time. |

23 December

December 10, 1966	*When I'm 64* is recorded. Paul wrote the song in 1962, but waited until this year, when his father turns 64, to record it.
December 14, 1966	Fan club members in the United Kingdom receive their Christmas present from the Beatles: *Everywhere It's Christmas*, with a cover designed by Paul.
December 16, 1966	*Strawberry Fields Forever* and three versions of *Penny Lane* are recorded.

| December 18, 1966 | World premiere of the film *The Family Way*, starring Hayley Mills, Hywel Bennett and Hayley's father John Mills. It was directed by Roy and John Boulting and based on Bill Naughton's play *All In Good Time*. |

26 December

| December 23, 1966 | The soundtrack album from *The Family Way*, with music by Paul, is released. |
| December 26, 1966 | John appears as a washroom attendant reading extracts from his books, in Peter Cook and Dudley Moore's programme, 'Not Only ... But Also', on BBC-2. |

PHOTO SESSIONS: 1966

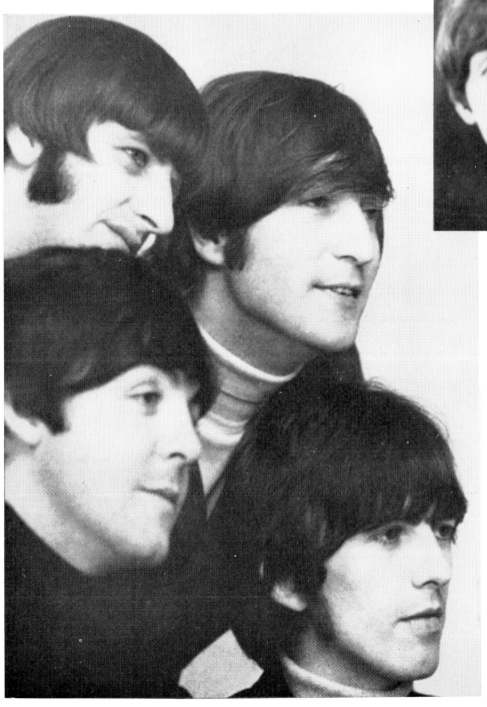

John posing with an award from the American magazine Harper's, *honouring the Beatles for their mod clothing.*

The photographs on these pages were taken in April 1966, and the middle photo in the upper row was used as the Beatles' official publicity shot for that year.

Shortly before the session which resulted in these pictures, Paul fell off a motorscooter while spending a weekend with his father in The Wirral, Cheshire, and chipped a piece from one of his front teeth. That bit of missing tooth explains why his smile here is not nearly as broad as the others' . . .

The photo session is over; the boys light up.

The original cover photo for the Yesterday . . . and Today *album.* Right: *two shots from the same session.* (*photos: R. Whittaker*)

The banned cover.

5 May 1966: Paul examines slides of the butcher cover.

In June 1966, in America, Capitol Records released a Beatle LP titled *The Beatles Yesterday And Today*. Capitol's Beatle albums were not simply duplicates of the albums organized by the group and released in England – they were collections of material culled from the Beatles' previously-released British records, selected and packaged by Capitol especially for the American market. *Yesterday And Today* included songs from the *Help!* and *Rubber Soul* LPs, plus, unusually, four numbers from *Revolver*, which would not be released in the United Kingdom for another three weeks. But this was not all that was unusual about *Yesterday And Today*. Also worthy of mention was the album's cover, which was not only unusual but downright controversial.

It had been John's idea to pose the band in butchers' overalls holding chunks of raw meat and the 'bloody' arms, legs, torso and heads of children's dolls. The photo was taken by Robert Whitaker in March or April, and first published on the cover of a British music paper called *Disc*. Brian Epstein's objections were ignored: as far as the Beatles were concerned, the butcher cover was to be used on their next American album. For some reason, Capitol Records agreed.

Some 750,000 copies of the album were printed and distributed (although some sources say it was only 60,000 and others claim the figure was as low as 6000) before the first indignant phone calls began coming in from distributors and retailers. The butcher cover, they complained, was too 'far out' for American tastes.

In a single weekend, all copies of the album still available and all promotional material featuring the

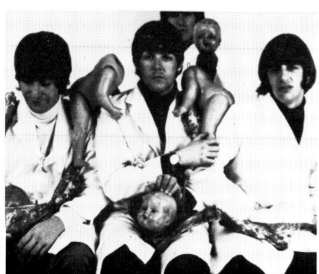

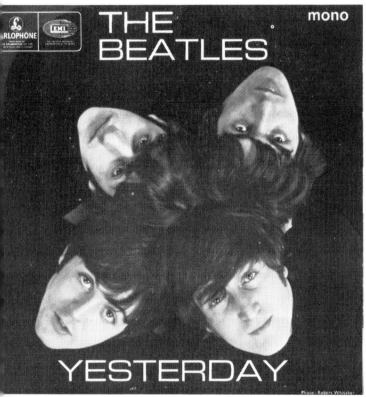

THE BEATLES

mono

YESTERDAY

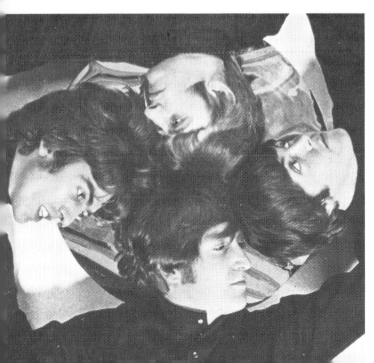

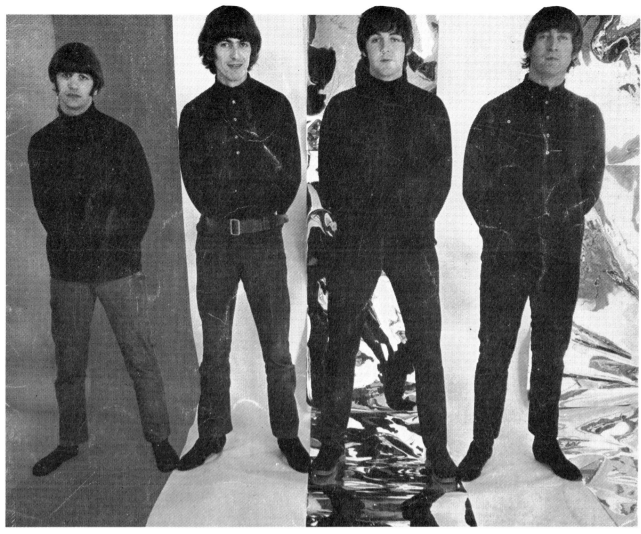

butcher photo were recalled by Capitol, and the offending picture was replaced by an innocent shot of the Beatles in a hotel room, gathered around a cabin trunk.

Most of the butcher covers were destroyed but, in order to save time, the new cover photo was simply pasted *over* the old one in some cases. When news of the switch was publicized, Beatle fans across America could be found beavering away in their kitchens, steaming cabin trunk photos off of their copies of *Yesterday And Today* in the hope of finding the original, rare butcher cover underneath.

Today, the butcher cover is still one of the most sought-after pieces of Beatle memorabilia.

John was very bitter about the switch. In his opinion, the issue was 'just as important as Vietnam'. He was serious when he said it.

These remarkable photos are part of a series by Robert Whitaker, taken in May of 1966 when the Beatles were busy recording tracks for their *Rubber Soul* album. It was not the first time the Fab Four had been shot from above, however. Two years earlier they had been photographed the same way in *A Hard Day's Night*.

Whitaker, who worked as a photographer for NEMS, supposedly took the pictures in a storage room at EMI's Abbey Road studios. There was a dog roaming around during the session, and it appeared in several of the shots, including one which was used as the cover for an EP released in Japan in 1967, which featured the songs *Bad Boy*, *Strawberry Fields Forever*, *Penny Lane* and *Good Day Sunshine*.

115

JOHN LENNON: MORE

Brian Epstein

In early August 1966, the world was shocked by the first major controversy involving the Beatles. It was a controversy which seemed serious enough to destroy the group's enormous popularity at a single stroke.

It all started when an interview with John Lennon was published in the American magazine *Datebook*: 'Christianity will disappear,' John was quoted as announcing, 'it will collapse. I don't have to argue about it. I'm right and you'll see that I'm right. We are more popular now than Jesus Christ. I don't know which will disappear first, rock-and-roll or Christianity.'

A number of influential American Christians considered these remarks to be the worst sort of blasphemy, and on August 4 the world's major press agencies broadcast news of the consequences: five radio stations in the American South had decided to eliminate all Beatle music from their programming.

The story appeared in papers around the globe, and most of the articles made it appear as though all America was up in arms against the group. In Spain, South Africa and the Philippines, the Beatles were completely banned from the airwaves.

It was the worst possible time for

POPULAR THAN JESUS

an American Beatle boycott, as the group was only days away from its departure for their fourth concert tour of the States. But fed by the worldwide publicity and the outrage of the Christian community, the movement was growing to dangerous proportions.

In Birmingham, Alabama, a radio station called on its listeners to make a giant pile of their Beatles records and photographs, and to set the pile ablaze if the boys dared to enter their city limits. In Oklahoma, the manager of an amusement park offered its grounds as the site for another Beatles bonfire. In Memphis, Tennessee, the birthplace of Elvis Presley, the City Council unanimously moved to request that the Beatles cancel their scheduled performance.

Meanwhile, in England, journalist Maureen Cleave (who had conducted the *Datebook* interview with John) hastened to reassure the world that John had not intended to be blasphemous and that his words had been taken out of context. In fact, the interview as printed in *Datebook* was a condensation of a longer article, which had appeared five months earlier in the *Evening Standard* in London, where it had not excited any particular comment. 'I don't believe for a moment that John was being irrev-

George during a 1967 recording session.

117

Press conference: 'I wish I'd kept me big mouth shut.'

erent or disrespectful,' Cleave explained. 'He was only saying that the position of Christianity has weakened, and that with most people the Beatles are more popular than the Church.' In her opinion, John was sorry about that state of affairs, not proud of it. 'We were talking about how much of its influence Christianity has lost in the modern world,' she went on, 'and his remarks were meant to illustrate that point.'

Brian Epstein was seriously worried that the Beatles might be faced with real trouble if they went to America, and he flew to the States himself to take a closer look at the situation there. While in the US, he asked the American promoter what it would cost simply to cancel the whole tour. 'A million dollars,' was the answer, and Brian was prepared to pay that sum out of his own pocket. After considerable deliberation, however, it was decided to take the risk and go ahead with the tour.

On August 11, a week after the controversy began, the Beatles boarded a plane at London Airport. Thousands of British fans were there, crying and begging the boys to change their minds: there had been threats from the Ku Klux Klan, and the fans were afraid. Even cooler heads were disturbed: the premiums on the boys' life insurance policies had been doubled at the last minute!

The Beatles themselves had remained silent about the matter, but on their arrival at Chicago's O'Hare Airport they held a major press conference. John read a carefully-prepared statement, which was published around the world within 24 hours:

'I'm sorry I opened my mouth. I'm not anti-God, anti-Christ or anti-religion. I wouldn't knock it. I didn't mean we were greater or better.'

Although most of the press conference was taken up by John's statement, the other three Beatles also had a chance to speak. They admitted that they too were concerned about the international reaction to the interview with John: 'I know John,' said George. 'He believes in Christianity. And I agree with him that it's going downhill at the moment.'

John's statement put an end to the worst manifestations of the hate campaign, and to everyone's great relief there were few problems during the American tour. Some minor disturbances were reported, though. The Ku Klux Klan attempted to disrupt the performance at the Memphis Coliseum, but the audience was more interested in the Beatles than in the Klan. During the performance there was a loud explosion in the hall and John, almost blind without his glasses on, fell to the stage thinking someone had taken a shot at him. And a clergyman in Cleveland declared: 'I will throw anyone out of my church who agrees with John Lennon's remarks about Christianity, or who attends the Beatles' concert'; disregarding the threat, some 20,000 fans turned up at the Cleveland show.

The Americans had been quick to condemn John for his remarks, and they were quick to forgive him. The rest of the world rapidly followed suit. The British Roman Catholic newspaper, *The Catholic Herald*, wrote: 'It was not Lennon's arrogance which was so shocking, but the difficult experience of hearing it said in public that many Christians are turning away from Christ.' The *Osservatore Romano*, official organ of the Vatican itself, which had originally reported its 'displeasure' at John's remarks, wrote after his clarification that 'there is some truth to his claim that Christianity's strong influence on mankind has

weakened'.

When the Beatles returned to England, their last American tour and their last appearance before a paying audience behind them, it seemed as if the religious controversy John had sparked was also, finally, over, and it seemed as if its ending had been, after all, a happy one.

But the controversy was *not* over; and when it finally did end, fourteen years later, it was tragically sad.

In 1966, Mark David Chapman, an eleven-year-old living in Atlanta, Georgia, was one of the Beatles' most devoted fans. In 1969 the boy ran away from home; a year later he became a born-again Christian and took to carrying a bible and a 'Jesus notebook' at all times. He wore a cross round his neck and quoted scriptures constantly. He became very upset about John's earlier comments, and remarked to a friend, 'Who are *they* to compare themselves to Jesus?' Chapman's Christianity led him to enroll with the YMCA as a counsellor in Arkansas. He met a woman at a prayer meeting and together they enrolled at Covenant College, a Presbyterian school of higher education in Tennessee, but he flunked out and his woman friend lost interest in him. He then suffered a mental breakdown, whereafter his religious fervour appeared to subside. As he grew older, the unstable young man alternately identified himself with John Lennon and with a god-like messenger whose duty it was to wreak the Lord's vengeance on John. It was the 'holy avenger' who finally gained the upper hand, and on December 8, 1980, John Lennon's unguarded remarks to an interviewer more than a decade earlier turned out to have been the first link in the terrible chain which led to his death.

January 19, 1967	Sections of *A Day In The Life* are recorded.
January 21, 1967	NEMS Enterprises merges with the Robert Stigwood Group, making Brian responsible for the management of the Who, Cream, the Merseys and Crispian St Peters.
January 30, 1967	Brian, John and Paul attend a concert at Brian's theatre, the Saville, in London. Performing are the Who and the Jimi Hendrix Experience.
February 1967	Patti Harrison joins the Maharishi Mahesh Yogi's Spiritual Regeneration Movement.
February 1, 1967	The title song for the new album, *Sgt. Pepper's Lonely Hearts Club Band*, is recorded by John, Paul and George.
February 6, 1967	The Beatles sign a new, nine-year recording contract with EMI. An EMI executive uses this opportunity to announce to the press that total worldwide sales of Beatles discs have now exceeded 180 million.
February 9, 1967	BBC-TV broadcasts promotional films for the *Penny Lane/Strawberry Fields Forever* single, shot previously in Liverpool by Swedish director Peter Goldmann. Because of a union ban against the use of lip-synch on British television, Goldmann may not simply show the Beatles mouthing the words of the songs. Instead, he uses the numbers as background music behind otherwise silent images – an idea which is quickly imitated by other directors of record promotions.
February 16, 1967	Recording of *Good Morning, Good Morning* begins. BBC-TV reruns the *Penny Lane/Strawberry Fields Forever* promotional films.
February 17, 1967	The *Penny Lane/Strawberry Fields Forever* single is released. In spite of the extensive and original television promotion, it peaks at No. 2 in the UK singles chart. It is the end of a run of eleven consecutive British number ones for the group, a sequence without precedent in chart history. Recording of *Being For The Benefit Of Mr Kite* begins.
February 20, 1967	John and Ringo attend a Chuck Berry concert at the Saville Theatre in London. During the show, a minor panic breaks loose when the fire curtain suddenly crashes to the floor.
February 21, 1967	*Fixing A Hole* is recorded.
February 22, 1967	*Lovely Rita* is recorded.
February 26, 1967	Brian buys a manor house in Rushlake Green, East Sussex. The house, used during the Second World War by Winston Churchill, costs him £35,000. Around this time and on Patti's advice, George has his first meeting with the Maharishi Mahesh Yogi.
March 2, 1967	Recording begins of *Lucy In The Sky With Diamonds*.
March 9, 1967	Recording begins on *Getting Better*.
March 11, 1967	The Beatles receive three Grammy Awards: for *Michelle*, for *Eleanor Rigby*, and for Klaus Voormann's cover for the *Revolver* LP.
March 15, 1967	*Within You, Without You* is recorded.
March 17, 1967	*She's Leaving Home* is recorded.
March 25, 1967	The band receives Ivor Novello Awards for *Michelle* and *Yellow Submarine*.
March 29, 1967	The reprise of *Sgt. Pepper's Lonely Hearts Club Band* is recorded.
March 30, 1967	In Michael Cooper's studio in Chelsea, the Beatles pose in military uniforms for the cover photograph for the *Sgt. Pepper* album. In an evening recording session, *Bad Finger Boogie* is recorded. The song is later retitled *With a Little Help From My Friends*.
April 2, 1967	The finishing touches are put on the *Sgt. Pepper* album. Three songs recorded for the LP but ultimately unused are George's *Pink Litmus Paper Shirt* and John's *Peace Of Mind* and *Colliding Circles*.
April 5, 1967	Paul, accompanied by Mal Evans, flies to Denver, Colorado, where Jane celebrates her 21st birthday with a party at the Quorum Restaurant. During the course of the day, Paul comes up with the idea for a film: *Magical Mystery Tour*. Jane is performing in America with a theatre group; at one point during the trip, she is quoted as saying, 'I want to be known as a Shakespearean actress, not as Paul McCartney's girlfriend.'
April 9, 1967	Paul flies from Denver to Los Angeles on Frank Sinatra's Lear jet.
April 10, 1967	Paul attends a Beach Boys recording session, where he produces the song *Vegetables* and plays bass on an unreleased version of *On Top Of Old Smokey*.

Early January

Late January

February

30 March

119

1 June

1 June

25 June

7 August

8 August

19 August

April 11, 1967	Flying back to London, Paul writes the title song for *Magical Mystery Tour* and sketches out a scenario for the film.
April 19, 1967	The Beatles become a corporation, officially registered as The Beatles & Co.
April 25, 1967	The instrumental tracks for the song *Magical Mystery Tour* are recorded.
April 27, 1967	Vocal tracks for *Magical Mystery Tour* are recorded.
May 3, 1967	The addition of a trumpet section completes work on the song *Magical Mystery Tour*. At the same session, recording begins on a number tentatively called *One Of The Beautiful People* (later retitled *Baby, You're A Rich Man*).
May 5, 1967	Paul shaves off his moustache.
May 11, 1967	Mick Jagger is present at the Olympic Studios in Barnes as recording on *Baby, You're A Rich Man* is completed. John plays an unusual instrument during the session: a clavioline.
May 25, 1967	John's Rolls Royce is painted in psychedelic colours.
May 27, 1967	In an interview published in the latest issue of *Melody Maker*, John announces: 'No more tours, no more moptops, We could never hear ourselves playing properly. Anyway, what more could we do after playing to 56,000 people? What next? More fame? More money? We were travelling all over the world – and we couldn't move outside our hotel.'
June 1, 1967	Release date of an album which will change the direction of rock music: *Sgt. Pepper's Lonely Hearts Club Band*. The LP, which has taken some 700 studio hours spread out over nine months of recording sessions and has cost £25,000 to produce, is packaged in a beautiful cover designed by Peter Blake. One song, *A Day In The Life*, is subjected to restrictions by BBC radio because its lyrics ('I'd love to turn you on') ostensibly promote the use of drugs. Two other songs from the same album undergo the same fate: critics claim the title of *Lucy In The Sky With Diamonds* is a not-too-subtle reference to LSD and its lyrics are an ode to that illegal and apparently dangerous substance; while the title of *Fixing A Hole* was construed as meaning shooting up with a hyperdermic. The Beatles themselves deny that either song contains references to or promotes the use of drugs.
June 14, 1967	At the Olympic Studios in Barnes, recording begins on *All You Need Is Love*.
June 19, 1967	In an interview with the *Daily Mirror*, Paul freely admits that he has used LSD on various occasions.
June 22, 1967	In the studio to record *All Together Now* and *It's All Too Much* for an upcoming animated film.
June 25, 1967	For the first time ever, a television programme is broadcast live across the world. An estimated 400 million people in 24 countries watch the show, 'Our World', which includes a sequence at one of EMI's recording studios in London, where the Beatles are putting *All You Need Is Love* on tape. 'Our World' was produced in Canada as part of Expo '67.
June 7, 1967	*All You Need Is Love* and *Baby, You're A Rich Man* are released as a single. John's voice on *All You Need Is Love* has been rerecorded, but otherwise the June 25 version is used. Because of the immense impact of the 'Our World' telecast, the single quickly becomes a number one hit in many countries.
July 24, 1967	The London *Times* carries a full-page advertisement calling for the legalization of marijuana, signed by all four Beatles, Brian Epstein, and many others.
July 31, 1967	John and Paul return from a vacation in Greece.
August 1, 1967	George and Patti fly to Los Angeles, where they stay in a house on Blue Jay Way (near Beverly Hills) and George writes a song named after that street.
August 7, 1967	George and Patti meet Ravi Shankar in Hollywood, then fly to San Francisco.
August 8, 1967	George and Patti walk through Golden Gate Park and Haight-Ashbury. George strolls around the streets of the area playing his guitar and singing *Baby, You're A Rich Man*.
August 9, 1967	Via New York, George and Patti return to England.
August 19, 1967	At 3.15 in the afternoon, Maureen gives birth to her second child, Jason Starkey, at Queen Charlotte's Hospital, Hammersmith, London.
August 22, 1967	At the Chappell Studios in London's Bond Street, the first version of *Your Mother Should Know* is recorded. The second (and final) version will be recorded during the first week in September.
August 24, 1967	John, Paul and George attend a lecture by the Maharishi Mahesh Yogi at the Hilton Hotel, Park Lane, London.
August 25, 1967	John, Paul, George, Ringo and assorted family members and camp followers take a train to Bangor, Wales, where they are to study Transcendental Meditation under the Maharishi. Cynthia is not on the train, though: a police constable thinks she is a fan and prevents her from boarding. Neil Aspinall subsequently drives her to Wales to join the others.
August 27, 1967	Brian Epstein, aged 32, is found dead in his bed. A post-mortem later establishes the cause of death as 'an accidental overdose of drugs and alcohol'. The Beatles hear the news in Bangor and immediately return to London.

Today's *Sunday Express* reports that Pete Best is currently working at a bakery for £18 per week.

26 August

August 30, 1967	A funeral service is held for Brian at the Greenbank Synagogue in Liverpool; afterwards, he is buried at Kirkdale (Jewish) Cemetery, Longmoore Lane, Liverpool 9.
September 1, 1967	Clive Epstein, Brian's brother, takes over the management of NEMS Enterprises. The Beatles, however, announce that they will manage themselves from now on, because 'no-one could possibly replace Brian'. NEMS currently retains 25 per cent royalties on all of the group's earnings, including record sales.
	A meeting to discuss the future of the Beatles is held at Paul's home. Plans for the filming of *Magical Mystery Tour* are made, and recording sessions for the film's songs are scheduled.
September 6, 1967	Two versions of *Blue Jay Way* are recorded.
September 7, 1967	The complex recording of *I Am The Walrus* begins (the necessary ingredients include three *cor anglais*, four cellos, six of the Mike Sammes Singers, eight violins, a mellotron and a BBC radio performance of *King Lear*).
September 8, 1967	Recording on *Flying* begins.
September 11, 1967	By 10.45 am, the participants in the Beatles' own magical mystery tour have gathered at Allsop Place in London. The bus shows up late, though, as the MMT logo has to be painted onto its sides at the last minute. Paul boards in London, while John, George and Ringo join up with the tour at Virginia Water. Filming begins inside the bus, on the way to Teignmouth.
September 12, 1967	Departure from Teignmouth. Scenes with tour hostess Wendy Winters (played by Mandy Weet) are filmed in transit. A bridge on the road to Widdicombe Fair is too narrow for the bus, and a traffic jam results. In Plymouth, a lunch break at the Grand Hotel's Berni Steak Bar. In the village of Bodmin, sequences with courier Jolly Jimmy Johnson (played by Derek Royle) are filmed as the rest of the company enjoys a round of ice lollies. The day's destination is the Atlantic Hotel, Newquay.
September 13, 1967	John and George direct a scene featuring Nat Jackley as Happy Nat the Rubber Man round the hotel pool. Meanwhile, Paul is in the bus directing Ringo, Auntie Jessie and Alf the chauffeur. The evening is passed playing billiards at the hotel; Spencer Davis drops in for a visit.
September 14, 1967	Filming around a tent in a field near Newquay. Lunch is eaten at four in the afternoon, and the meal is filmed for use in the movie. In the evening, Spencer Davis organizes a party in a nearby pub.
September 15, 1967	Back in the bus, there are stops for filming at a snack bar in Taunton and for tea at a roadside restaurant. Singing to accordion accompaniment, the company returns to London.
September 19–24, 1967	A week of filming at the RAF base in West Malling, Kent. With unused hangars serving as studios, some of the most important sequences of *Magical Mystery Tour* are shot.
September 25, 1967	*The Fool On The Hill* is recorded, with Paul accompanying himself on recorder.
September 27–29, 1967	Recording of *I Am The Walrus* is completed.
September 30, 1967	John, George and the Maharishi appear on David Frost's TV show 'The Frost Programme' to discuss Transcendental Meditation.
October 7, 1967	Promoter Sid Bernstein offers the Beatles $1,000,000 to do two shows at New York's Shea Stadium. The band turns him down.
October 13, 1967	United Artists releases a single titled *How I Won The War*, which consists entirely of dialogue from the film. According to its label, the disc has been recorded by 'Musketeer Gripweed and the Third Troop'. Musketeer Gripweed, however, turns out to be none other than John Lennon; it is the name of the character he plays in the movie.
October 18, 1967	World premiere of the film *How I Won The War*.
October 20, 1967	The Chris Barber Band releases a single titled *Cat Call*, composed by Paul.
November 1–2, 1967	Paul is in Nice filming *The Fool On The Hill* for *Magical Mystery Tour*. His trip to France had not been without its problems, as he accidentally left home without money or a passport!
November 4–5, 1967	In the studio to record the new single: *Hello, Goodbye*.
November 10, 1967	Paul directs the shooting of a promotional film for the new single at the Saville Theatre in London. The Beatles wear their Sgt. Pepper costumes and lip-sync *Hello, Goodbye*; because of the ban on lip-sync by British unions, the film can only be shown outside the United Kingdom.
November 14, 1967	The *Hello, Goodbye* single is released, with *I Am The Walrus* on the flip side.
November 27, 1967	In America, the *Magical Mystery Tour* LP is released, with songs from the film on Side One and other selections on Side Two. Inside the cover are lyrics to the film songs, plus a 32-page booklet consisting of photographs from the film and the entire *Magical Mystery Tour* plot presented in comic-strip form. *Not Unknown, Anything* and *India* (all by George) and *Annie* (by Paul), all of which were recorded during the *Magical Mystery Tour* sessions in May and June, do not appear on the album.

Mid September

30 September

18 October

1 December

2 December

4 December

November 28, 1967	For the fifth time, the Beatles enter the studio to record a Christmas single for their British fan club members.
December 1, 1967	The songs from the *Magical Mystery Tour* film (Side One of the American LP) are released in England as a double EP, Britain's first. A lyric sheet and the 32-page booklet are included, although everything has been scaled down. The EP has advance orders of 400,000 and by the end of January 1968, sales will have topped 600,000. The LP is not released in Britain until November 19, 1976; in the interim the US album sells 50,000 copies in Britain as an official import. (Two of the numbers heard in the film, *Shirley's Wild Accordion* and *Jessie's Dream*, appear neither on the LP nor the EP, but the latter is bootlegged as *Aunt Jessie's Nightmare*.)
December 2, 1967	Ringo, Maureen and Ewa Aulin leave for Rome. Ringo and Ewa have roles in the film *Candy*, which is being filmed there: Ewa plays Candy and Ringo is Emanuel the gardener. The script is by Terry Southern, the director Christian Marquand. On BBC Radio, John is interviewed by Kenny Everett about the *Magical Mystery Tour* songs, in a programme titled 'Where It's At'.
December 4, 1967	At 94 Baker Street in London, the Beatles open the Apple, the first of a projected empire of Apple Boutiques. One wall of the shop is covered by an enormous mural, painted by Simon Posthuma, Josje Leeger and Marijke Koger, members of a Dutch artists' co-operative called The Fool. The boutique's manager is John's friend Pete Shotton who, more than a decade earlier, had been one of the original Quarrymen.
December 11, 1967	Members of the British Beatles fan club receive their annual Christmas present from the band. This year's single is titled *Christmas Time Is Here Again*, and comes in a cover with its front designed by John and Ringo and its back 'designed' by 4½-year-old Julian Lennon.
December 15, 1967	Shooting on *Wonderwall* begins, directed by Joe Massot. George will write the music for the film.
December 17, 1967	Press review of *Magical Mystery Tour*. Linda Eastman is present as a photographer.
December 21, 1967	The Beatles throw a Christmas party for friends, Apple employees, and the cast and crew of *Magical Mystery Tour*.
December 25, 1967	Jane Asher receives a diamond ring as she and Paul officially announce their engagement. John and his father, in an attempt at a reconciliation, spend Christmas Day together in Weybridge. The elder Lennon is currently employed as a dishwasher.
December 26, 1967	BBC-1 broadcasts *Magical Mystery Tour* in black-and-white, having paid £20,000 for the right to do so.
December 27, 1967	English critics are almost unanimous in blasting *Magical Mystery Tour*. Paul puts in an appearance on David Frost's 'The Frost Programme' to discuss the apparent failure of the film.
December 29, 1967	John, Cynthia and actor Victor Spinetti leave for a six-day vacation in Casablanca, Morocco.

10 December 1966: The Beatles arrive at the recording studio.

RECORDING 'SGT. PEPPER'

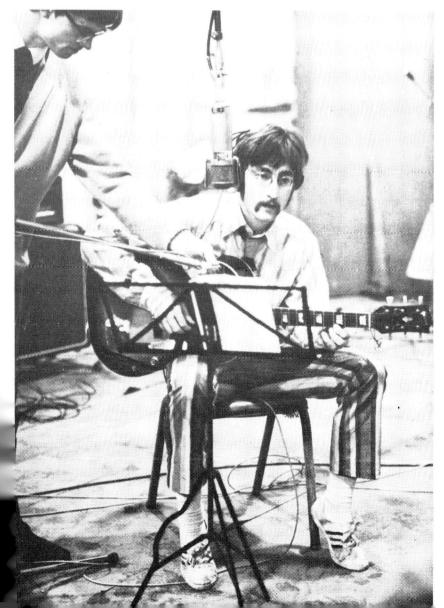

The most talked-about, most remarkable, most complex record album made in the sixties was, unquestionably, the Beatles' *Sgt. Pepper's Lonely Hearts Club Band*. It is a record which made musical history, which turned the recording industry upside-down, which served as a glittering example for almost every LP to follow it and almost every band to come along after the Beatles.

Sgt. Pepper is not your typical 1967 album. It is more than a simple throwing-together of a dozen unconnected songs – it is a unified whole, and its numbers *belong* together. It is a concert, a musical.

Recording began on December 10, 1966, and lasted until April 2, 1967. For four long months, the expensive EMI studios were inhabited by the Beatles, George Martin, and a host of sound engineers and studio musicians. The engineers, of whom Geoffrey Emerick was the most important, provided the technical wizardry: the sound effects, the speeded-up and slowed-down segments. The musicians handled the dozens of extra instruments which the boys wanted: piano, organ, violins, cellos, clarinets, saxophones,

123

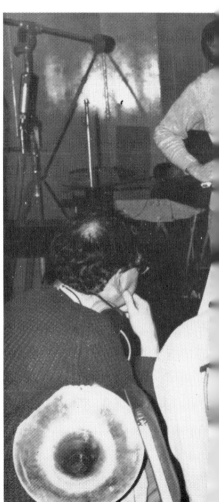

trumpets, trombones, Indian instruments (like the tampura, the tabla and the dilruba) and, for *A Day In The Life*, a 41-piece orchestra.

Today, with 32-track recording equipment an industry standard, the achievement which was *Sgt. Pepper* does not perhaps seem so astonishing – but in 1967, when the album was released, it came as a complete and overwhelming shock. No one was prepared for it, not even the most fervent Beatle fans.

When the surprise finally began to wear off, the reaction set in. The record was *so* unusual, the music and lyrics *so* bizarre, that critics used *Sgt. Pepper* as evidence to back up the rumour that the Beatles were heavily involved with LSD and other drugs. 'Found my way upstairs and had a smoke, somebody spoke and I went into a dream,' Paul sang in *A Day In The Life*, and since smoking combined with dreaming 'obviously' indicated drug abuse, the BBC was quick to ban the song. A few weeks later, when someone noticed that the first letters of the three key words in the title of *Lucy In The Sky With Diamonds* formed the common

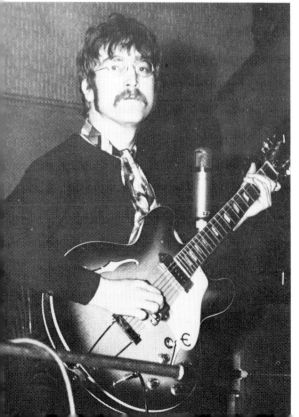

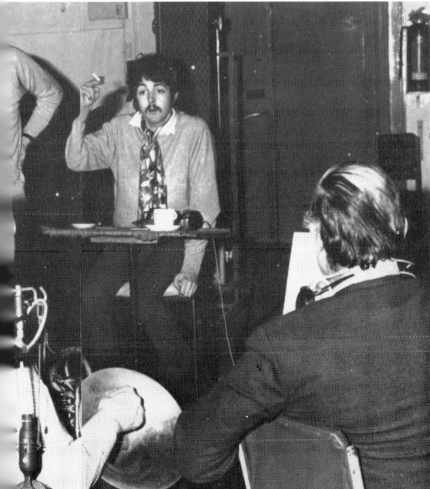

abbreviation for the hallucinogenic substance lysergic acid diethyl-amide (LSD), that song was also banned from the air.

But in spite of such consider-ations, the album became an enor-mous bestseller. Although it cost 20 times as much to produce as the first Beatle LP – some £25,000 and a record for its time – it quickly pro-duced a profit. And today, fifteen years after its initial release, it is still considered to be one of the all-time masterpieces of popular music.

Two weeks before the official release date of *Sgt. Pepper's Lonely Hearts Club Band*, the complete album was played as Radio London's 'LP of the Week' at five in the afternoon on May 12, 1967. Radio London was one of the most successful off-shore pirate radio stations of the late sixties.

Although EMI had already made several cuts from the album avail-able for radio broadcast, no station had yet been given a tape of the entire disc – and the pressing of copies for commercial distribution had not yet begun! This made Radio London's May 12 broadcast a major musical scoop and, at the same time, a major mystery. Who had given them their tapes?

The question has never been conclusively answered, but it is possible to venture an educated guess. About a week before Radio London gave *Sgt. Pepper* its un-authorized world premiere, there had been a break-in at the home of Paul McCartney. And among the items discovered to be missing were two proof pressings of the Beatles' newest album. . . .

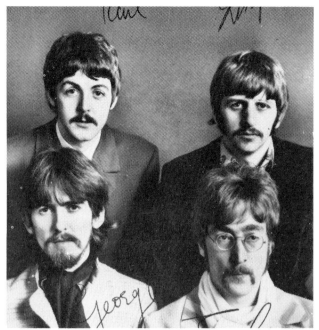

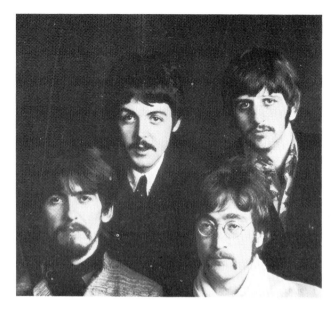

PHOTO SESSIONS: 1967

The photograph printed above was used as the Beatles' official publicity shot for 1967. It was taken in January, during a recording session for the *Sgt. Pepper* album; the pictures to the right and below were taken during the same session. Many newspapers and magazines reprinted these images, as the Beatles' new beards and moustaches were considered Big News. Some publications claimed that the facial hair clearly proved that the group was breaking up, or that they were recording their last album, or simply that they had all gone crazy. . . .

This picture appeared in the music press at the beginning of 1967, and on the cover of the Penny Lane/Strawberry Fields Forever *single in February of the same year. The Beatles' 'moptop' image had radically changed.*

One of the pictures from this session appeared on the back cover of the *Penny Lane/Strawberry Fields Forever* single, released on February 17. The single's front cover featured pictures of the four Beatles as children.

THE 'SGT. PEPPER ALBUM COVER

As with the album itself, the *Sgt. Pepper* cover was a unique and daring idea, carried out masterfully and at high cost.

The Beatles felt that the Lonely Hearts Club Band was a representation of everyone, everywhere. For the album cover, they decided to have themselves photographed in the midst of the people they most admired in world history.

They selected some 60 writers, actors, artists, comedians, gurus, singers, teachers and sports figures, including Stu Sutcliffe, the Beatle who had not lived to share their greatest successes. Peter Blake made life-size photo blow ups of most of the characters, and wax statues of Sonny Liston, Dr David Livingstone, Diana Dors, George Bernard Shaw; the Beatles themselves were borrowed from Madame Tussaud's; Blake and Jann Haworth arranged the figures against the wall of Michael Cooper's photo studio in Chelsea. (Under the warm studio lighting, the wax statues soon turned soft!)

The living Beatles dressed up in uniforms rented from Burman's, a theatrical costumer. (Naturally, within two months of the album's release date, Sgt. Pepper uniforms were available in most of London's boutiques.)

Simon Posthuma and Marijke Koger, Dutch artists belonging to the collective known as The Fool, painted the Sgt. Pepper logo on the big bass drum. And Blake and Haworth set up the garden, with flowers, plants, statuettes, trophies, candles, a portable television set, a hookah, and the word Beatles spelled out in hyacinths.

The finished photo cost £1000 to produce, but it was worth it. It was a perfect visualization of the spirit of *Sgt. Pepper* and, together with the group portrait on the inside of the foldout cover, the inset of Sgt. Pepper cut-outs, the complete lyrics on the back cover and even the inner sleeve (innovatively designed by The Fool), it turned what might have been a simple record package into a party – and an integral part of one of the most interesting and important LPs in the history of pop music.

Photographer Michael Cooper's son helps set the scene.

The collage motif was used more than once. Above: Robert Freeman's picture from 1964. Below: Ringo and John, 26 November 1967.

Who's Who?

1. a guru
2. Aleister Crowley
3. Mae West
4. Lenny Bruce
5. Karlheinz Stockhausen
6. W. C. Fields
7. Carl Jung
8. Edgar Allan Poe
9. Fred Astaire
10. Merkin
11. an actress
12. Huntz Hall
13. Simon Rodia
14. Bob Dylan
15. Aubrey Beardsley
16. Sir Robert Peel
17. Aldous Huxley
18. Dylan Thomas
19. Terry Southern
20. Dion
21. Tony Curtis
22. Wallace Berman

23. Tommy Handley
24. Marilyn Monroe
25. William Burroughs
26. a guru
27. Stan Laurel
28. Richard Lindner
29. Oliver Hardy
30. Karl Marx
31. H. G. Wells
32. a guru
33. Stuart Sutcliffe
34. drawing ot a girl
35. Max Miller
36. drawing of a girl
37. Marlon Brando
38. Tom Mix
39. Oscar Wilde

40. Tyrone Power
41. Larry Bell
42. Dr David Livingstone
43. Johnny Weissmuller
44. Stephen Crane
45. Issy Bonn
46. George Bernard Shaw
47. Albert Stubbins
48. a guru
49. Albert Einstein
50. Lewis Carroll
51. Sonny Liston
52. George Harrison
53. John Lennon
54. Ringo Starr
55. Paul McCartney
56. a guru
57. Marlene Dietrich
58. Diana Dors
59. Shirley Temple
60. Bobby Breen
61. Lawrence of Arabia
62. a man

24 June 1967: Posing for the press.

World' cameras would follow the group into the studio and capture on film the recording of a new Beatles song. Plans for a *Sgt. Pepper* TV special and the *Magical Mystery Tour* project were postponed, and the boys began work on a song for 'Our World' immediately.

By the end of the month, John had written the music and lyrics for *All You Need Is Love*, a powerful number with a message which would have universal appeal. Recording of the musical tracks began at the Olympic Studios in Barnes on June 14, with John playing clavichord, George on violin and Paul running a violin bow across the strings of an Arco bass guitar. Several days later, back at EMI's Abbey Road studios, the musical tracks were completed: George Martin played piano and an assortment of session musicians added two trumpets, two trombones, two saxophones, two cellos, four more violins and an accordion.

The song was now ready – except for the vocals, which would be sung live during the 'Our World' broadcast.

On June 24, the Beatles received the press in EMI's Studio 1, transformed for the occasion into a setting appropriate for a world-wide party. There were hundreds of streamers, balloons painted to look like globes, and the Beatles themselves wearing signboards which bore the slogan 'Love is all you need' in five languages.

The next day, June 25, some 400 million people in 26 countries watched the images of 'Our World' unfold on their television screens – although the programme's title was changed to 'Across the World'

In May 1967, the Beatles were invited to participate in an unprecedented television event: the world-wide broadcast of a variety programme to be titled 'Our World', which was being produced in conjunction with the Canadian World's Fair Expo '67. Many countries were to be represented in the show, and the Beatles were asked to appear for the United Kingdom.

The idea for their contribution was an obvious one: the 'Our

at the very last moment, when five Communist countries suddenly withdrew their co-operation.

After segments about lady streetcar conductors in Australia and eccentric painters in France, and a Van Cliburn piano recital from the United States, the scene shifted to EMI's Studio 1. John and Paul sat on high stools wearing headphones, George and Ringo were seated a bit further back. The mob of background vocalists included Jane Asher, Patti Boyd, Brian Epstein, Mick Jagger, Marianne Faithfull, Keith Richard, Keith Moon, Mike McGear, Eric Clapton, Gary Leeds and Graham Nash. George Martin was visible in the control booth, and Mal Evans appeared handing out sandwiches.

Thirteen musicians strolled into the studio and struck up the opening bars of the *Marseillaise* . . . and the world listened as the Beatles began to sing.

From the studio in Abbey Road, BBC-TV transmitted the images to the Early Bird satellite above the Atlantic Ocean, from which they were passed onto the Lana Bird satellite and then to the ATS/B above the Pacific. . . .

That same evening, the tapes of *All You Need Is Love* were jetted to America, Japan, Australia and Canada, and the single went on sale around the world a scant two weeks later. On the B-side was *Baby, You're A Rich Man*, which had been recorded early in May for the *Yellow Submarine* cartoon. With the audience for its television debut numbering 400 million, it should come as no surprise that the single became a number one hit throughout most of the free world.

John, after the broadcast.

TELEVISION: OUR WORLD

131

THE APPLE BOUTIQUE

In the 'Swinging Sixties', London's Carnaby Street boutiques were quick to copy and mass-market whatever styles of clothing the trendsetting Beatles chose to wear. It seemed reasonable therefore to take the merchandizing of Beatlewear into the group's own hands.

For some months during 1967, the Beatles had been involved with Simon Posthuma, Marijke Koger and Josje Leeger, three Dutch artists who had formed a collective known as The Fool. Simon, Marijke and Josje had already worked on the cover design for the *Sgt. Pepper* album, and had painted both John's Rolls Royce and his piano in wild psychedelic colours.

Now, Josje was set to work designing a line of Beatle clothing: bizarre belled clown suits, purple velvet witches' cloaks, nuns' habits, Mexican sheepskin coats, satin harem robes. Marijke created a series of posters and, together with Simon, led 20 art students in painting the inside and outside walls of a shop at 94 Baker Street. The painting on the front of the shop was some 20 yards high, and was reproduced on the front pages of all major British newspapers. Most of the other traders in Baker Street signed an angry petition protesting at the new eyesore in their midst.

The mural is almost finished. Below: *just before the opening.*

Josje Leeger (left) *and Marijke Koger of The Fool.*

Cynthia and John with George and Patti at the opening of the Apple Boutique.

Jenny Boyd, George's sister-in-law, in the boutique. Below: cash register and salesgirl.

On December 5, 1967, a gala reception was held at the boutique. It was called an 'applejuice party', and the guest list included the Rolling Stones, Twiggy, Rudolf Nureyev and an army of journalists. John and George announced the planned opening of more Apple boutiques all over England: shops selling leisurewear, theatrical costumes, gifts and so on.

Two days later, on December 7, the Apple Boutique opened its doors to the public. Its manager was Pete Shotton – the same Pete Shotton who, twelve years earlier in Liverpool, had been one of the founding members of a skiffle group called the Quarrymen.

The Apple Boutique became a place of worship for Beatles fans, clothing fanatics and hippies in general. Thousands of people flocked to Baker Street to gape at the building's exterior, its interior, the exotic robes of its salesladies (one of whom was Jenny Boyd, George's sister-in-law), its inflatable furniture, its clouds of incense, its fountain filled with plastic dahlias, its Beatle mannequins and rainbow-coloured cash registers.

Unfortunately, not much money ever found its way into those rainbow tills, and new branches of the Apple empire did not spring from the ground as rapidly as John and George had predicted.

A second shop, specializing in theatrical clothing, did in fact open up on May 22, 1968, but the end of Apple's experiment with the retail trade was already in sight. On July 31, 1968, only eight months after its grand opening, the Apple celebrated its grand closing. It was indeed an extraordinary celebration the kind of event which only the Beatles could have stage-managed.

John, Paul, George and Ringo went through the shop's inventory and selected items to keep for themselves. Then the Apple's doors were flung open for one last spree – and all of the remaining stock was given away to anyone who happened to walk by! It was an expensive, but unforgettable, way to say farewell.

Lennon-McCartney

Brecht and Weil, Rogers and Hammerstein, Bacharach and David, Goffin and King, Cahn and Van Heusen. Song-writing teams are not unusual in the world of popular music but, usually, one of the partners writes the lyrics and the other composes the music. John Lennon and Paul McCartney were an exception to that rule: each of them was capable of writing both words *and* music. And although most Beatle songs were officially credited to 'Lennon-McCartney', there were in fact only a few dozen numbers which were truly co-productions.

Normally, either Lennon or McCartney came up with a more or less complete idea, including melody, refrain and partial lyrics; the other partner then helped out with the central section of the number, the middle eight. Many of Paul's songs, for example, which would otherwise have been too sweet and sentimental, became genuine Beatles songs with the addition of a few critical or cynical lines by John. Similarly, Paul also often helped John out. What follows is an overview of those songs where the identity of the sole or principal author is known.

JOHN   PAUL

1962

Please Please Me, Ask Me Why

Love Me Do, P.S. I Love You

1963

From Me to You, Misery, She Loves You, I'll Get You, I Want to Hold Your Hand, Little Child

Do You Want to Know a Secret, There's a Place, This Boy, It Won't Be Long, All I've Got to Do, Not a Second Time

Thank You Girl, I Saw Her Standing There, I Wanna Be Your Man (with John), All My Loving, Hold Me Tight

1964

Baby's in Black

You Can't Do That, I Call Your Name, A Hard Day's Night, I Should Have Known Better, If I Fell, I'm Happy Just to Dance with You, Tell Me Why, Anytime at All, I'll Cry Instead, When I Get Home, I'll Be Back, I Feel Fine, No Reply, I'm a Loser, It's Only Love, I Don't Want to Spoil the Party

Can't Buy Me Love, Things We Said Today, And I Love Her, She's a Woman (with John), I've Just Seen a Face, I'll Follow the Sun, Eight Days a Week, Every Little Thing, What You're Doing

1965

The Word, We Can Work It Out

Ticket to Ride, Yes It Is, Help!, You've Got to Hide Your Love Away, You're Going to Lose That Girl, It's Only Love, Norwegian Wood, Nowhere Man, What Goes On, Girl In My Life, Run for Your Life

I'm Down, The Night Before, Another Girl, I'm Looking Through You, Tell Me What You See, I've Just Seen a Face, Yesterday, Drive My Car, You Won't See Me, Michelle, Day Tripper

1966

Rain, I'm Only Sleeping, She Said She Said, And Your Bird Can Sing, Dr. Robert, Tomorrow Never Knows, Strawberry Fields Forever

Paperback Writer, Eleanor Rigby (with John), Here, There and Everywhere, Yellow Submarine, Good Day Sunshine, For No One, Got to Get You into My Life, When I'm 64 (with John), Penny Lane (with John)

1967

With a Little Help From My Friends, A Day in the Life, Baby You're a Rich Man

Lucy in the Sky with Diamonds (with Paul), Being for the Benefit of Mr. Kite, Good Morning, Good Morning, All You Need Is Love, I am the Walrus

Sergeant Pepper's Lonely Hearts Club Band, Getting Better, Fixing a Hole, She's Leaving Home, Lovely Rita, Hello Goodbye, Magical Mystery Tour, Your Mother Should Know, The Fool on the Hill

1968

Hey Bulldog, Across the Universe, Dear Prudence, Glass Onion, Bungalow Bill, Happiness is a Warm Gun, I'm So Tired, Julia, Yer Blues, Everybody's Got Something to Hide Except Me and My Monkey, Sexy Sadie, Revolution, Goodnight, Polythene Pam, Cry Baby Cry

Lady Madonna, Hey Jude, Back in the U.S.S.R., Ob-La-Di, Ob-La-Da, Honey Pie, Martha My Dear, Blackbird, Rocky Raccoon, Why Don't We Do It in the Road, I Will, Birthday (with John, George and Ringo), Mother Nature's Son, Helter Skelter, Maxwell's Silver Hammer, All Together Now

1969

I've Got a Feeling, Two of Us

Don't Let Me Down, Dig a Pony, Dig It, You Know My Name, The Ballad of John and Yoko, Come Together, I Want You/She's So Heavy, Because, Sun King, Mean Mister Mustard

Get Back. Let It Be, The Long and Winding Road, She Came In Through the Bathroom Window, Teddy Boy, Oh Darling, You Never Give Me Your Money, Golden Slumbers, Carry That Weight, Her Majesty, The End

1968

3 February

3 February

19 February

January 5, 1968	In spite of the negative reviews, *Magical Mystery Tour* is re-broadcast, this time in colour, on BBC-2.
January 9, 1968	George and Patti leave for Bombay, where George will write, arrange and record the music for *Wonderwall* in a total of ten days.
January 11, 1968	George records the instrumental track for *The Inner Light* at the De Lane Lea Studios in Bombay.
January 19, 1968	*Dear Delilah*, by a group called Grapefruit, is released on the RCA label. The group is managed by Terry Doran, George's personal assistant, and is the first act signed to Apple Publishing, also run by Doran. It sells more copies than it deserves to, mainly because a large number of Beatle fans automatically begin collecting anything connected with Apple.
January 20, 1968	Paul is in the studio to produce an album entitled *McGough And McGear*, by two members of the Scaffold. 'McGear' is, of course, Paul's brother Michael; McGough is Liverpool poet, Roger McGough.
February 3, 1968	At EMI's Abbey Road studios, Paul and a group of session musicians record *Lady Madonna*.
February 4, 1968	At the Abbey Road studios, John begins recording *Across The Universe*.
February 5, 1968	At the request of a student, Paul holds a press conference at the Royal Garden Hotel in London in connection with the Leicester Arts Festival. Other than this one press conference, Paul's involvement with the festival is non-existent.
February 6, 1968	At the Abbey Road studios, the vocals are recorded for *The Inner Light*. Ringo appears as a guest on the BBC-1 television series 'Cilla', which stars Cilla Black. They sing *Act Naturally* and several other numbers together.
February 8, 1968	A BBC film crew joins the Beatles in the Abbey Road studios to shoot a promotional film for *Lady Madonna*. During the same session, John completes work on *Across The Universe*.
February 10, 1968	*Magical Mystery Tour* is broadcast on Dutch television. Holland is one of the many countries outside the UK to buy the film, which cost £30,000 to make and brings in over £1,000,000 in overseas sales. Most countries screen the film once they have bought it, but a few bother to re-screen it later.
February 11, 1968	*Only A Northern Song* and *Hey Bulldog* are recorded at EMI's Abbey Road studios. It is the first Beatles recording session to be attended by Yoko Ono.
February 13, 1968	Ringo appears again on BBC-1's 'Cilla'.
February 16, 1968	George, Patti, John, Cynthia and assorted camp followers arrive in Rishikesh, India, to study Transcendental Meditation with the Maharishi. Their fellow students include Mia Farrow and the Beach Boys' Mike Love.
February 17, 1968	Hunter Davies is commissioned to write the authorized biography of the Beatles.
February 19, 1968	Paul, Jane, Ringo and Maureen fly to India to join the Rishikesh meditation programme.
March 1, 1968	Ringo and Maureen drop out of the Maharishi's meditation programme in India and fly back to England, explaining that they miss their children too much to continue.
March 8, 1968	Release date of Cilla Black's new single, *Step Inside Love*. The song, which is also used as the theme music for her television series, is a Paul McCartney composition.
March 9, 1968	For the *Sgt. Pepper* album, the Beatles are awarded four Grammy awards.
March 14, 1968	The *Lady Madonna* promotional film is shown on BBC-1's 'Top of the Pops'.
March 15, 1968	The new single, *Lady Madonna/The Inner Light*, is released. *The Inner Light* is the first of George's songs to be used on a Beatles single.
March 26, 1968	Paul and Jane leave Rishikesh for England.

March 29, 1968	Derek Taylor is appointed as Apple's Press Officer.
April 3, 1968	Apple Corps Ltd. officially opens it doors at 95 Wigmore Street, London.
April 7, 1968	*Magical Mystery Tour* is broadcast on Japanese television.
April 20, 1968	Apple Corps has a large advertisement in the latest issue of the *New Musical Express*, inviting unknown songwriters and musicians to submit material for consideration. John and Cynthia arrive back in England, having walked out on the Maharishi's meditation programme in Rishikesh. George and Patti also quit the programme, but spend a day in Madras (where George appears in a film about Ravi Shankar) before returning to England on April 22.
April 30, 1968	Paul is on stage in Bradford, England, conducting the Black Dyke Mills Band. *Thingummybob*, composed by Paul and played by the band, is later used as the theme tune for a television series with the same name.
May 1, 1968	Cynthia, Julian and Donovan leave for a short vacation in Greece.
May 4, 1968	Mary Hopkin wins the most votes on the Thames Television talent contest 'Opportunity Knocks'.
May 5, 1968	Twiggy calls Paul to tell him about Mary Hopkin's win.
May 11, 1968	After John's refusal to take her along on his forthcoming business trip to America, Cynthia leaves for a vacation in Italy with Julian and her mother. They stay at the Bassanini family's Hotel Cruiser in Rome.
May 13, 1968	John and Paul leave for New York, where they hold a press conference at the Americana Hotel to announce the establishment of an American branch of Apple. Paul meets Linda Eastman again, and writes (about her?) *She Came In Through The Bathroom Window*.
May 15, 1968	John and Paul are guests on 'The Tonight Show', and talk about Apple's activities.
May 16, 1968	John sends Cynthia a telegram, telling her he wants a divorce.
May 17, 1968	George and Patti are in Cannes, along with Ringo and Maureen, to attend the world premiere of *Wonderwall*.
May 20, 1968	John and Paul are back from America, George and Ringo are back from France, and the four of them are in the studio to begin recording sessions for the new album. The sessions will continue until early October. The same day, John and Yoko do some experimental recording in John's private studio. Some of the resulting tracks will later appear on their *Two Virgins* LP.
May 21, 1968	Paul and Jane have lunch with Andy Williams, attend his concert at the Royal Albert Hall and, afterwards, are present at a party held in Williams' honour.
May 22, 1968	John, Yoko, George and Patti hold a press conference to announce the opening of Apple's second shop, Apple Tailoring (Civil and Theatrical), at 161 King's Road, Chelsea. The store will specialize in theatrical costumes.
May 23, 1968	Apple Tailoring officially opens. Its manager is fashion designer John Crittle.
May 30, 1968	The Beatles are in EMI's Studio 3 to begin recording work on *Revolution* and *Revolution 9*. During the week, recording also begins on a number with the working title *This Is Some Friendly*, written by Ringo in India, which will ultimately appear as *Don't Pass Me By*.
June 7, 1968	George is in California to appear in *Messenger Of The East*, a film about Ravi Shankar. Ringo and Maureen are also present.
June 8, 1968	Paul and Jane attend the wedding of Paul's brother Mike and Angela Fishwick. Paul serves as his brother's best man.
June 11, 1968	Paul records *Blackbird* at EMI's Abbey Road studios.
June 15, 1968	On the occasion of the National Sculpture Exhibit, John and Yoko plant acorns in front of Coventry Cathedral in the name of peace.
June 18, 1968	In the Old Vic Theatre in London, the National Theatre Company premieres a play based on John's *In His Own Write*, under the direction of Victor Spinetti, who previously appeared in *A Hard Day's Night, Help!* and *Magical Mystery Tour*.
June 20, 1968	EMI and Apple Records agree that all future Beatle discs will appear on the Apple label with Parlophone catalogue numbers, while EMI will handle Apple's distribution.
June 21, 1968	Paul visits the Capitol Records Convention in Los Angeles to promote the Apple label, and stays at the Beverly Hills Hotel with Linda Eastman.
June 22, 1968	John is interviewed about the theatrical interpretation of his book on the BBC-TV programme 'Release'. The Beatles buy new offices for Apple at 3 Savile Row in London. The stately building, which formerly housed the Jack Hylton Organisation, costs £500,000.
June 24, 1968	George is in the Trident Studios in London with Jackie Lomax to produce Jackie's *Sour Milk Sea* single.
June 30, 1968	Paul is in the studio with the Black Dyke Mills Band to produce and conduct *Thingummybob* and *Yellow Submarine*, to be released as a single.

13 May

17 May

8 June

29 June

1 July

July 1, 1968	John's first art exhibition, 'You Are Here', organized in collaboration with Yoko, opens at the Robert Fraser Gallery in London. John and Yoko, dressed completely in white, release helium-filled white balloons with messages attached to them. As he launches his balloons, John says, 'I declare these balloons high.' In the studio, the Beatles are joined by a 30-piece orchestra to begin recording work on *Goodnight*.
July 2, 1968	*Ob-La-Di, Ob-La-Da* is recorded.
July 7, 1968	Patti Harrison opens an antique shop, Juniper, in the Chelsea Antique Market.
July 12, 1968	Recording of *Don't Pass Me By* is completed.
July 15, 1968	*Cry Baby Cry* is recorded, with George Martin playing harmonium.
July 17, 1968	Thousands of fans mob the street in front of the London Pavilion, Piccadilly Circus, where all four Beatles, Yoko, Maureen and Patti are in attendance at the world premiere of the animated cartoon *Yellow Submarine*: 100 policemen have their hands full keeping the fans from overwhelming the guests. After the show, the Beatles host a party at the Royal Lancaster Hotel.
July 18, 1968	*Helter Skelter* is recorded. The first version of the song runs to 24 minutes.
July 19, 1968	*Sexy Sadie* is recorded.
July 20, 1968	In the BBC-TV programme 'Dee Time', Jane reveals that her engagement to Paul has been broken off. 'New hope for millions of girls,' the newspapers announce.
July 23, 1968	*Come On, Come On* is recorded. By the time the song is released on the white double album, however, it is retitled *Everybody's Got Something To Hide Except Me And My Monkey*.
July 25, 1968	*While My Guitar Gently Weeps* is recorded, with John on organ.
July 26, 1968	At Paul's house, John and Paul polish off the writing of *Hey Jude*; the bulk of the song was written earlier by Paul alone. Paul later says that the song was written for Julian Lennon shortly after John and Cynthia's divorce, but John always maintained that the lyrics were really a message from Paul to him.
July 29, 1968	*Hey Jude* is recorded, with a camera crew filming the session for a BBC project called 'Experiment in Television'.
July 31, 1968	The Apple Boutique closes its doors: after John, Paul, George and Ringo have picked out items to keep for themselves, all other merchandise in stock (worth approximately £20,000) is given away to passers-by.
August 1, 1968	A 40-piece orchestra is brought into the studio to complete the recording work on *Hey Jude*.
August 2, 1968	George and Patti leave for a vacation in Los Angeles. BBC-TV broadcasts the first episode of a new series, 'Thingummybob', with theme music composed by Paul and played by the Black Dyke Mills Band.
August 7, 1968	Paul and several friends paint the windows of the Apple Boutique white, then cover them with song titles (*Hey Jude*, *Revolution*) and slogans. In the studio, George's song *Not Guilty* is recorded, with a guitar solo by Eric Clapton. The track never appears on a Beatle album, but eleven years later a newly-recorded version (without Clapton) turns up on George's solo LP, *George Harrison*.
August 9, 1968	Paul begins recording *Mother Nature's Son*.
August 11, 1968	Apple announces the beginning of 'National Apple Week', during which extensive advertising in the media publicizes the release of the first discs on the Apple label: the *Thingummybob* single by the Black Dyke Mills Band, and the *Wonderwall* soundtrack album with music written, arranged and produced by George.
August 13, 1968	*Yer Blues* is recorded.
August 14, 1968	*What's The New Mary Jane* is recorded.
August 15, 1968	*Rocky Raccoon* is recorded.
August 16, 1968	Release date of the Apple single (and the first Apple success): *Those Were The Days* by Mary Hopkin. Within a few short months, worldwide sales of this simple tune exceed four million copies. The melody is based on a Russian folk song, *Darogoi Dlimmoyo (Dear For Me)*, written in the twenties by Alexander Wertinsky; lyrics are by American singer/songwriter Gene Raskin in 1962. The choice of this song for the first-ever release on the Apple label was Paul's.
August 20, 1968	Paul records *Wild Honey Pie*.
August 22, 1968	*Back In The USSR* is recorded.
August 24, 1968	Ronan O'Rahilly, founder and former owner of off-shore radio station Radio Caroline and a friend of John's, is named financial advisor to Apple.
August 28, 1968	At the Trident Studios in London, recording begins on *Dear Prudence*, a song written by John for Mia's sister, Prudence Farrow, during the last trip to India. Background voices include Jackie Lomax, Mal Evans, and Paul's nephew John.
August 30, 1968	*Hey Jude* and *Revolution* are released as the first Beatle single on the Apple label.
September 1, 1968	The final version of *Helter Skelter* is recorded.

1 July

17 July

28 July

11 August

August

September 4, 1968	At Twickenham Studios, in the presence of about 60 fans, a crew films the Beatles singing *Hey Jude* for broadcast later this week on David Frost's TV programme, 'Frost on Sunday'.
September 6, 1968	Jackie Lomax's *Sour Milk Sea* single is released on the Apple label.
September 8, 1968	'Frost on Sunday' is broadcast, including *Hey Jude*.
September 11, 1968	John and Paul record *Glass Onion*.
September 14, 1968	Worldwide sales of *Hey Jude* pass the two million mark.
September 16, 1968	John, Paul and George record *I Will*.
September 18, 1968	*Birthday*, written in the studios by all four Beatles, is recorded; the vocalists are John, Paul, Linda, Yoko and Patti. During a break in the session, the band watch the film *The Girl Can't Help It* on television at Paul's house.
September 19, 1968	*Piggies* is recorded. The same evening, the Beatles can be seen singing *Revolution* on BBC-TV's 'Top of the Pops'.
September 23, 1968	*Happiness Is A Warm Gun* is recorded.
September 30, 1968	Heinemann Publishers issues the first authorized biography of the Beatles: *The Beatles* by Hunter Davies.
October 1, 1968	*Honey Pie* is recorded without Ringo, at the Trident Studios in London. Ringo claims that he has left the group, but returns after a week's vacation.
October 3, 1968	*Savoy Truffle* is recorded (without Ringo) at the Trident Studios.
October 4, 1968	Paul records *Martha My Dear* (a song which, contrary to popular opinion, is *not* about his dog), at the Trident Studios.
October 6, 1968	In Los Angeles, George makes an unscheduled and unexpected appearance on 'The Smothers Brothers' Comedy Hour' to promote *Hey Jude*.
October 8, 1968	George is back in England and in the EMI studios with John and Paul, *Long, Long, Long* is recorded. Ringo has not yet returned to the group.
October 9, 1968	John records *I'm So Tired* in one take, and recording of *Bungalow Bill* begins.
October 10, 1968	*Why Don't We Do It In The Road?* is recorded.
October 11, 1968	Release date of the Bonzo Dog Doo-Dah Band's *I'm The Urban Spaceman* single, produced by 'Apollo C. Vermouth', otherwise known as Paul McCartney.
October 13, 1968	John records *Julia*.
October 14, 1968	The Starr family leaves for a vacation in Sardinia as John, Paul and George Martin begin work on the mixing of the double album. Two of the numbers originally planned for inclusion (*Maxwell's Silver Hammer* and *Polythene Pam*) have not yet been recorded; they are eventually released, almost a year later, on *Abbey Road*.
October 17, 1968	George is back in Los Angeles with Jackie Lomax and Mal Evans, to promote Jackie's *Sour Milk Sea* single and to record four new Lomax numbers.
October 18, 1968	It requires the presence of 40 uniformed policemen to raid Ringo's flat in Montague Square, Marylebone, where John and Yoko, who are living there at the time, are arrested for possession of 219 grammes of cannabis resin. They are later released on bail; at the eventual trial they are found guilty and fined £150 with 20 guineas (£21) costs.
October 31, 1968	Linda Eastman flies to England and moves in with Paul.
November 3, 1968	The Beatles appear on BBC-TV with Lulu, Donovan and George's mother.
November 5, 1968	Paul and Linda leave for a vacation in Scotland.
November 8, 1968	Full-page advertisements appear in several London papers, soliciting donations for Abie Nathan's 'peace ship', which will beam radio programmes promoting peace in the Middle East to Israel and the Arab nations. The ads are paid for by John and Yoko. John and Cynthia's decree absolute, finalizing their divorce, is announced.
November 9, 1968	Apple releases an album of experimental music by John and Yoko: *Unfinished Music Number 1: Two Virgins*. John and Yoko appear on the cover in the nude, reason enough for EMI to refuse to distribute the disc. After a stand-off lasting several months, a compromise is finally reached: the cover is hidden behind a plain brown wrapper, except for the faces of John and Yoko, who peer out through two holes cut through the paper bag. Retailers in Holland, apparently a more progressive country than England, are allowed to sell the record without the brown paper figleaf. However, they *are* supplied with green Apple stickers and encouraged to use them to cover up all visible private parts. Few retailers bother to take advantage of the opportunity.
November 21, 1968	Yoko has a miscarriage. During her stay at Queen Charlotte's Maternity Hospital, John sleeps in her room.
November 22, 1968	The double album *The Beatles* is released; it is generally referred to as 'the white album', on account of its plain white cover which only has 'The Beatles' embossed on it.
November 24, 1968	Grapefruit drops away from Apple Publishing's tree of artists, claiming that too little attention is being paid to it. Manager Terry Doran comments: 'I like the Beatles as friends, but not as bosses. . . . There is too much driftwood at Apple.'

14 August

30 August

9 November

28 November

11 December

20 December

November 28, 1968	Six days after the appearance of the white album, the *Yellow Submarine* LP is released.
December 7, 1968	*Disc and Music Echo*, a weekly British music paper, publishes a scoop: Paul's new steady girlfriend is Linda Eastman, photographer for *Rolling Stone* and *The New York Times*.
December 11, 1968	Under the direction of Michael Lindsay-Hogg, the Rolling Stones shoot a TV film titled *The Rolling Stones' Rock and Roll Circus*. The film is, unfortunately, never broadcast, but a bootleg soundtrack album includes a nine-minute version of *Yer Blues*, performed by John, Yoko, Eric Clapton, Keith Richard and Mitch Mitchell.
December 17, 1968	World premiere of the film *Candy*, in which Ringo plays Emmanuel the Gardener.
December 18, 1968	John and Yoko hold another 'event', titled 'Alchemical Wedding' – for 1½ hours they are on stage at the Royal Albert Hall, writhing within a large white sack.
December 20, 1968	British fan club members receive their traditional gift from the band, this year titled *The Beatles' 1968 Christmas Record*. Unlike previous years, however, the messages from John, Paul, George and Ringo have been recorded separately, then edited together by Kenny Everett. John and Yoko make a film called *Rape* for March 1970 broadcast on Austrian television.
December 23, 1968	John and Yoko, both dressed as Santa Claus, pass round the presents at the Apple Christmas party.

Apple Scruffs

During the sixties, many Beatle fans used their holiday time to make devout pilgrimages to various of Beatledom's holy spots. Every Beatle house had its own guard of honour of fans, armed with cameras and autograph books, waiting patiently for even the briefest glimpse of their idols. Whenever the group was known to be recording, the EMI studios in Abbey Road were also besieged by crowds, and the Apple offices in Savile Row were another natural hang-out for hard-core fans.

Some pilgrims made Beatle-watching their life's work. Month after month, they spent every spare moment on duty. They began to know one another, affectionately called themselves the Apple Scruffs. In 1970, they published their own magazine, *The Apple Scruffs Monthly Book*. And they became internationally known when George wrote a tribute to them for his *All Things Must Pass* album.

It was not easy being a Scruff. Neither rain, hail, sleet nor snow would hold these dedicated lunatics back from putting in at least three or four hours a day at their posts. Naturally, they owned all albums and singles on which one or more members of the group put in an appearance. Obviously, they bought all magazines and newspapers which so much as mentioned the word Beatle. It goes without saying that they had little time left over for any other pursuit.

In addition to the Apple Scruffs, there were thousands of other fans who, although somewhat less fanatic than the Scruffs, were hooked enough to make special trips to London for the express purpose of staring hungrily at the assorted houses, studios and offices which had connections with the group and of – hopefully! – coming face-to-face with a Beatle.

The locations were there to be gazed at, but a personal encounter was a rarer experience. From the files of the Official Dutch Beatles Fan Club come the following accounts:

Ton Hoofwijk of Grevenbricht visited London in 1968. 'It was July 30,' he later reported, 'and I was walking through St John's Wood looking for Paul's house. It wasn't hard to find, because there were maybe 30 fans with cameras standing in front of the gate. Around three in the afternoon a green mini-Cooper appeared, driven by a man with a beard. (Author's note: probably Neil Aspinall.) He said a kind of password into the microphone next to the gate, and then the gate opened up quickly to let the car in. A minute later Paul came out of the house, walked to the mini, called "Hello, there!" to us and climbed in. Before I knew it, the car, the man with the beard and Paul were gone.'

Brigitte Jonkers was in the Apple Boutique the day before its gala closing. 'Somebody whispered that I should come back the next day, because they were going to give everything away. I didn't believe it, and so I didn't go. The stupidest mistake I ever made in my life! I'll never forgive myself. . . .'

When Irene Crul of Heemstede was in London, she went to Paul's house and – an inspired thought! – rang the doorbell. A housekeeper informed her via intercom that Paul was asleep, and she decided to wait. Later, she heard a car start up somewhere inside the grounds. The gate swung open, and a grey-green Jaguar headed towards the street. 'It was Paul,' Irene remembers. 'I shouted and held my hand up like a traffic cop, and sure

The entrance to EMI's studio complex at 3 Abbey Road, photographed by fans.

The Apple offices in Savile Row.

enough he stopped. I had my camera ready, but I was so nervous that all the pictures came out blurred. I got his autograph: "Love, Paul." Isn't that the end? His car licence number is LLO 840D, in case you ever see him on the road. That night I was so happy I couldn't sleep.'

Grada van der Vught, of The Hague, has a miracle worker for a father. In 1967 he told her that she was going to London for a vacation, and that while there she would have a chance to meet with Paul. On May 17, her parents brought her to the well-known house on Cavendish Avenue and rang the bell. To Grada's great surprise, a woman's voice responded that they were expected, and the heavy metal gate swung wide to admit them. They met Paul in the garden, and Grada introduced herself. 'At least, I tried to,' she recalls, 'but I was completely tongue-tied. "Mr McCar – Mr – Mr Paul – Paul Mc – Sir Paul – " Finally he winked at me and said, "Just call me Paul."'

We talked for a bit and he gave me his autograph, and then the other three Beatles came out of the house! My mother was taking pictures, and then someone said, "Are you coming, Paul? We can't keep George Martin waiting much longer." Paul and I said good-bye, and then the four of them climbed into his Mini and drove off.' To this day, Grada still doesn't know how her father arranged it all. . . .

Max Bokking of Zeist climbed over the fence surrounding John's manor in Tittenhurst Park, was discovered within the grounds and brought into the house itself, where he managed to see John for a few moments, and snap a few photographs.

Sylvia and Corinne Nelissen of Soestdijk were in London on July 22, 1969, and were standing in front of the EMI studios when two cars pulled up to the curb. 'We looked . . . and there was George! We were taking pictures like a pair of madwomen as he struggled to get through the crowd of fans. He was wearing a strawberry-red shirt and he had sunglasses on. He disappeared through the door in less than no time. *But we had seen him!* We didn't have much time to recover from the shock, because Ringo showed up about ten minutes later. I was at the top of the steps and I wanted him to look into my camera lens, so I called to him. He looked, and he said "Hello!" to me alone. He was really very friendly.'

It was George who summed it all up the best: 'In the fog and in the rain/Through the pleasures and the pain/On the step outside you stand/With your flowers in your hand/My Apple Scruffs. . . .'

17 May 1967: Grada van der Vught meets Paul.

23 March 1969: Yoko signs a Beatle fan's wrist. (photo:
H. V. Fulpen)

1971: John and Yoko at Tittenhurst Park. (photo: Max
Bokking)

When it comes to singles, *Hey Jude* is one of the Beatles' masterpieces: it was one of the few songs of the late sixties written by John and Paul in true collaboration; it was the longest single the boys ever released; it was the first Beatle disc to appear on the group's own Apple label; it was an enormous technical challenge skilfully handled (involving two recording studios, four days of sessions and 40 musicians); and it was – and is – above all else, a brilliant statement and a brilliant song.

The idea for *Hey Jude* was Paul's. He began to write it on his way to visit Cynthia Lennon, shortly after her divorce from John, and originally meant it to be a comfort to the couple's only child, Julian. In 1973 John Lennon said of *Hey Jude* 'That's [Paul's] best song. It started off as a song about my son, Julian. Then it turned into "Hey Jude". I always thought it was about me and Yoko, but he said it was about him and his.'

Paul found himself unable to complete the tune satisfactorily and asked John for assistance. On Friday, July 26, 1968, the two of them finished off the song at Paul's house. Two days later, Paul played *Hey Jude* for George and Ringo. And the next day, July 29, rehearsals began in an EMI studio. Rehearsals continued on July 30, and were filmed by a BBC crew for inclusion in a fifteen-minute documentary titled 'An Experiment in Television'.

On Wednesday, July 31, all the Beatles' sound equipment and instruments were moved to the Trident Studios, where work began anew. First the music tracks were laid down, with Paul playing piano, George on electric piano and Ringo shaking a tambourine. Then came the vocals: Paul singing lead and the other three Beatles providing a background chorus.

Yellow Matter Custard (also released as *As Sweet As You Are*) includes an excellent series of recordings from the boys' weekly radio programme, broadcast by the BBC in 1963. The Beatles played live, in a BBC studio, but without an audience, and performed not only original numbers, but many tunes by other composers as well. This is the Beatles at their very best, with songs which can be found nowhere but on illegal LPs: *I Got A*

BIRTH OF A SINGLE:

Woman, Glad All Over, A Shot Of Rhythm 'n' Blues, Crying Waiting Hoping, To Know Her Is To Love Her and a dozen more.

To Know Her Is To Love Her was already a part of the group's repertoire on January 1, 1962, when they auditioned for Decca Records in London. They played fifteen songs, and the tapes miraculously survived the slings and arrows of outrageous fortune, most of them being released on a bootleg as *The Decca Audition Tapes* in 1979. The pre-Beatlemania Beatles sing *Sheik Of Araby, September In The Rain, Three Cool Cats, Red Sail In The Sun-*

set, Like Dreamers Do, Love Of The Loved and six others. Probably in response to this very popular bootleg a legitimate album of twelve of the fifteen songs recorded was released in the UK in Autumn 1982. The album, entitled *The Complete Silver Beatles*, contains twelve songs; the only tracks from the audition not included are *Love Of The Loved, Hello Little Girl* and *Like Dreamers Do*. These were all Lennon-McCartney compositions and were left off to avoid possible legal problems.

But with music and instruments on tape, the recording was still

'HEY JUDE'

incomplete. Paul and John saw *Hey Jude* beginning as a tender ballad, then working its way up to an intense and lengthy climax. On August 1 it was decided that, in order to build to and maintain that climax, a full 40-piece orchestra would be needed.

Producer George Martin spent most of the day translating what the Beatles wanted onto musical scores for the 40 musicians, and John and Paul took each musician aside to explain when they were and were not supposed to be playing. Most of them were only needed to contribute one or two long-held notes.

Recording went on through the night. Early in the morning of August 2, as the number neared completion, the 40 musicians were asked to underscore its closing minutes by clapping their hands and joining in on the repeated *na-na-na* chorus. The orchestra co-operated vigorously.

John, Paul, George Martin and several technicians worked on through the morning and afternoon, remixing the various tracks. And by the late afternoon on August 2, the first rough proof-pressing of *Hey Jude* was in Apple's hands.

Originally, the song had been planned as the B side of a single whose A side was to be *Revolution* (which had been written in February while the Beatles were with the Maharishi in India, and recorded in June), but eventually these plans were reversed and *Hey Jude* was used as the single's A side. A total of four versions of *Revolution* had been recorded: the first version ran over ten minutes in length; the second version was released in November on the white double album *The Beatles* as *Revolution No. 1*, and the fourth version was used as the flip side for *Hey Jude*. Finally, the complete single was released on August 30, 1968.

Photo Sessions: 1968

After the *Hey Jude* single was recorded, the Beatles held a special photo session to produce an unusual series of pictures to celebrate the disc's August 30 release date. The series was to be used for publicity purposes, and copies would also be provided to the group's fan clubs throughout the world.

Around lunchtime on August 11, a Sunday, the boys gathered at Paul's house in Cavendish Avenue, London. From there they left for their first location, the *Sunday Times* building in Gray's Inn Road, with a number of photographers (including Don McCullin, Jeremy Banks and Stephen Goldblatt) and a truck-load of costumes. On the roof of the building, John, Paul, George and Ringo posed:

one set of pictures was taken against a white wall, with a wind machine providing a stiff breeze and allowing, for the first time in years, all four Beatle foreheads to be simultaneously visible; a second set of pictures had the group against a blue background, dressed in red capes, crash helmets and motorcycle goggles – and, at one point, a boot on Ringo's head. Two months later, one of these rooftop shots appeared on the cover of *Life* magazine.

The second location was the Mercury Theatre in Bayswater, near Paddington Station, where, after a tea break in the theatre bar, the Beatles donned weird costumes and posed around a piano. This time, Ringo had a parrot on his shoulder instead of a boot on his head.

Next came a series of pictures taken on the opposite side of London from Bayswater, in a resi-

dential neighbourhood in East London, where the boys were photographed in front of a row of houses, in a park, amongst high bushes, and with a group of children in front of a fence.

The fourth location was a deserted section of the London Docks, where John and Paul performed a striptease in front of the assembled cameras.

And the marathon photo session was not yet over: the final pictures were taken in the soundproofed glass meditation chapel in Paul's garden designed by Digby Bridges, which Paul had purchased for $30,000 in October 1967. (He described it as his 'glass thingy'.) The chapel was more than four yards high and some nine yards in diameter; its glass roof was supported by four pillars and there was a hydraulic lift in the middle. In these shots, Paul's dog Martha played a major role.

Angus McBean took this photograph in the spring of 1969, to match his earlier shot for the cover of Please Please Me. *(see page 39)*

January 2, 1969	At the Twickenham Film Studios in London, the Beatles begin recording sessions for their next album. A camera crew under the direction of Michael Lindsay-Hogg captures these sessions on film for the next Beatle movie, which is to be a documentary about the band. Thus, the new year, the new album and the new film begin simultaneously.
January 3, 1969	In New Jersey, 30,000 copies of the *Two Virgins* album cover are confiscated by the police as pornographic material.
January 10, 1969	During a recording session, George and Paul get into an argument and George announces that he wants to leave the group. The argument itself is not caught by Michael Lindsay-Hogg's cameras, but when the completed documentary, *Let It Be*, is released, we get to see and hear its aftermath, as a cynical George tells Paul, 'All right, I'll play whatever you want me to play, or I won't play at all if you don't want me to play.'
January 18, 1968	In an interview with *Disc and Music Echo*, John reveals that Apple is having serious financial difficulties. 'If it carries on like this,' he says, 'we'll be broke in six months.'
January 20, 1969	*Wonderwall* has its London premiere.
January 30, 1969	Around lunchtime, the Beatles perform live on the roof of Apple's Savile Row headquarters. The proceedings are filmed, up to and including the arrival of the police, who call a halt to the show after receiving complaints about the noise.
January 31, 1969	After 30 days during which 28 hours of film have been shot and more than 100 hours of music have been recorded, the studio work on *Let It Be* is completed. Of the approximately 70 old and new songs recorded, twelve will appear on the *Let It Be* album in 1970 and dozens more will crop up on various bootleg LPs.
February 2, 1969	Yoko's divorce from Anthony Cox is finalized.
February 3, 1969	Paul plays drums and bass guitar and sings as the Steve Miller Band records *My Dark Hour*; he is later credited on the album cover as Paul Ramon. Apple announces that the Beatles' business affairs will, in the future, be handled by Allen Klein.
February 4, 1969	The New York law firm Eastman & Eastman is hired to advise Apple on legal matters. The elder Eastman is Linda's father, the younger is her brother.
February 7, 1969	George is admitted to a hospital with a throat infection. Paul is fined £19 for his refusal to pay a speeding ticket issued in July of 1969.
February 20, 1969	*Candy* premieres at the Odeon Theatre in Kensington, London.
February 21, 1969	Apple releases Mary Hopkin's *Postcard* album, produced by Paul. Paul also has designed the album's cover, for which Linda has done the photography. One of the tunes Mary sings on this record, *Honeymoon Song*, was in the Beatles' repertoire during the Cavern Club days.
February 22, 1969	After 88 consecutive weeks in the *Billboard* Hot 100, *Sgt. Pepper's Lonely Hearts Club Band* finally drops from the list.
February 24, 1969	NEMS is purchased by Triumph Investments.
February 28, 1969	John meets Allen Klein at the Dorchester Hotel in London. In an interview years later he recalls: 'I remember that he knew all about the Beatles and their music. It was more than the Eastmans knew. As soon as we had spoken for half an hour I knew he was the man to get us out of the rut.' John decides to make Klein his personal manager, an example which George and Ringo later follow. Paul, however, chooses the Eastmans to handle his affairs.
March 1, 1969	Shooting begins on *The Magic Christian*, starring Ringo and Peter Sellers. Paul is in the studio with Mary Hopkin to record *Goodbye*, a McCartney composition.
March 2, 1969	John and Yoko perform in an avant-garde jazz concert at the Lady Mitchell Hall in Cambridge. Portions of their appearance are recorded, and released two months later on the *Unfinished Music Number 2* LP.
March 3, 1969	Allen Klein begins negotiations to release the Beatles from their contracts with NEMS, a firm which no longer offers the group any services yet still earns millions in royalties from all their sales.

January

30 January

March

20 March

23 March

15 April

March 4, 1969	The *Magic Christian* set is visited by Paul, Linda, Mary Hopkin and Princess Margaret.
March 11, 1969	Paul and Linda announce that their wedding will take place the following day. While Paul is in the studio assisting with the recording of Jackie Lomax' *Thumbin' A Ride*, Linda is at the Marylebone Registry Office to take care of the necessary paperwork. That evening, Paul searches for a jeweller to sell him a ring after closing time; the ring he finally buys costs £12.
March 12, 1969	Paul and Linda are married at the Marylebone Registry Office in London, in the presence of Paul's brother Mike, Linda's six-year-old daughter Heather, Mal Evans and Peter Brown. To avoid fans and photographers, the wedding party enters the building via a rear door. The civil ceremony is followed by a religious one, at St John's Wood Church, and then by a reception at the Ritz Hotel. Meanwhile, *chez* Harrison is raided by police. Yogi, a specially trained Labrador retriever, sniffs out a small quantity of marijuana, so George and Patti are arrested, detained for several hours at Esher police station, and are eventually released on bail of £250 each.
March 16, 1969	Paul, Linda and Heather fly to New York for a three-week stay with Linda's parents. John and Yoko are also airborne, for a short vacation in Paris.
March 17, 1969	Dick James sells all of his shares in Northern Songs to Sir Lew Grade of ATV. The sale, which takes five minutes to complete, gives ATV 37½ per cent ownership of Northern Songs.
March 20, 1969	John and Yoko fly to Gibraltar, where they are quietly married in the presence of Apple's David Nuttall and Peter Brown. After the ceremony, they all return to Paris. During the course of the day, John writes *The Ballad Of John And Yoko*.
March 21, 1969	John and Yoko travel to Amsterdam, where they begin a bed-in for peace at the Hilton Hotel. Except for visits to the bathroom, they will remain in bed for eight days: the point of the exercise is to draw media attention to the cause of peace. In fact, they spend much of the week talking with journalists from around the world about peace.
March 28, 1969	The sale of Dick James' 37½ per cent of Northern Songs to ATV is announced by the press, and the Beatles hear about it for the first time. Apple releases Mary Hopkin's *Goodbye* single and makes a promotional film of Mary and Paul in the recording studio available to television stations. John and Yoko end their Amsterdam bed-in.
March 31, 1969	John and Yoko's film *Rape* is broadcast on Austrian television. Before the show goes on the air, they hold a press conference at the Hotel Sacher in Vienna, throughout which they are seated in large white bags. At Esher and Watton Magistrates' Court, George and Patti are each fined £250, with 10 guineas (£10.50) costs, for possession and use of marijuana.
April 1, 1969	John and Paul call Allen Klein to discuss the implications of the recent sale of Dick James' Northern Songs shares to ATV. After the conversation, all three of them head for London, where John says in an interview that he will continue recording with the Beatles because he needs the money, his available capital having shrunk to £50,000. In the same interview, John announces his plan to send two acorns to all world leaders, inviting them to grow 'peace oaks' in their gardens.
April 2, 1969	Allen Klein and the Beatles meet with Bruce Ormrod of Henry Ansbacher and Company, a London banking firm, to discuss ways that the group can maintain control over Northern Songs.
April 3, 1969	Billy Preston signs a recording contract with Apple.
April 7, 1969	John and Paul remix *Get Back*, after airplay of the song by the disc jockeys convinces them it needs additional work.
April 10, 1969	The Beatles refuse an ATV bid for their shares in Northern Songs, which amount to 30 per cent of the total number of shares in the company. On the contrary, they announce their intention to buy up all available shares from minor stockholders in an attempt to gain majority ownership.
April 15, 1969	A new Beatle single is released: *Get Back* and *Don't Let Me Down*. Among the musicians is Billy Preston.
April 22, 1969	John and Paul are in EMI's Abbey Road studio to record *The Ballad Of John And Yoko*. In a short ceremony at the top of Apple's Savile Row building, John Winston Lennon officially changes his name to John Ono Lennon.
April 24, 1969	The Beatles offer just over £2,000,000 for one million shares of Northern Songs currently in the hands of small shareholders. The purchase price will be covered by a loan from Henry Ansbacher and Company, with the shares already owned by John, George and Ringo as collateral. Paul refuses to allow his own shares to be used as a part of the loan package.
April 25, 1969	*Rape* is shown at the Montreux Film Festival.
May 1, 1969	Apple announces the establishment of a new label for experimental music and spoken-word recordings: Zapple.
May 2, 1969	The first Zapple record is released: John and Yoko's *Unfinished Music, Number 2: Life With The Lions*. Recording begins on *Something*.

May 4, 1969	Ringo and Peter Sellers throw a party at Les Ambassadeurs to celebrate the completion of shooting on *The Magic Christian*. The guest list includes John and Yoko, Paul and Linda, Richard Harris, Roger Moore, Sean Connery, Stanley Baker and Christopher Lee.
May 5, 1969	John and Yoko buy Tittenhurst Park, an eighteenth-century Georgian mansion in Ascot, for £150,000.
May 6, 1969	Ringo and Maureen leave for a short vacation in the Bahamas.
May 7, 1969	John, Paul and Allen Klein meet with Sir Joseph Lockwood of EMI to discuss a sizeable increase in the band's record royalties, but Lockwood refuses to make any changes until the royalty problems between the Beatles and NEMS have been resolved.
May 8, 1969	John, George and Ringo name Allen Klein's Abkco Industries, Inc. as the official manager of the Beatles; Abkco is to receive 20 per cent of the group's net income as payment for services rendered. Paul, however, refuses to accept this new state of affairs. Alistair Taylor, Brian's personal assistant as early as 1961 and currently general manager of Apple, is fired.
May 9, 1969	The second album on the Zapple label is released: George's *Electronic Sound*.
May 10, 1969	Artist Alan Aldridge presents John and Yoko with a small sculpture of the two of them naked, in their *Two Virgins* pose.
May 16, 1969	Ringo, Maureen and Peter Sellers sail for New York on the S.S. *Queen Elizabeth II*. George, Patti, John and Yoko, who had originally planned to go along on the cruise, stay behind after they are refused US visas because of their convictions on drug-related charges.
May 17, 1969	Paul and Linda announce that Linda is expecting a child, then leave for a vacation in Cannes and Pampelonne, France.
May 18, 1969	John and Yoko discuss their 'You Are Here' exhibition with David Frost on London Weekend TV.
May 19, 1969	The Beatles receive an Ivor Novello Award for *Hey Jude*.
May 22, 1969	The *QE II* arrives in New York, where some additional shooting for *The Magic Christian* takes place.
May 23, 1969	ATV puts Jack Gill onto the board of directors of Northern Songs. They offer to put a director chosen by the Beatles on the board as well, but the group refuses. The release of the third Zapple LP, *Listening To Richard Brautigan*, is indefinitely postponed.
May 24, 1969	John and Yoko found their own film production company and publishing house: Bag Productions. Together with Yoko's five-year-old daughter, Kyoko, they fly to the Bahamas to hold a new bed-in.
May 25, 1969	In order to be closer to the American border, John and Yoko decide to hold their bed-in in Canada instead of the Bahamas, and fly with Kyoko to Toronto. At the Toronto airport, they are held for two hours by immigration officials.
May 26, 1969	John and Yoko begin their bed-in in room 1742 of the Queen Elizabeth Hotel in Montreal. This time they spend ten days in bed, but reap less publicity than they received during their eight days in Amsterdam.
May 29, 1969	Ringo and his family return to England by plane.
May 30, 1969	*The Ballad Of John And Yoko* is released as a single, with *Old Brown Shoe* on the flip side. Although the cover and the label identify the Beatles as the recording artists, *Ballad* was recorded without George and Ringo.
June 1, 1969	During their Montreal bed-in, John and Yoko record *Give Peace A Chance*, with a background chorus including Timothy Leary, the Radha Krishna Temple and assorted journalists. George leaves for a holiday on Sardinia.
June 3, 1969	John and Yoko end their bed-in and travel to Toronto, where they attempt to extend their Canadian visas.
June 7, 1969	John and Yoko leave Canada and return to England.
June 14, 1969	John and Yoko appear on London Weekend TV's 'The David Frost Show'.
June 15, 1969	Recording continues on the new album. Sessions will last through the middle of August.
June 22, 1969	Radio Luxembourg broadcasts an interview with John and Yoko. The main topic of discussion is the experimental *Life With The Lions* album.
June 27, 1969	Ringo and Maureen leave for a holiday in the south of France.
June 29, 1969	John, Yoko, Julian and Kyoko leave for a holiday in Scotland.
July 1, 1969	In Scotland, John loses control of his car and is involved in a collision near the tiny Highland hamlet of Golspie. Although none of them are seriously injured, the four holidaymakers are admitted to a local hospital.
July 2, 1969	Cynthia picks up Julian from the hospital in Scotland and leaves with him for Greece.

9 May

May

151

30 May

4 July

8 August

	Paul is in the studio to work on the new album, and records *Her Majesty*.
July 3, 1969	In connection with the Plastic Ono Band's new single, *Give Peace A Chance*, a press conference is held at the Chelsea Town Hall in London. Ringo and Maureen fill in for John and Yoko, who are still in hospital in Scotland.
July 4, 1969	*Give Peace A Chance* is released, with *Remember Love* on the flip side.
July 6, 1969	John, Yoko and Kyoko are discharged from hospital and fly back to London.
July 7, 1969	The Plastic Ono Band performs at the Chelsea Town Hall, King's Road, London.
July 8, 1969	John Eastman writes letters to all four Beatles, seriously criticizing the financial arrangements which Allen Klein has been making in the group's name.
July 9–11, 1969	Several versions of *Maxwell's Silver Hammer* are recorded.
July 12, 1969	George records the vocals for *Something*.
July 15, 1969	The Beatles are in the studio together to begin work on *You Never Give Me Your Money*. The song was written by Paul, ostensibly about the group's current financial difficulties.
July 17, 1969	Ringo records *Octopus's Garden*.
July 18, 1969	*Oh! Darling* is recorded by Paul, George and Ringo. Paul has been screaming for a week in order to make his voice completely raw for this session. Two separate versions of *Penina*, a McCartney composition, are released: one by Carlos Mendes in Portugal and one by the group Jotta Here in Holland. Mendes and Jotta Here both claim to have been given the song during Paul's last vacation in Portugal.
July 21, 1969	Recording begins on *Come Together*.
July 24, 1969	Recording begins on *Mean Mr Mustard, Here Comes The Sun* and *Sun King*.
July 25, 1969	*She Came In Through The Bathroom Window* is recorded.
July 28, 1969	*Polythene Pam* is recorded.
July 31, 1969	*Golden Slumbers, Carry That Weight* and *The End* are recorded.
August 3, 1969	Ringo, Maureen and Mal Evans attend a Hank Snow concert at the London Palladium Theatre.
August 8, 1969	At 10 am, the cover photograph for the *Abbey Road* album is shot by Ian MacMillan.
August 9, 1969	At the EMI studios in Abbey Road, Mary Hopkin records *Que Sera, Sera* with Paul on guitar and Ringo on drums. She sings the song in French, and the single is later released in France only. The single includes a new middle eight written by McCartney and is subsequently covered by Karen Young for UK release.
August 21, 1969	The Beatles are present at Apple's annual general meeting.
August 28, 1969	Linda gives birth to a daughter, named Mary after Paul's mother. George holds a press conference to promote the single which he has produced for the Radha Krishna Temple: *Hare Krishna*.
August 31, 1969	George and Patti, Ringo and Maureen, John and Yoko, Neil Aspinall and Mal Evans are all on the Isle of Wight to see Bob Dylan in concert. After the show the nine of them (including Dylan) go by helicopter to Tittenhurst Park.
September 5, 1969	Allen Klein negotiates changes in the Beatles' recording contracts with EMI. On the one hand, the group's royalties are almost doubled, but on the other hand EMI receives permission to put together new albums of previously-released Beatle material without first consulting the band.
September 9, 1969	Ringo is admitted to the Middlesex Hospital with an intestinal complaint.
September 10, 1969	*Self Portrait*, a film by John and Yoko, has its world premiere at the Institute of Contemporary Arts in London.
September 13, 1969	John, Yoko, Eric Clapton, Klaus Voormann and Alan White leave for Canada, to perform at Varsity Stadium, Toronto, in the Toronto Rock'n'Roll Revival Festival; on the way, they rehearse in the airplane. John is so nervous before the show that he throws up in his dressing room.
September 20, 1969	According to today's *Daily Express*, ATV now owns almost 50 per cent of Northern Songs. Paul still owns 751,000 shares (worth approximately £1.5 million), John has 694,000 shares (worth approximately £1.4 million) and Ringo has 40,000 shares (worth approximately £80,000). George has by this time sold all his shares.
September 25, 1969	Apple releases a single by White Trash: *Golden Slumbers*, a Lennon/McCartney composition which the Beatles themselves have also recorded for their *Abbey Road* album, to be released the next day, September 26. John and Yoko appear as guests at the press conference Apple holds to promote the White Trash single. At ATV's annual shareholders' meeting, Lord Renwick announces that the firm now holds 54 per cent of the shares in Northern Songs, an absolute majority.
September 26, 1969	*Abbey Road* is released.
September 30, 1969	John and Yoko are in the studio to record the new Plastic Ono Band single: *Cold Turkey* and *Don't Worry Kyoko (Mummy's Only Looking For A Hand In The Snow)*.
October 2, 1969	In the new issue of *Record Mirror*, John claims that the Beatles' financial situation is not exactly rosy. 'Most of what I earn goes into Apple,' he says, 'and it never

comes back.'

October 9, 1969	Yoko is admitted to King's College Hospital in London, where she has her second miscarriage.
October 12, 1969	On radio station WKNR in Detroit, disc jockey Russ Gibbs reports that Paul has been dead for several years, and that a lookalike has taken his place. Numerous clues in support of this theory are apparently to be found on the covers of various Beatle albums, beginning with *Revolver*, and in the lyrics to many of the group's songs. Gibbs, who claims to have received his information from a mysterious and anonymous telephone caller, presents his case convincingly, and a huge number of his listeners believe him. The rumour is quickly picked up by the local press, by the national press, and finally by the international press. New 'proofs' of Paul's death follow closely on each other's heels, and the rumour grows steadily stronger.
October 15, 1969	Ringo and Maureen fly to Los Angeles to deal with a number of business matters, including the possibility of an American television special starring Ringo, to be titled *Starr Time*.
October 16, 1969	The Beatles admit that they have been beaten, and give up the battle for Northern Songs. John, Paul and Ringo sell their remaining shares to ATV.
October 20, 1969	George and Patti attend a Ravi Shankar concert at the London Festival Hall.
October 22, 1969	The 'Paul is dead' rumour reaches the pages of *Time* magazine. Several radio stations announce the name of Paul's supposed replacement, William Campbell, who is claimed to have undergone plastic surgery to increase his already-strong resemblance to the 'late' McCartney. Paul himself makes his first comment on the rumour: 'I'm dead, am I? Why does nobody ever tell me anything?' Surprisingly active for a corpse, Paul leaves for a vacation in Scotland.
October 27, 1969	In the studio, Ringo begins work on his first solo album, *Sentimental Journey*.
October 24, 1969	Release date of the Plastic Ono Band's *Cold Turkey* single, which carries the instruction 'Play Loud' on its label. This time round, the band consists of John and Yoko, Eric Clapton, Klaus Voormann and Alan White.
October 31, 1969	On Allen Klein's advice, *Something* and *Come Together* are released as the new Beatle single.
November 1, 1969	John and Yoko leave for a vacation in Greece.
November 4, 1969	The New York *Daily News* publishes the first article refuting the 'Paul is dead' rumour.
November 6, 1969	John and Yoko's film, *Rape, Part II*, is shown at the Mannheim Film Festival in West Germany.
November 7, 1969	Paul is on the cover of the current issue of *Life*; in an interview printed in the magazine, he echoes Mark Twain's comment that the reports of his death have been greatly exaggerated.
November 8, 1969	Capitol Records announces that the sales of Beatle singles and albums have risen sizeably since the beginning of the 'Paul is dead' controversy.
November 9, 1969	John and Yoko film *Apotheosis*, in which they soar above Hampshire in a hot-air balloon.
November 13, 1969	John buys an island, Dorinish, off the coast of Ireland, and donates it to the hippie community to be used as a testing ground for the hippie lifestyle.
November 14, 1969	John and Yoko's *Wedding Album* is released, in a box filled with mementos and souvenirs. Side Two of the LP consists of tapes from the Amsterdam bed-in.
November 15, 1969	In an interview with the *Disc and Music Echo*, John declares that John Lennon the Beatle is a different person than John Lennon the artist: 'I am an artist and my art is peace and I happen to be a musician. My music is done with the Beatles – that's where I get my wages from.'
November 25, 1969	John returns his MBE to the Queen to protest at the British government's position regarding the Vietnam war and the situation in Biafra – and to protest at the fact that his *Cold Turkey* single is not doing well in the charts.
December 1, 1969	George, Patti, Ringo and Maureen are at the Royal Albert Hall in London to attend a concert by Delaney and Bonnie and Friends, the first show of the group's current tour of England and Scandinavia.
December 2, 1969	George performs in Bristol as one of Delaney and Bonnie's Friends. He will continue to appear with the band through the remainder of their tour.
December 4, 1969	George performs with Delaney and Bonnie and Friends in Birmingham.
December 5, 1969	*Come And Get It*, which is used to accompany the credits in Ringo's film, *The Magic Christian*, is released as a single by Apple. Written and produced by Paul, it has been recorded by a group formerly known as the Iveys but now calling themselves Badfinger. Apple has previously announced another single for December 5 release: *What's The New Mary Jane/You Know My Name (Look Up The Number)*, by the Plastic Ono Band. Although sample copies of the disc are pressed, its release is first postponed and finally cancelled. *What's The New Mary Jane* ultimately appears on a number of bootleg albums, and *You Know My Name* turns up in March of 1970 as the B side of the Beatles' *Let It Be* single.

August/September

14 November

153

December 6, 1969	Ringo is a guest on LWT's 'The David Frost Show', talking about his solo LP and his role in *The Magic Christian*. George performs with Delaney and Bonnie and Friends at the Empire Theatre in Liverpool.
December 7, 1969	George performs with Delaney and Bonnie and Friends at the Fairfield Hall in Croydon. Several numbers from this concert later appear on the *Delaney And Bonnie On Tour* album.
December 8, 1969	*The Magic Christian* is previewed for the press at the Odeon Theatre, Leicester Square, London.
December 10, 1969	John and Yoko join a committee demanding a new trial for convicted murderer James Hanratty, who has been sentenced to death. They announce their intention to film a documentary concerning the Hanratty case. Ringo appears in BBC-TV's 'Late Night Line Up'. George performs with Delaney and Bonnie and Friends at the Falconer Theatre in Copenhagen, Denmark.
December 11, 1969	Promoter Mike Belkin offers the Beatles at least $2.4 million to play twelve concerts in the United States. They turn him down.
December 12, 1969	*The Magic Christian* has its world premiere at the Odeon Theatre, Kensington in London. Ringo, Maureen, John, Yoko and Princess Margaret are among those present. Release date of the Plastic Ono Band's *Live Peace In Toronto* album, recorded at the September 13 concert.
December 14, 1969	Ringo participates in the shooting of 'With A Little Help From My Friends', a television documentary about George Martin.
December 15, 1969	The BBC films an hour-long documentary about John for its '24 Hours' TV programme. At the Lyceum Ballroom in London, John, George, Billy Preston, Keith Moon, Eric Clapton and Delaney and Bonnie and Friends put on a charity concert for UNICEF under the title 'Peace For Christmas'. The slogan for the Benefit is 'War is over, if you want it'.
December 16, 1969	John and Yoko fly to Canada, where they announce plans for a music festival for peace to be held the following July in Toronto. They put up at Ronnie Hawkins' farm, and wind up staying for five days.
December 17, 1969	John holds a press conference at the Ontario Science Center in Toronto.
December 19, 1969	British members of the Beatles Fan Club receive *The Beatles' Seventh Christmas Record*, again consisting of separately-recorded messages from John, Paul, George and Ringo. John talks with Marshall McLuhan in a 45-minute interview on CBC-TV. Enormous posters reading 'WAR IS OVER! If You Want It – Happy Christmas from John & Yoko' appear on billboards in New York, Los Angeles, Montreal, Toronto, London, Paris, Amsterdam, Berlin, Rome, Athens and Tokyo.
December 21, 1969	A special train carries John and Yoko to Montreal, where they hold a press conference at the Chateau Champlain Hotel.
December 22, 1969	John and Yoko meet Pierre Trudeau, the Prime Minister of Canada, and John Munro, the Canadian Minister of Health.
December 23, 1969	John and Yoko return to England by air.
December 24, 1969	Ringo sings *Octopus's Garden*, accompanied by the George Martin Orchestra, on BBC-TV's 'Live'. Ringo can also be seen on the box in 'With A Little Help From My Friends', the George Martin documentary filmed earlier this month.
December 29, 1969	John and Yoko leave for Aalborg in Denmark, where they visit Kyoko and Anthony Cox, Yoko's ex-husband, and are visited by Hammrick and Leonard (two Canadian hypnotists who attempt to stop them from smoking) and by Ritchie York, John Brower and Allen Klein (who come to talk over plans for the Toronto Peace Festival).
December 31, 1969	As the sixties draw to a close, British television broadcasts a documentary called 'Men of the Decade'. Twenty minutes of the programme are devoted to John.

12 December

19 December

15 December

1961: Paul plays dead while George, John and Pete gather round him.

WAS PAUL DEAD?

The Beatles always enjoyed peppering their albums with in-jokes and hidden messages, and Beatle fans old and new still enjoy playing the game of unravelling the myriad clues and codes and uncovering the secrets behind them. By listening to the records over and over again, by spinning them faster or slower than normal, by playing them backwards or extremely loud, the dedicated fan may be richly rewarded: he hears snatches of sound which the average listener never notices, bits of song and lines of speech, and begins to feel himself a part of that select group of insiders at whom the boys' private humour was originally aimed.

Of course, there's always the danger that reading too much between the lines may lead to 'revelations' never planned or intended by the Beatles. In 1969, an otherwise tame year in the music world, one American Beatle fan spent an enormous amount of time poring through his collection of albums and album covers, looking for 'evidence' to back up his theory that Paul McCartney had been killed in an automobile smashup late in 1966, and that his place in the group had since been filled by a McCartney lookalike. He presented his theory, complete with 'proofs' from *Sgt. Pepper, Magical Mystery Tour* and the white double LP *The Beatles*, in a telephone call to Russ Gibbs, a disc jockey on Detroit's underground radio station, WKNR-FM. On October 12, Gibbs passed the information on to his listeners.

Most of the indications which purportedly proved that Paul was dead came from *Sgt. Pepper*, the album which had also been used two years earlier to 'prove' that the Beatles had become nothing more than a quartet of drug fiends. Now, though, Gibbs claimed that the *Sgt. Pepper* project had in fact been conceived as a means of communicating the facts of Paul's death and replacement to all who were clever enough to decipher it.

On the record's front cover we see a crowd of mourners gathered around a grave. There are two funeral wreaths: red hyacinths spell-

The floral bass . . .

ing out the word 'Beatles' – and yellow hyacinths in the form of a bass guitar, a clear reference to Paul. The Beatles themselves are in the front row of mourners: John, Ringo and George hold golden instruments – but Paul's clarinet is black, the colour of death. There is a hand held above Paul's head, with its palm facing forward: claimed to be an Eastern symbol of death, and behind this *particular* hand can be seen the face of Stephen Crane, author of *The Red Badge of Courage*, who died in 1900 at the age of 28 – Paul's age in 1970.

On the back cover the Lonely Hearts Club Band appears again, but Paul's back is turned to us as if he is no longer with us. George's thumb points to the first line of the *She's Leaving Home* lyrics: 'Wednesday morning at five o'clock as the day begins.' The date of Paul's allegedly fatal car crash – November 9, 1966 – was indeed a Wednesday, and the accident indeed occurred at 5 am, after an all-night recording session. At the time, only a few newspapers reported the incident: had an attempt been made to suppress the story altogether?

A hand over his head . . .

The inside of the foldout cover shows a large close-up shot of the four Beatles. Paul wears a black patch on his arm, and the patch bears the letters 'OPD'. Doctors, Russ Gibbs pointed out, use those letters to abbreviate the phrase 'Officially Pronounced Dead.'

Musically, the most important clue on the *Sgt. Pepper* album is the song *A Day In The Life*, where John sings: 'He blew his mind out in a car.' Although John was repeatedly to explain that the line was a reference to the death of Tara Browne, one of the heirs to the Guinness Brewery fortune, it would prove impossible to convince the fans, who would simply return to the disc's front cover and point to the doll on the far right. She wears a shirt or sweater which says 'Welcome the Rolling Stones', and balanced on her leg, butting up against the word 'Stones', is a small model car. The inference is clear: it is Paul's car we see, smashed into the stones of a stone wall or bridge.

'Wednesday morning at five o'clock . . .'

'Officially Pronounced Dead'?

Paul's desk notice: 'I was' . . .

Only Paul's rose was black . . .

The *Magical Mystery Tour* album, Gibbs went on, is also rife with obvious symbolism and tantalizing hints. On the front cover, for example, we see three white animals and one black one, a walrus. In certain parts of Scandinavia a black walrus is looked on as a symbol of death and, as John informed us in the song *Glass Onion*, 'Here's another clue for you all: the walrus was Paul.' If you turn the cover upside-down, the yellow stars spelling out the word 'Beatles' become a telephone number: 537-1438. But where was the telephone? Russ Gibbs decided that London was the most likely place, and dialled the number. A journalist answered, and claimed to know nothing at all about the story of Paul's death. Yet, a week later, when Gibbs placed the call again, the number had mysteriously been disconnected. (No wonder, if thousands of fans started ringing it up to check the rumour!) The 32-page booklet which accompanies *Magical Mystery Tour* shows Paul with a hand above his head on pages 7, 14, 15, 18 and 24. On page 23, three Beatles wear red carnations in their lapels, while Paul's is black. On pages 10 and 13 Paul is the only member of the group not wearing shoes – corpses are usually buried without their shoes on, and the pair of shoes standing next to Paul on page 13 is covered with blood. On page 3 we see Paul in a military uniform, with a sign in front of him reading 'I WaS.' And then there are the songs: a voice quite plainly asking 'Is he dead?' towards the end of *I Am The Walrus*, and at the end of *Strawberry Fields Forever* John mumbling 'I buried Paul.'

Taken individually, of course, each of these clues seems much too far-fetched to be worthy of serious attention. But as Russ Gibbs piled on more and more of them, their collective weight caused even the most sceptical listeners to wonder if there might not be some truth to the theory after all. WKNR was swamped with thousands of telephone calls, and other radio stations began to broadcast the story. All Beatle records stretching back to 1966 were played backwards, all album covers and publicity pictures were searched for additional evidence. An official Is-Paul-McCartney-Dead Society was founded to collect the information as it was reported and to investigate the clues.

Ten days after Russ Gibbs' original broadcast, an article on the 'Is Paul dead?' question appeared in *Time* magazine, bringing international attention to the controversy. By now, some radio stations had even ferreted out the name of Paul's alleged replacement, a certain William Campbell who had once won a McCartney lookalike contest.

Was Paul really dead? It seemed logical to ask the man himself. In an interview with the London *Evening Standard*, Paul said: 'I'm dead, am I? Why does nobody ever tell me anything?' And after that cryptic statement, he left London for a vacation on his farm in Scotland.

The rumours continued to spread – and to grow. Even the most devoted Beatle fans began believing them, or at least began wondering, 'Could it be? ... Finally, Paul issued a press release, hoping to put an end to the entire issue. But the journalists and disc jockeys were not to be denied their sport. They waited hungrily for the release of the new Beatle album, anticipating a wealth of new evidence. When *Abbey Road* finally became available, they were not disappointed.

On the cover, the Beatles are walking away from EMI's Abbey Road studios in what is obviously a funeral procession: John is in the lead and wears priestly white, Ringo follows in black mourning clothes, Paul wears a baggy grey suit – a suit to be buried in – and George brings up the rear in the worn denim of a gravedigger. Paul is out of step with the rest of the group, and he is barefoot. Parked on the left side of the street is an off-white Volkswagen with the licence number LMW 281F – and Paul would have been '28' back in 1970, '1F' only he had lived. On the right side of the street is a black police van, the type of van which, it was said, was generally sent to the scenes of serious traffic accidents in England. Lewis Yager, chairman of the Is-Paul-McCartney-Dead Society, treated the van's licence number as a telephone number and dialled it: his call was answered by an old woman who insisted that she knew nothing at all about Paul McCartney – in a voice which sounded strangely like the voice of Ringo Starr. (Poor woman!)

And it was on the *Abbey Road* cover that Paul's lookalike

Abbey Road: *a funeral procession?*

replacement made his first mistake: as he crosses the street between Ringo and George, he holds a cigarette loosely between the index and middle fingers of his right hand. The 'real' Paul, however, had been left-handed. . . .

In an interview in the November 7 issue of *Life* magazine, Paul again tried to convince the world that he was not dead. The same week, Capitol Records announced that sales of Beatle albums and singles had gone sky-high since the beginning of the rumour. And it was not only Capitol and the Beatles who were reaping the benefits of all this free publicity: Silver Fox Records released a single titled *Brother Paul* by Billy Shears and the All-Americans, MGM Records came out with the Mystery Tour's *The Ballad Of Paul*, José Feliciano waxed *Dear Paul* for RCA. Not to be outdone by the competition, Capitol went so far as to canonize its 'dead' Beatle, putting out a single called *Saint Paul* by Terry Knight.

However, slowly but slowly, as John would have put it, the news of Paul's death became stale and the flow of rumours bled itself dry. Yet the story still resurfaces from time to time, and small groups of fans convince themselves anew that Paul McCartney was fatally injured in an automobile accident on November 9, 1966.

After all, all four members of the group had suddenly started to wear moustaches and beards at the end of that year, for no particular reason. Unless of course it was to conceal the fact that *one* Beatle's face, the face of 'Paul McCartney', had undergone some subtle – and sinister – changes. . . .

Bare feet, out of step, and right handed . . .

Police van: an accident?

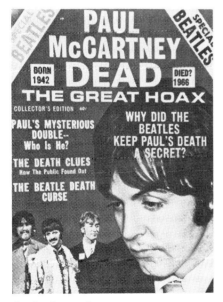
American fan magazine cover.

Licence plate: Paul's age?

ABBEY ROAD

August 8, 1969. 10 am. Abbey Road, St John's Wood, London. John, Ringo, Paul and George cross the street, single-file, at a pedestrian crossing, and are photographed by Ian Macmillan for the cover of their final album. Abbey Road has been closed off to vehicles and pedestrians for the past hour, but even so some amateur photographers manage to get into the area with their cameras.

Why Abbey Road, rather than one of London's myriad other streets? Simple: Abbey Road is the location of EMI's Studio 2, where almost all Beatles singles and albums have been recorded since October 1962.

The Beatles waiting for a picture to be taken. Paul's sandals can be seen on the right.

WAR IS OVER!

IF YOU WANT IT

John: 'I'm going to sell peace like Coca-Cola.'

Late in March 1969, the world first came to know John Lennon as an apostle of peace. After their wedding on March 20, John and Yoko travelled to the Netherlands and began a week-long 'bed-in' in their room at the Amsterdam Hilton. It was an unusual and effective publicity stunt, and the newlyweds were visited by hundreds of journalists from around the world during their week in bed. They may have come to talk about John's marriage or about the Beatles, but the couple made sure that the subject of every conversation was peace.

'I'm going to sell peace the way they sell Coca-Cola,' John declared, and he proved himself a capable and intelligent salesman, using his name and fame to manipulate the words 'peace' and 'love' from newspapers' crossword puzzles onto their front pages.

Naturally, there was also a great deal of criticism. 'He's only doing it to make himself more popular', was an often-heard comment, or 'Why does he need to waste all that money on a room at the Hilton?'

John and Yoko began a second bed-in on May 25, in Montreal, Canada. While in bed they recorded the single *Give Peace A Chance* as the Plastic Ono Band. The song became a hit, reaching the number two spot on the British charts and fourteenth place in America. More importantly, it put the Lennons' message of peace on Earth in front of millions of listeners and was immediately adopted as a theme song of the anti-Vietnam movement.

While George toured England and Scandinavia with Delaney and Bonnie and Ringo was caught up in

the filming of *The Magic Christian*, John set to work on a project which would indeed market peace as if it were a soft drink or a new washing powder. On December 16, 1969, a series of giant billboards appeared in downtown New York, Los Angeles, Montreal, Toronto, London, Paris, Amsterdam, Berlin, Rome, Athens and Tokyo – billboards reading 'War Is Over If You Want It' and signed, with Christ-

mas greetings, by John and Yoko. Preparing and placing the hoardings was expensive, but John later announced, in all seriousness, that he had sent the bills to Richard Nixon!

Again, the stunt led to front-page photos in dozens of newspapers, and dozens of interviews in which John and Yoko discoursed lengthily and cogently on peace. And again they provided a move-

John and Yoko with mini-posters and a 'Bag of Laughter'.

162

The posters in London . . .

. . . in Paris

ment with a rallying cry: 'War is over if you want it' became a frequently-used slogan at demonstrations and protest marches.

Why were the posters only hung in eleven cities, and why were such places as Washington, Moscow, Saigon and Tel Aviv left off the list, places closely involved in hostilities at that time? Quite simple, really: John and Yoko organized the project with the help of a network of friends spread around the world, and the billboards were set up only in the cities where there were people interested in participating. In Holland, for example, the contact was photographer John de Rooy, who had met the Lennons during their bed-in at the Amsterdam Hilton, where he took the 'Hair Peace' photo which was later used on the cover of their *Wedding Album*.

. . . and in Amsterdam

John and Yoko at Tittenhurst Park in 1969. (photo: J. de Rooy)

163

1970

1 January

16 January

30 January

LENNON

INSTANT KARMA!

APPLES 1003

6 February

12 February

3 April

January 1, 1970	In Denmark, John and Yoko welcome in the seventies by having their hair clipped short. 'We can travel unrecognized,' says John. The chopped-off hair is donated to Michael X, who uses it to raise money for his Blackhouse in North London.

January 14, 1970	Paul buys Low Ranadran Farm, which lies next to his own farm in Scotland.
	    An exhibition of fourteen of John's lithographs of himself and Yoko opens at the London Arts Gallery. The drawings, praised by some critics and condemned as pornographic by others, are available for purchase under the title *Bag One*.
	    George pays well over £100,000 for Friar Park, a 30-room mansion in Henley-on-Thames. The property includes three guest houses and 40 acres of land.

January 16, 1970	Scotland Yard raids the London Arts Gallery and confiscates eight of John's 'pornographic' lithographs.
January 25, 1970	John and Yoko issue a press release in which they refer to 1970 as 'Year One'.
January 26, 1970	In the studio, John writes and records *Instant Karma*. Ringo, Maureen and Peter Brown fly to Los Angeles for the American premiere of *The Magic Christian*. On their arrival, they hold an airport press conference.
January 27, 1970	Ringo tapes an appearance for Dan Rowan and Dick Martin's 'Laugh-In'. John and Yoko leave for Paris.
January 28, 1970	*The Magic Christian* has its American premiere at the Four Star Theater in Los Angeles. Ringo attends both the premiere and the party which is held afterwards at the Beverly Hills Hotel.
January 30, 1970	In Burbank, Ringo appears on the television programme 'Philiben's People' and tapes more material for 'Laugh-In'.
February 6, 1970	*Instant Karma* is released as the Plastic Ono Band's new single. *Who Has Seen The Wind*, on the flip side, features guitar solos by George. Both songs have been mixed by Phil Spector.
February 12, 1970	John sings *Instant Karma* on BBC-TV's 'Top of the Pops'.
February 26, 1970	In America, the *Hey Jude* album is released. It is a collection of Beatle singles which have not previously appeared on LPs. John cancels his plans to participate in the upcoming Toronto Peace Festival, having discovered that the proceeds from the event will not be used to promote world peace after all.
March 1, 1970	In America, film of the Beatles singing *Two Of Us* and *Let It Be* are shown on 'The Ed Sullivan Show'.
March 6, 1970	The new single, *Let It Be/You Know My Name*, is released.
March 8, 1970	Ringo records *It Don't Come Easy* with Klaus Voormann, Stephen Stills and George.
March 15, 1970	A promotional film for Ringo's *Sentimental Journey* album is shot.
March 29, 1970	Ringo sings *Sentimental Journey*, accompanied by the George Martin Orchestra, on 'The David Frost Show'.
April 3, 1970	The *Sentimental Journey* LP is released. 'I did it for me Mum,' says Ringo about this collection of old-time melodies.
April 7, 1970	The *Delaney And Bonnie On Tour* album is released, with George as one of the guitarists.
April 9, 1970	Paul sings *Maybe I'm Amazed* in a five-minute spot on London Weekend TV.
April 10, 1970	Paul's interview of himself, intended for the press kit promoting his *McCartney* solo album, leaks out. In the interview, Paul declares that he is estranged from the Beatles, and will work on his own in the future. An article announcing the end of the Beatles appears in the *Daily Mirror*, and the news quickly spreads through the British and then the world press. Although the London *Times* contradicts the story, it seems clear that the band has breathed its last.
April 12, 1970	Paul establishes his own production company: McCartney Productions Ltd (MPL).
April 14, 1970	McCartney Productions purchases the film rights to the *Rupert Bear* children's cartoon strip from the Express Newspapers group. Although no film has been released at the time of going to press, it seems likely that an animated version of Rupert Bear will appear in the UK in 1983–84 as support for the third 'Star Wars' epic, *Return Of The Jedi*.

April 17, 1970	Paul's solo album, *McCartney*, is released. In a lengthy interview in *Rolling Stone*, John dismisses the announcement that Paul has left the Beatles as a publicity stunt and reveals that he himself left the band months earlier, although an agreement had been made to keep the break-up secret.
April 27, 1970	A London judge rules that John's lithographs are not pornographic, and the drawings are returned. George arrives in New York and announces to the press that, in his opinion, the break-up of the Beatles is only temporary.
May 1, 1970	In New York, George records a number of songs with Bob Dylan. Although the material is never legally released, two numbers (*I'd Have You Anytime* and *When Everybody's Come To Town*) ultimately appear on bootlegs. During the course of the day, George also visits the office of the American Beatles Fan Club.
May 4, 1970	George flies back to England.
May 8, 1970	The *Let It Be* album, recorded prior to *Abbey Road*, is finally released.
May 13, 1970	The *Let It Be* film has its world premiere. Intended as a documentary about the recording of an album, it is instead a documentary about the end of an era. At the premiere, the Beatles themselves are conspicuous by their absence.
May 20, 1970	George begins recording sessions for a new solo album, *All Things Must Pass*, which will be released on November 30. *Let It Be* has its British premiere in Liverpool. Again, neither John, Paul, George nor Ringo puts in an appearance. The implication is clear: as a group, the Beatles no longer exist.
June 11, 1970	John, who has now been in America for some time, announces that he has no plans to return to England.
June 15, 1970	In a letter to Allen Klein written at Paul's request, John Eastman suggests that, although the Beatles are contractually obliged to remain together till April 1976, the group now be officially dissolved.
July 7, 1970	Louise Harrison, George's mother, dies of cancer in a Liverpool hospital, with George at her side.
July 10, 1970	Louise Harrison is cremated.
July 31, 1970	Cynthia Powell marries Roberto Bassanini.
August 4, 1970	Apple's press department is shut down, and its staff of two is fired.
August 8, 1970	Paul writes a letter to John, asking for an official end to the existence of the Beatles. John later replies that he will take Paul's request under consideration when Paul receives the approval of George and Ringo.
September 18, 1970	Stella McCartney, Paul's second child, is born.
September 25, 1970	Ringo's second solo album, *Beaucoups Of Blues*, is released.
September 28, 1970	John and Paul file suit against Northern Songs. In accordance with a contract dating back to 1963, they demand half the firm's income and capital.
November 11, 1970	Lee Starkey, Ringo's third child, is born.
November 15, 1970	Paul files a suit against John, George, Ringo, Allen Klein and Apple, in an attempt officially to dissolve the band. (The case takes just over four years to decide, but on January 9, 1975, a judge finally rules that the entity once known as the Beatles no longer exists.)

17 April

8 May

29 August

Ringo and Maureen in 1965

BEATLE WIVES AND LOVERS

Paul and Jane

George and Patti

John and Cynthia in 1967

On August 23, 1962, John Lennon married Cynthia Powell, a girl he met at art school, at the Mount Pleasant Registry Office in Liverpool. At the time, it was felt that a male pop star's image was somehow tarnished the moment he took himself a wife, and so the existence of a Mrs Lennon was carefully kept from the press and John and Cynthia were never seen together in public. Even when their son Julian was born, on April 8, 1963, John's 'other life' as husband and father was held secret.

The news finally leaked out late in 1963, and from January 1964 the Lennons were at last able to be seen in public together. Unexpectedly, the fans immediately accepted Cynthia and Julian, and John's popularity was undiminished. After all, there were still three unmarried Beatles left, weren't there?

Not for long.

On February 11, 1965, Richard Starkey married Maureen Cox, a Liverpool hairdresser, and on January 21, 1966, George Harrison married fashion model Patricia Anne Boyd. Paul McCartney, meanwhile, has been 'going steady' with actress Jane Asher since the middle of 1963, and it was taken for granted that they would eventually get around to tying the knot.

Up to now, matrimony – or any permanent relationship – had proved disastrous to the career of every pop star who had ever dared to say 'I do', but the Beatles were clearly the exception to the rule. John and Cynthia, Paul and Jane, Ringo and Maureen, George and Patti – none of it seemed to have the slightest effect on the group's

166

unprecedented success.

Success had its own effect on the relationships, however. Only a few short months after Paul and Jane officially announced their engagement, on Christmas Day, 1967, the Lennons' marriage was on the rocks. To the dismay of both Cynthia and the other Beatles, John began falling deeper under the influence of Japanese-born avant-garde artist Yoko Ono; in May 1968, he asked Cynthia for a divorce. And two months later, on July 22, Paul and Jane suddenly broke off their short-lived engagement.

While Paul played the field for a while – including a brief fling with Francie Schwartz, who sold the story of her love affair with a Beatle to a number of magazines and published it in book form as *Body Count* in 1972 – John and Yoko were inseparable. They shocked the world by posing nude for the cover of their experimental *Two Virgins* album, they were arrested for possession of drugs, they held exhibitions and 'happenings' which, in Paul's opinion, were bad for the group's image.

On March 12, 1969, Paul married American photographer Linda Eastman. A little over a week later, on March 20, John and Yoko were married on Gibraltar. Yoko was not well accepted by the other Beatles and their women and, perhaps with a touch of vengeance, she and John never really accepted Linda, either. On August 29, five months after Paul became the last Beatle to

Paul and Linda in 1971

John and Yoko with pictures of Julian and Kyoko, their children from their first marriages.

give up his bachelor status, Linda gave birth to their daughter Mary.

The Beatles were already having problems with their music, their ideas, their new album, even – finally – with their popularity. Now, with the tensions surrounding Yoko and Linda, the group had still more to worry about.

John spent more time travelling with his wife and less time working with the Beatles, and he began to perform and record with other musicians. And in April 1970, Paul announced that he had left the group, and that the Beatles no longer existed.

The international press, quick to seek out a scapegoat, pinned the blame on the two new Beatle wives, with Yoko receiving the brunt of the criticism.

WILL THE BEATLES EVER PLAY TOGETHER AGAIN?

New Musical Express *17 October 1970*

NEW YORK POST, MONDAY, A

When Yok
McCartne

By DAVID LANCASHIRE

LONDON (AP)—The official biogr
of the Beatles says the major cause
breakup of the pop quartet appeared
John Lennon's marriage to Yoko Ono.

"If there was one single element
split, I'd say it was the arrival of
said Hunter Davies, author of "The B
An Official Biography."

While he was writing the book,
was the most intimate confidant
Beatles outside their own music and
ness organization.

Melody Maker *17 July 197*

Georg
B

Dear mailbag,

In order to put out of its misery the limping dog of a news story which has been dragging itself across your pages for the past year, my answer to the question, "will the Beatles get together again?"....

is no.

Paul McCartney

Melody Maker *29 August 1970*

Record Mirror *30 August 1970*

JOHN & PAUL TOGETHER ?

RUMOURS OF a reconciliation between John Lennon and
MaCartney swept the pop world this week, and sparked off fee
that the Beatles might come together again as a recording gr

However, although it would make commercial sense for
Beatles to remain a recording force, Record Mirror underst
that Paul MaCartney has been so inflexible in his position to
Klein that he cannot bring himself to climb down except on
understanding that Klein would no longer be involved in
handling of the affairs of Apple.

Contacts close to the Beatles seem to think basically that
rumours were over-optimistic.

In an answer to a question about the possible reconcilia
between John and Paul, both Peter Brown (Apple's acting
officer) and Neil Aspinall said: "I didn't know they had split

But the fact remains that they still do not see eye to
regarding the management of the Beatles' financial affairs.

alked In,
id 'O No!'

e inside out, so we're tied forever,
r happens."

artney did not clarify in detail his
for breaking away from the group.
Davies maintained that under Yoko's
e, Lennon began taking charge at
he Beatles' business headquarters,
"was a blow to Paul's pride . . .
by the wayside and . . . they were
r bosom buddies . . . George Harri-
Ringo Starr [the other two Beatles]
exactly dotty over or endeared to
her."

THE NEW BEATLE

go set charity appearance

TLES FOR U.N. GIG

THE first-ever scheduled performance
by a Beatle since the group
stopped touring in 1966 will take
place at New York's Madison Square
Gardens on August 1.

George Harrison and Friends — including
Ringo Starr, Leon Russell, and Klaus Voorman — will play two shows, and the pro-
ceeds will go to the United Nations fund
for the refugee children of Bangla Desh.

Ravi Shankar, Harrison's friend and former sitar-
teacher, asked George to play the concert, and
may himself appear on the bill.

Although John Lennon has given three un-
scheduled public performances — in Toronto,
London's Lyceum, and most recently with Frank
Zappa at Fillmore East — this will be the first time

John, George, Ringo .. now comes Klaus

THE Beatles are back. But from now on
it's John, George, Ringo . . . and
Klaus.

The new Beatle, in place of Paul
McCartney, is 29-year-old German-born
guitarist Klaus Voorman.

The surprise move comes in the middle of a
court fight by Paul to
get the group broken
up.

Last night, for the first
time in a year, John,
George and Ringo were
back together at their
Apple offices discussing
future recordings. And
with them was Klaus. The
new Beatle has always
been close to the group.

He was once a member
of a trio known as Paddy.
Klaus and Gibson, which
was also under the management of the late Brian
Epstein, manager of the
Beatles.

Albums

Later, he joined Manfred
Mann as bass guitarist.

Recently, he has played
as a session guitarist on
George Harrison's albums
and with John Lennon and
the Plastic Ono band.

He is also a close friend
of Ringo Starr.

Klaus is married to
actress Christine Har-
greaves of "Coronation
Street" fame and lives in
Hampstead.

He is a fine artist as well
as musician and designed
the cover of the Beatles'
album, "Revolver."

An associate said: "Paul

refuses to return to the
group and so what are they
to do?

"When Ringo was ill
once in Beatlemania days,
they took on Jimmy
Nichol. It worked then —
why shouldn't it work
now?"

Paul McCartney and his
wife Linda are in America.
He could not be contacted
last night for an opinion
on the new line-up.

The other Beatles refused
to comment.

But the move and the
copyright of the Beatles'
name with a new face in
the line-up may well lead to
further legal action.

Solicitors for John,
George and Ringo said
yesterday that they would
appeal against last week's
High Court decision in
Paul's favour appointing a
Receiver and manager to
look after their affairs in
place of Allen Klein.

Daily Mirror 20 March 1971

169

XMAS

1963

1964

1965

In October 1963, the Beatles recorded a special single which was sent as a Christmas present to members of the British Beatles Fan Club and was not available commercially. This 'Beatles' Christmas Record' was such a hit with the fans that it was followed in 1964 by 'Another Beatles' Christmas Record', and by five more Christmas singles every year till 1969. In 1970, after the break-up of the group, Apple Records prepared one final Christmas disc for the fans, an album including all seven of the 1963–69 singles.

The Beatles' Christmas records provide the listener with a unique opportunity to hear John, Paul, George and Ringo at their wise-cracking, spontaneous best. For those of you who have never been lucky enough to enjoy the singles themselves, the following extracts will hopefully allow you to get a sense of their atmosphere and charm.

Sincere Good Wishes for Christmas and the New Year from John, Paul, George and Ringo

Recorded in EMI's Studio 2 on October 19, 1963, after a session during which *I Want To Hold Your Hand* and *This Boy* were recorded. Engineer: Norman Smith. Length: 5 minutes, 10 seconds.

This first Christmas record is, simply, a spoken letter from the Beatles to the members of their British fan club. Each member of the group has a turn at speaking, and there is a great deal of clowning around and interrupting.

The single begins with a few notes of *From Me To You*, which turns into a weird version of *Good King Wenceslaus* with John singing lead.

John: 'Hello, this is John speaking to you with his voice.' He talks about the success of the Beatles' first two singles, *Love Me Do* and *Please Please Me*, and about the boys' 'biggest thrill of the year', their performances at the London Palladium and in the Royal Variety Show (at which point all four Beatles merrily whistle *God Save The Queen*). He thanks the fans for their letters, and for the gifts and cards he received on his birthday: 'I'd love to reply personally to everyone but I just haven't enough pens.'

Paul agrees with John's thank-you's and adds that the Beatles no longer like jelly babies: after announcing once that they were their favourite sweets, they were swamped with 'boxes, packets and crates' of them. He says that the group is often asked which they enjoy the most, concerts or stage shows or recording, and answers: '. . . going into the recording studio to make new records, which is what we've been doing all day before we started on this special message.' He ends with a pseudo-German version of *Good King Wenceslaus*.

Ringo introduces himself as the group's drummer and newest member, and sings a jazz version of *Good King Wenceslaus*.

George: 'Thank you, Ringo – *we'll* phone *you*. I'm George Harrison. Nobody has said anything yet about our fan club secretaries, Anne Collingham and Bettina Rose. Not to mention Freda Kelly in Liverpool.' (All: 'Good old Freda!') George also closes with a rendition of *Good King Wenceslaus*.

Together, the Beatles sing an improvised and bastardized version of *Rudolph, The Red-Nosed Reindeer*: 'Doo-dah, the red-nosed reindeer, had a very shiny nose; when anybody picked it. . . .'

Another Beatles Christmas Record

Recorded in EMI's Studio 2 on October 26 and 27, 1964. Engineer: Norman Smith. Length: 4 minutes, 7 seconds.

Again, a spoken letter with personal messages from each Beatle: Paul talks about the recording and sales success of the records, John about his book, George about *A Hard Day's Night* and *Help!* and Ringo about the band's travels during the past year. They are reading from scripts, although there is also a great deal of improvisation.

The single begins with the sound of approaching footsteps. A piano breaks out into *Jingle Bells*, and is quickly joined by humming, a kazoo, a harmonica and John singing the first two words of the song.

Paul thanks the fans for buying Beatle records. 'Don't know where we'd be without you, really.' (John: 'In the Army, perhaps.') 'We hope you've enjoyed listening to the records as much as we've enjoyed melting them. No, no – no, that's wrong! – *making* them!' He talks about Studio 2 and concludes by wishing everyone 'a happy Christmas and a *very* New Year!'

John: 'John-John speaking. Thanks all of you who bought me book . . . it was very handy. And there's another one out pretty soon, it says here – hope you'll buy that, too. It'll be the usual rubbish, but it won't cost much, you see. . . . I write them in my spare time, it says here.' (Paul: 'Did you write this yourself?') 'No, it's somebody's bad handwroter.'

George: 'Hi, there! I'd like to thank all of you for going to see the film. 'Spect a lot of you saw it more than once.' (John: 'I did.') 'Did you? So did I. Thanks, anyway, 'cos it makes us very pleased, you know. We had a quiet time making it – actually we didn't. We had a great time making it, and we're glad it turned out okay. The next one should be completely different. We start shooting it in February. This time, it's a-gonna be in colour.' (John: 'Green.') 'It'll be a big laugh, we hope.' (John, Paul and Ringo laugh uproariously.)

Ringo: 'I'd like to thank you just for being fans. . . . 'Spect you're wondering where we've been. Well, Beatle people, we've been to Australia, and America, and New Zealand, and Australia, and New Zealand! . . . Those airport receptions knocked us out man, great!'

After a verse of *Oh, Can You Wash Your Father's Hair?*, the boys all shout 'Happy Christmas!' while running off into the distance.

The Beatles' Third Christmas Record

Recorded in EMI's Studio 2 on October 19, 1965, during the *Rubber Soul* sessions. Engineer: Norman Smith. Length: 6 minutes, 35 seconds. Cover photo: taken on November 1 during the taping of Granada-TV's 'The Music of Lennon and McCartney'.

This time the Beatles improvise together around a studio microphone, rather than reading from a script and taking turns.

The single begins with an off-key rendition of *Yesterday*, then goes on to a rambling conversation in which the fans are repetitively thanked for the cards and presents which they have sent the group for Christmas and for their birthdays. 'Especially the chewed-up pieces of chewing gum and the playing cards made out of knickers,' says John.

John sings a nonsense Christmas song with a comic Scots accent, then switches to a minstrel-show send-up. He is accompanied by guitar and tambourine and, as he switches again – this time to a speeded-up version of *Auld Lang Syne* – by Ringo singing along.

Paul: 'Last year, we was here, around the same old mike. . . .'
Ringo: '. . . same old guitar, same old faces. . . .'
John (singing): 'It's the same old song, but with a different meaning –'
George: 'Copyright, Johnny!'
Paul: 'Yeah, what're we gonna do that's out of copyright?'
John: 'Let's play a request for all the boys in B.A.O.R.E.'
Ringo: 'What shall we play for them, 'cos we got some fans in the forces. . . .'
John (in a radio announcer's voice): 'Well, here in Munich it's not quite as fine as it is in London. . . . Oh, it's not bad over here, but a bit of rain and all that.'
Ringo: 'Stay tuned in! It's a five-way linkup!'
John: 'If you've enjoyed this programme, tune to 29314567 megacycles. If you can't find that – drop it!'

Together, the band sings *Auld Lang Syne* as an angry protest song, sprinkled with references to Vietnam, China and Israel, then runs into *Christmas Comes But Once A Year* and finally into a seemingly endless reprise of *Yesterday*, again horribly off-key. By playing with the lyrics, *Yesterday* too becomes a Christmas song: 'Bless you all on Christmas Day.' As the others sing and whistle, John announces that 'this year's turned out to be a big year for us, one of our biggest years since we can remember.'

1966

Pantomime (Everywhere it's Christmas)

Recorded in Dick James Music's studio on November 25, 1966. Producer: George Martin. Length: 6 minutes, 50 seconds. Cover: designed by Paul.

This year's single is a collection of carefully rehearsed and recorded skits. Except for the song which opens and closes the record and a quick comment by Mal Evans, it is a Christmas disc which has nothing whatsoever to do with Christmas.

Song: *Everywhere It's Christmas*

Orowayna (Corsican Choir and Small Choir)
Paul: 'Our story opens in Corsica. On the veranda is a bearded man in glasses, conducting a small choir....'

A Rare Cheese (Two Elderly Scotsmen)
Ringo: 'Meanwhile, high in the Swiss Alps, two elderly Scotchmen munch on a rare cheese.'
Paul: 'Mmmmm. Wonderful stuff, this, Angus!'
John: 'Aye. Wonderful stuff!'

The Feast
John: I'm standing in the entrance to the Main Tent. Immediately behind me, the festivities have already begun.'

The Loyal Toast
George: 'At the same time as this, in the Captain's Mess, on board HMS Tremendous, a toast is being proposed.'

Paul: 'To Her Majesty!'
All: 'To Her Majesty!'

Podgy the Bear and Jasper
Paul: 'Podgy the Bear and Jasper were huddled around the unlit fire in the centre of the room....'

Felpin Mansions: Part One (Count Balder and Butler)
Felpin Mansions: Part Two (The Count and the Pianist)
Paul: 'Come in!'
Ringo: 'May I come in?'
Paul: 'Come in, Count!'
Ringo: 'May I?'
Paul: 'Yes, come in!'
Paul plays a piano and sings *Please, Don't Bring Your Banjo Back*.

Mal Evans: 'Yes, everywhere it's Christmas!'

Reprise: *Everywhere It's Christmas*

1967

Christmas Time (Is Here Again)

Recorded in EMI's Studio 2 on November 28, 1967. The script was written earlier in the day by the band.

Producer: George Martin. Special guest: Victor Spinetti. Length: 6 minutes, 19 seconds. Cover: designed on November 29 by John and Ringo (front cover) and by Julian Lennon (back cover).

Again a collection of short sketches, carefully mixed (by George Martin and John) in the spirit of *Sgt. Pepper* and *Magical Mystery Tour*.

John: 'Interplanetary remix, take 444!'

Song: *Christmas Time Is Here Again*
The song is sung by John, Paul, George, George Martin and Victor Spinetti, with John playing drums, Paul at the piano and George on guitar.

Paul: 'The boys arrive at BBC House.'
Victor: 'What do you want?'
All: 'We have been granted permission, O Wise One!'
Victor: 'Ahhhhh! Pass in peace!'
Ringo and Victor do a wild tapdance.
Mal Evans: 'Are you 13 Amp?'

John and Paul do an interview sketch.
Paul: 'Sitting with me in the studio tonight is a cross-section of British youth....'

George introduces a number requested by Mrs G. Evans 'for all the people in hospital' – *Plenty of Jamjars* by the Ravellers.

John and George do a quiz show send-up.
John: 'And how old are you?'
George: 'Thirty-two.'
John: 'Never!'
George: 'I am.'
John: 'Get away!'
George: 'I am!'
John: 'Well, you've just won a trip to Denver and five others. And also – wait for it! – you have been elected as Independant candidate for Paddington!'

Theatre Hour
Ringo: 'Hello, operator! I've been cut off! Emergency!'

Reprise: *Christmas Time Is Here Again*

All: 'Thank you for a wonderful year!'

The Poetic Scotsman
This bit, with John reciting incomprehensible poetry in a heavy Scots burr and George Martin playing a Hammond organ, was added to the single after Paul, George and Ringo had left the studio.

1968

Happy Christmas

Recorded in November in four different locations: at John's home in London, at Paul's home in London, in the back of Ringo's 'diesel-powered removal van' in Surrey, and with George in America. Additional material was recorded at George's house in Esher during rehearsals for the white album, *The Beatles*. Producer and sound editor: Kenny Everett. Special guest: Tiny Tim. Length: 8 minutes, 2 seconds. Cover: designed by Paul.

Kenny Everett created this year's single by editing together separately-recorded messages from John, Paul, George and Ringo, and intercutting random musical fragments and distorted snippets from the white album.

Ringo: 'Hello, this is a big "Hi!" and a sincere Merry Christmas from yours truly, Ringo Starr!'

John: 'Once upon a time there were two balloons called Jock and Yono. They were strictly in love, bound to happen in a million years. They were together, man. Unfortunatimetable, they seemed to have previous experience, which kept calling them one way or another. You know how it is. But they battled on against overwhelming oddities, including some of their beast friends. Being in love, they cloong together even more, man, but some of the monster outdated bus lorry hip throwers did stick slightly, and they occasionally had to resort to the dry cleaners....'

George introduces Mal Evans.
Mal: 'Merry Christmas, children, everywhere.'

Ringo does a sketch in which he has a telephone conversation with himself.

Paul sings again.

John: 'Once upon a pool table there lived a short-haired butcher's boy by the way of Ostigrad. It comes in scent and cesspoolorawick airport. Her father was in a long story cut short in the middle of his life sentence. We're indebted to the colloquial office for its immediate disposaloronowitz, including, I might add, hot patella watootem. On the other handbag, I mean to say, l'amour nous sommes toujourealistic. Free speaking, for this film, is about an hourglass houseboat. The full meaning of Winchester Cathedral defies description; their loss was our gainsborough nil....'

George introduces Tiny Tim, who sings a lengthy and frighteningly off-key version of *Nowhere Man* to close the single.

1969

Happy Christmas 1969

Recorded late in 1969 in four locations: at John and Yoko's home in Ascot, Ringo's home in Weybridge, Paul's home in London, and the London offices of Apple. Sound editor: Maurice Cole (Kenny Everett's original name). Length: 7 minutes, 55 seconds. Cover: designed by Ringo (front cover) and Zak Starkey (back cover).

This is the seventh and last *new* Christmas record, although in 1970 fans received an album including all seven of the previously-released Christmas singles. The contributions from Paul, George and Ringo are brief and uninspired; John and Yoko provide a lengthy sketch and sing a song. No-one refers to the Beatles at all.

Yoko: '... strolling in Ascot garden with your wife, Yoko. Do you have any special thoughts for Christmas?'
John: 'Well, Yoko, it *is* Christmas, and my special thoughts, of course, tend towards eating.'
Yoko: 'Alright, so eating. What do you like to eat?'
John: 'Well, I'd like some cornflakes, prepared by Persian hands, and I'd like it blessed by Hare Krishna Mantra.'

A strange montage of George giving Christmas greetings in a number of different voices.

Ringo (singing): 'Oh, good evening to you, gentlemen....'

John: 'How do you see your place in the seventies to come? We've had the swinging sixties, and I was wondering, Mrs Lennon, how you saw your place in the seventies?'
Yoko: 'Quite peaceful seventies, hopefully, you know.'
John: 'You think there's gonna be peace, do you?'
Yoko: 'Yes, and freedom.'

John and Yoko sing two versions of *Happy Christmas*.

Ringo says 'Merry Christmas' over and over again. The tape is speeded up until the words become incomprehensible, then slowed down again. When the words again are distinguishable, we hear that he is now saying 'Magic Christian' over and over again.
Ringo: 'Just a plug for the film, Ken – try and keep it on.'

In a short skit, John plays a little boy telling Yoko, his mother, what he wants for Christmas: a teddy bear, a train set, a man on the moon....

171

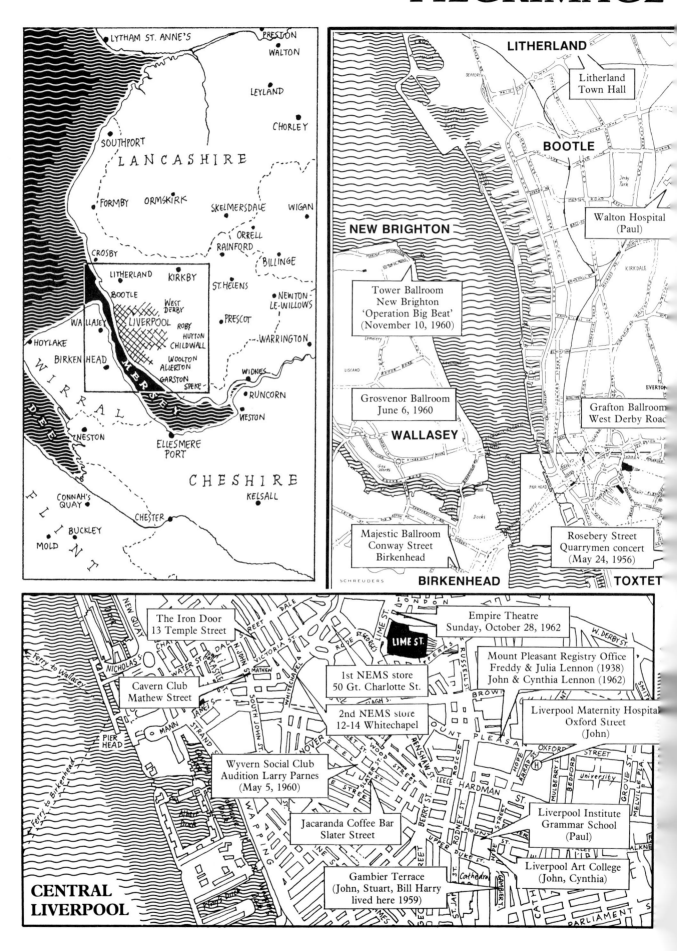

LYTHAM ST. ANNE'S
PRESTON
WALTON
LEYLAND
CHORLEY
SOUTHPORT
L A N C A S H I R E
FORMBY ORMSKIRK
SKELMERSDALE WIGAN
ORRELL
RAINFORD
CROSBY BILLINGE
LITHERLAND KIRKBY
BOOTLE ST. HELENS
WEST DERBY
WALLASEY LIVERPOOL NEWTON-LE-WILLOWS
ROBY
HOYLAKE HUYTON
CHILDWALL PRESCOT
BIRKENHEAD
WARRINGTON
WOOLTON
ALLERTON
GARSTON
SPEKE WIDNES
W I R R A L
RUNCORN
WESTON
NESTON
ELLESMERE PORT
C H E S H I R E
CONNAH'S QUAY KELSALL
FLINT
BUCKLEY CHESTER
MOLD

LITHERLAND
Litherland Town Hall
BOOTLE
Walton Hospital (Paul)
NEW BRIGHTON
Tower Ballroom
New Brighton
'Operation Big Beat'
(November 10, 1960)
Grafton Ballroom
West Derby Road
Grosvenor Ballroom
June 6, 1960
WALLASEY
Majestic Ballroom
Conway Street
Birkenhead
Rosebery Street
Quarrymen concert
(May 24, 1956)
SCHREUDERS BIRKENHEAD TOXTET

CENTRAL LIVERPOOL

The Iron Door
13 Temple Street
Empire Theatre
Sunday, October 28, 1962
Mount Pleasant Registry Office
Freddy & Julia Lennon (1938)
John & Cynthia Lennon (1962)
Cavern Club
Mathew Street
1st NEMS store
50 Gt. Charlotte St.
2nd NEMS store
12-14 Whitechapel
Liverpool Maternity Hospital
Oxford Street
(John)
Wyvern Social Club
Audition Larry Parnes
(May 5, 1960)
Jacaranda Coffee Bar
Slater Street
Liverpool Institute
Grammar School
(Paul)
Gambier Terrace
(John, Stuart, Bill Harry
lived here 1959)
Liverpool Art College
(John, Cynthia)

TO LIVERPOOL

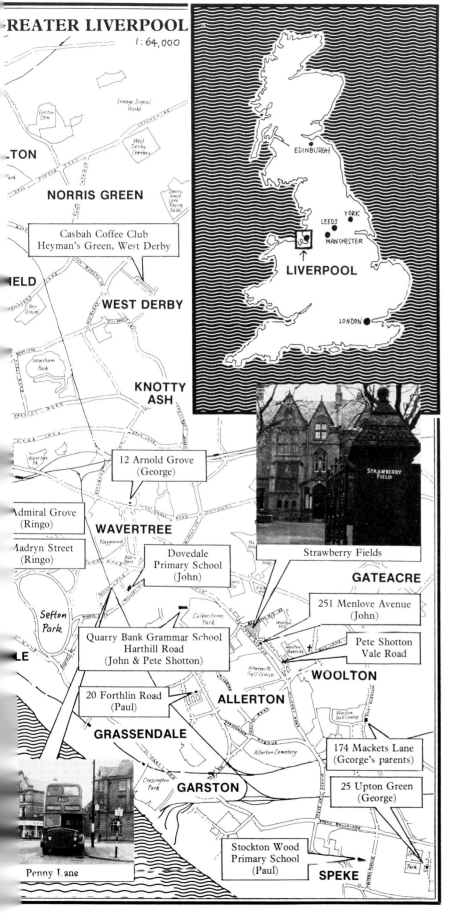

GREATER LIVERPOOL
1:64,000

NORRIS GREEN

Casbah Coffee Club
Heyman's Green, West Derby

WEST DERBY

KNOTTY ASH

12 Arnold Grove
(George)

Admiral Grove
(Ringo)

WAVERTREE

Madryn Street
(Ringo)

Dovedale
Primary School
(John)

Strawberry Fields

GATEACRE

251 Menlove Avenue
(John)

Quarry Bank Grammar School
Harthill Road
(John & Pete Shotton)

Pete Shotton
Vale Road

Sefton
Park

WOOLTON

20 Forthlin Road
(Paul)

ALLERTON

GRASSENDALE

174 Mackets Lane
(George's parents)

25 Upton Green
(George)

GARSTON

Stockton Wood
Primary School
(Paul)

SPEKE

Penny Lane

Penny Lane and Strawberry Fields really exist. Just look at any map of Liverpool.

Penny Lane, a shopping street, is clearly marked – in fact more clearly on the map than on the street itself, where there have been no identifying Penny Lane signs since 1967. Souvenir hunters stole the signs shortly after the Beatles' single was released on February 17 of that year; they were replaced and restolen several times, before the city fathers finally gave up and left the street unmarked. It's there, though, for the pilgrims to find, along with its legendary barber's shop, bank and fire station.

Strawberry Fields, a Salvation Army Children's Home, is also shown on the map. Around the corner, at 251 Menlove Avenue, John Lennon lived as a boy. Paul lived a few streets away, at 20 Forthlin Road. Nearby is Mackets Lane, where George bought a house for his parents; George grew up in Upton Green, Speke (lower right), an area where Paul also lived, but he was born in Wavertree, where his parents had a house at 12 Arnold Grove. While John, Paul and George came from the suburbs, Ringo was raised in Dingle, in the city centre: he was born at 9 Madryn Street and, three years later, moved to 10 Admiral Grove.

The map also shows the outlying areas where the Quarrymen, Johnny and the Moondogs, the Silver Beatles and, finally, the Beatles had their early successes: New Brighton, Wallasey and Birkenhead, for example, all of which are situated across the Mersey from Liverpool.

In the heart of town (at the lower left of the map) are the grammar school Paul attended, the art academy where John was a student, the Cavern Club and other important Beatle shrines.

When Penny Lane and Strawberry Fields were immortalized by the group in 1967, baby pictures of John, Paul, George and Ringo appeared on the single's cover. The photos were not labelled, though, so fans could only guess at who was who. For those of you who still have not figured it out, here's the solution.

Get Back to Toronto: *the first Beatle bootleg*

Get Back: *the first Dutch bootleg*

Sweet Apple Trax: *accept no substitutes!*

BOOTLEGGING THE BEATLES

A bootleg is an illegal album which is pressed and distributed outside of the official recording company channels. There are two different types of bootlegs: first, counterfeit editions of existing albums, which are illicitly copied and then sold for a lower price than the original (but at a higher profit, since no artists' royalties are paid); secondly, pirated collections of material not released by the group in question's recording company (such as interviews, tapes of rehearsals, or concert performances).

The manufacture of counterfeit bootlegs is nothing more than theft, and the albums themselves are of little or no interest to fans. The second type of bootleg is equally illegal, but often much more interesting: these records present fans with material they would otherwise never have the opportunity to hear. And although the manufacture and sale of both sorts of bootleg is a money-making business, the Type I manufacturers are usually *only* motivated by profit, while the Type II manufacturers are often fans themselves.

In the jazz world, bootlegging has become a more or less acceptable practice. Because jazz is improvisational, a combo rarely plays the same piece exactly the same way twice, and for that reason many concerts are taped and made available to jazz-lovers as bootlegs. Since legitimate jazz albums tend not to be very commercial anyway, recording companies don't usually bother making a fuss about jazz bootlegging.

Pop performances, of course, also differ from night to night,

although the differences may only be in the introductions of the songs and the reactions of the crowd. But a fan who attends one particular concert may well want to have a recording of that concert as a souvenir, and the hard-core fan may even want records of the concerts he missed. Interviews, rehearsal tapes and the like are also musts for the devotee, especially when they provide a behind-the-scenes look at a star or a group.

The first Beatle bootlegs appeared around 1970 and featured tapes of rehearsals for the *Let It Be* album. The tapes were recorded openly: the *Let It Be* sessions were being filmed, anyway, and the studio was so filled with sound equipment and cameras that a few more tape recorders here and there were probably not even noticed.

A flood of additional bootlegs followed quickly: over the years, thousands of fans had recorded hundreds of Beatle concerts, radio and television broadcasts, interviews and so forth, and many of these fans now began releasing pirate albums of the best and unique material.

Unlike jazz, though, pop music is extremely commercial, and the dozens of Beatle bootlegs which streamed onto the market sold heavily. Even though the official recording companies had no plans to market the bootlegged material themselves, they felt that the illegal albums were cutting into their own sales and they rapidly began legal actions in an attempt to shut the bootleggers down. In spite of the lawsuits and the court orders, boot-

leg albums by the Beatles (and other popular groups) remained available, and many of them remain available to this day. They have become harder to find, however, and they have become more expensive. Some of them were well-recorded and some were poorly-recorded, some were well-pressed and some badly-pressed, some contain fascinating material and some contain dross – but the fans continue to hunt them down, and no self-respecting Beatlemaniac can consider his or her collection complete without at least a few of them.

Which of the many Beatle bootlegs are the best, the most interesting and important? The following paragraphs are a guide to the cream of the crop:

The very first pirated Beatle album was titled *Get Back To Toronto* and released by I.P.F. Records. Anyone who has seen the *Let It Be* film knows what to expect: rehearsal sessions, half-finished songs, old rockers, musical fragments, jokes, conversations and more. But the best material from the numerous *Let It Be* bootlegs was collected on two double albums and issued on the Instant Analysis label as *Sweet Apple Trax*; the eight sides of music and talk were later squeezed onto four sides, which, in a spoof on the Beatles' own double-white album, were released as the double-black album.

Of the many bootleg concert albums available, three stand out: *Last Live Show, First United States Performance* and *Beatles In Japan/Five Nights In A Judo Arena*. Although the albums are well worth owning,

174

Last Live Show: *only not really . . .*

First US performance: *hoarse voices*

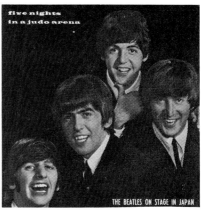
Beatles in Japan: *rare performances*

the titles (like the titles of and cover information on a large number of bootlegs) are all inaccurate.

Last Live Show is *not* a recording of the Beatles' final concert, held at San Francisco's Candlestick Park on August 29, 1966 – that performance was in fact recorded, but the tapes have not yet been released. *Last Live Show* is actually the soundtrack of the television documentary made during the boys' Shea Stadium concert over a year earlier, on August 15, 1965. The bootleg transmits the feel of the Beatles' American appearances excellently, with the screams of the fans, the typically American introductions ('Ladies and Gentlemen! Honoured by their country, decorated by their Queen and loved here in America! Here they are: the Beatles!') and the humorous banter by John and Paul. An added attraction in an interview with the group, recorded in the helicopter which transported

them from downtown Manhattan to Shea Stadium. Unfortunately, the interview and the concert itself have been snipped into separate sequences and intercut, which detracts from the live atmosphere.

That atmosphere is thoroughly maintained on *First United States Performance*, although again the album title is misleading: what we hear on this bootleg is the Beatles' September 15, 1964 concert in Cleveland, which took place during – but *not* at the beginning of – their first American tour. Amateurishly taped by a member of the audience with a simple portable recorder, the set is a unique documentation of the Beatles' early years. The well-known songs – *Love Me Do, Please Please Me, Twist And Shout, Can't Buy Me Love, Roll Over Beethoven* – take on a different and exciting flavour as they pour forth from hoarse Beatles throats.

These last two bootlegs are much

more interesting to the collector than the officially-released *The Beatles At The Hollywood Bowl*, put out in 1977 in an attempt to stem the tide of illegal concert albums. *Hollywood Bowl* was beautifully recorded in stereo by EMI, but thoughtlessly produced: numbers from two performances held a year apart (in 1964 and 1965) were indiscriminately combined to create the disc.

Five Nights In A Judo Arena, released by Weintraub Records, features recordings made for broadcast on Japanese television, which explains its excellent sound quality. The Beatles only performed in the Budokan Arena for *three* nights, though – June 30, July 1 and July 2, 1966 – and the album contains numbers from only *one* of those three dates. Regardless of the misleading title, it is perhaps the most important of the live bootlegs, including a rare opportunity to hear the group do *Yesterday, Day Tripper, Nowhere Man* and *Paperback Writer* on stage. It is also historically interesting, as it was the last Beatle concert to have yet been released on an album.

In the BBC studios with presenter Lee Peters: *Pop Go the Beatles.*

Yellow Matter Custard: *cover versions*

THANKS YOU FAB
GEAR WACKERS
FROM THE BOYS
THE MEN - . . . .
. . . . THE BEATLS

JohLennon Nov '68